Petronius Arbiter was the Arbiter of Elegance at the court of the extravagant young Nero. Little is known of his life except for the extraordinary way he ended it, described in telling detail by the historian Tacitus. Petronius' comic masterpiece, the *Satyrica* – famous not least for its namesake, *Fellini Satyricon* (1969) – is generally recognized as one of the most original and engaging works to survive from classical antiquity. Whether read as the first European novel, a parody of classical romance, a sophisticated example of pagan pornography or a gay classic, Petronius' picaresque account of the Priapic adventures of Encolpius and his beautiful lover, Giton, takes us deep into the underworld of the Roman empire. Told in the first-person by Encolpius, the *Satyrica* offers a brilliant comic exploration of an ancient empire in decline and of the energies released by its decay. Since it was first translated into English by William Burnaby in 1694, the *Satyrica* has never ceased to delight and scandalize. This new translation attempts to capture the comic vigor and literary cunning of the original in the idioms of contemporary American English.

R. Bracht Branham is the author of *Unruly Eloquence: Lucian and the Comedy of Traditions* (Harvard University Press, 1989), awarded the Wilson Prize by Harvard University Press. He is co-editor with M.-O Goulet-Cazé of the forthcoming *The Cynics: The Cynic Movement in Antiquity and Its Legacy for Europe* (University of California Press, 1996). He teaches classics and comparative literature at Emory University.

Daniel Kinney is an Associate Professor of English and Director of the comparative literature program at the University of Virginia. He has written several studies of Medieval and Renaissance genres and modes of reception and is a prize-winning translator and editor.

Petronius

SATYRICA

Edited and translated by
R. BRACHT BRANHAM
Emory University
and
DANIEL KINNEY
University of Virginia

University of California Press
Berkeley   *Los Angeles*

Consultant Editor for this volume
RICHARD STONEMAN

University of California Press
Berkeley and Los Angeles, California

Published by arrangement with J. M. Dent,
a division of the Orion Publishing Group

First paperback printing 1997

Translation and other critical material
copyright © J. M. Dent 1996

Library of Congress Cataloging-in-Publication Data

Petronius Arbiter,
    [Satyricon, English]
    Satyrica / by Petronius; translated and with a new commentary by
R. Bracht Branham and Daniel Kinney.
       p.   cm.
    Includes bibliographical references (p.   ).
    ISBN 0-520-20599-5   ISBN 0-520-21118-9 (pbk.)
    1. Satire, Latin—Translations into English.   2. Rome—Fiction.
I. Branham, Robert Bracht.   II. Kinney, Daniel.   III. Title.
PA6558.E5B73   1996
873'.01—dc20
                                     95-53110
                                        CIP

9   8   7   6   5   4   3   2   1
Printed in the United Kingdom

CONTENTS

Who, finally, would venture a German translation of Petronius, who was, to a greater degree than any great musician has hitherto been, a master of *presto* in invention, ideas, words – what do all the swamps of the sick wicked world, even of the 'antique world', matter when one has, like him, the feet of a wind, the blast and breath, the liberating scorn of a wind that makes everything healthy by making everything *run*.

Nietzsche, *Beyond Good and Evil* 2.28 (trans. Hollingdale)

NOTE ON THE AUTHOR AND TRANSLATORS

PETRONIUS ARBITER was the Arbiter of Elegance at the court of the extravagant young Nero. Little is known of his life except for the extraordinary way he ended it, described in telling detail by the historian Tacitus. Petronius' comic masterpiece, the *Satyrica* – famous not least for its namesake, *Fellini Satyricon* (1969) – is generally recognized as one of the most original and engaging works to survive from classical antiquity. Whether read as the first European novel, a parody of classical romance, a sophisticated example of pagan pornography or a gay classic, Petronius' picaresque account of the Priapic adventures of Encolpius and his beautiful lover, Giton, takes us deep into the underworld of the Roman empire. Told in the first-person by Encolpius, the *Satyrica* offers a brilliant comic exploration of an ancient empire in decline and of the energies released by its decay. Since it was first translated into English by William Burnaby in 1694, the *Satyrica* has never ceased to delight and scandalize. This new translation attempts to capture the comic vigor and literary cunning of the original in the idioms of contemporary American English.

R. BRACHT BRANHAM is the author of *Unruly Eloquence: Lucian and the Comedy of Traditions* (Cambridge, Massachusetts: Harvard University Press, 1989), awarded the Wilson Prize by Harvard University Press. He is co-editor with M.-O. Goulet-Cazé of the forthcoming *The Cynics: The Cynic Movement in Antiquity and Its Legacy* (Berkeley: University of California Press, 1996). He teaches classics and comparative literature at Emory University.

DANIEL KINNEY is an Associate Professor of English and Director of the comparative literature program at the University of Virginia. He has written several studies of Medieval and Renaissance genres and modes of reception and is a prize-winning translator and editor.

CHRONOLOGY OF PETRONIUS' TIMES

BC
49 Caesar crosses the Rubicon. Roman Civil Wars begin
48 Pompey defeated by Caesar at the battle of Pharsalus
48 Pompey assassinated (born 106)
44 Caesar assassinated (born c. 100)
43 Cicero assassinated (born 106)
43 Birth of Ovid
42 Birth of Tiberius
31 Augustus defeats Antony at the battle of Actium
30 Antony (born c. 83) and Cleopatra (born 69) commit suicide
27 Augustus becomes the first Roman emperor
19 Death of Vergil (born 70)
10 Birth of Claudius
 8 Death of Horace (born 65)

AD
  Chariton's *Chaereas and Callirhoe* (mid-first century BC/AD?)
  Xenophon of Ephesus' *Anthia and Habrocomes* (mid-second century BC?)
4BC-1 Birth of Seneca
 4 Death of Herod the Great (born c. 73 BC)
12 Birth of Caligula
14 Tiberius succeeds Augustus (born 63 BC) as emperor
18 Death of Ovid
20 Birth of Cornutus the Philosopher
27 Tiberius retires to Capri
34 Birth of Persius
37 Caligula succeeds Tiberius as emperor
37 Birth of Nero
39 Birth of Lucan, nephew of Seneca
41 Claudius succeeds Caligula as emperor
50 Seneca acts as tutor and advisor to Nero
54 Nero succeeds Claudius as emperor
?55 Birth of Tacitus (the historian). Dies after 116
59 Nero has his mother, Agrippina (born 15), killed
62 Titus Petronius Niger serves as consul suffectus; traditionally identified with
   Petronius Arbiter, author of the *Satyrica*

62   Seneca retires from Nero's court
62   Persius dies
63   Cornutus the philosopher exiled (63–5?)
64   The burning of Rome; Christians burned, crucified and fed to dogs
65   Pisonian conspiracy against Nero fails
65   Seneca commits suicide
65   Lucan, nephew of Seneca, commits suicide
66   Petronius commits suicide (birthdate unknown)
68   Nero commits suicide

INTRODUCTION

Author

The remarkable sketch of Petronius by the Roman historian Tacitus (*c.* 56–115) remains the best introduction to him:

> With regard to [Caius] Petronius, I ought to dwell a little on his antecedents. His days he passed in sleep, his nights in the business and pleasures of life. Others achieved greatness by the sweat of their brows; Petronius idled into fame, and he was reckoned not a debauchee and spendthrift, like most of those who squander their substance, but a man learned in luxury. And indeed his talk and his doings, the freer they were and the more show of carelessness they exhibited, were the better liked, for their look of natural simplicity. Yet as proconsul of Bithynia and soon afterwards as consul, he showed himself a man of vigour and equal to business. Then falling back into vice or affecting vice, he was chosen by Nero to be one of his few intimate associates – as Arbiter of Elegance – since the emperor thought nothing charming or elegant unless it won the approval of Petronius. Hence jealousy on the part of Tigellinus, who looked on him as a rival and even his superior in the science of pleasure. And so Tigellinus worked on Nero's cruelty, which dominated every other passion, charging Petronius with having been the friend of Scaevinus, bribing a slave to become informer, robbing him of the means of defence, and hurrying into prison the greater part of his domestics.
>
> It happened at the time that the emperor was on his way to Campania and that Petronius, after going as far as Cumae, was there detained. He bore no longer the suspense of fear or of hope. Yet he did not fling away life with precipitate haste, but having made an incision in his veins and then, according to his humour, bound them up, he again opened them, while he conversed with his friends, not in a serious strain or on topics that might win for him the glory of courage. And he listened to them as they repeated, not thoughts on the immortality of the soul or on the theories of philosophers, but

light poetry and playful verses. To some of his slaves he gave liberal presents, a flogging to others. He dined, and indulged himself in sleep, that death, though forced on him, might have a natural appearance. Even in his will he did not, as did many in their last moments, flatter Nero or Tigellinus or any other of the men in power. On the contrary, he described fully the prince's shameful excesses, with the names of his male and female companions and their novelties in debauchery, and sent the account under seal to Nero. Then he broke his signet-ring, that it might not be subsequently available for imperiling others.

(*Ann.* 16. 18–19: After A. J. Church and W. J. Brodribb)

While scholars have puzzled over the fact that Tacitus here refers to a C. Petronius, while most manuscripts of the *Satyrica* refer to the author as Petronius Arbiter or simply Arbiter, most are now persuaded that these references are to one and the same person for two reasons: i) the few datable references in the *Satyrica* fit the early imperial period (mid-first century AD) in which Tacitus' Petronius lived; ii) both the manuscripts of the *Satyrica* and Tacitus associate the very rare name Arbiter with that of Petronius. In the manuscripts Arbiter is a cognomen, in Tacitus it is part of Petronius' sobriquet at the court of Nero – *elegantiae arbiter* or Arbiter of Elegance.[1]

In fact, it is far easier to explain how Tacitus or his sources (or the transmission of the text of Tacitus or of the *Satyrica*) might have jumbled the names than it is to explain the uncanny congruity of Tacitus' sketch of Petronius' character and death with the aesthetics of Petronius' masterpiece. In both we find a systematic and paradoxical inversion of Roman norms. Day and night, work and play, virtue and vice are displaced and re-evaluated, as Tacitus' portrait of the author repeatedly counter-points values real and apparent. For example, Petronius is described as lazy but yet as earning the same reputation as the industrious; he sleeps all day but at night 'shows himself a man of vigor and equal to business' – including the business of pleasure. While squandering his resources makes him sound like a 'debauchee and a spendthrift', Tacitus introduces these strongly pejorative terms[2] only to negate them (*non*) in favor of the memorable oxymoron 'learned in luxury' (*erudito luxu*). Similarly, Petronius' words and deeds are described as artfully contrived but precisely to produce the appearance of simplicity, not of artifice. Indeed, Tacitus, usually so firm in his moral judgments, seems unsure whether he wishes to censure Petronius as a self-indulgent eccentric or to praise him as a brave courtier, just as he admits to not knowing whether Petronius was actually vicious or merely pretended to be to survive at Nero's court (Tacitus, 16.18.2). What could be more Petronian than this narrative situation where the narrator, the sober historian interested in the facts, is not sure what to count as real and what is merely pretended? If Tacitus' Petronius did not write the *Satyrica*, he should have.

This impression is reinforced by the fact that Tacitus focuses his account on Petronius' response to his own impending death, a topic central to the *Satyrica*. Petronius' accomplishments in the 'science of pleasure' evidently excited the jealousy of another powerful courtier, Tigellinus, the commander of the Imperial Bodyguard. In the context of court intrigue this led to denunciations and finally to Petronius' detention. We are not explicitly told that Petronius was invited to commit suicide, only that he rejected the possibility of reprieve and would not play the emperor's game of hope and fear. Instead, faced with the same grim choice forced on so many others by Nero, he took control of the situation by opening his own veins. By refusing to cultivate a reputation for courage or to discourse on high-minded subjects such as the immortality of the soul, and preferring instead to listen to 'light poetry' and 'playful verses'; – and even to sleep and dine – Petronius deliberately turned his own death scene into a veritable parody of the traditional philosophical stance toward death associated most famously with Socrates (in Plato's *Phaedo*) and, more recently, with Seneca, who had been given a death sentence by Nero only the year before and whose heroic death is also described by Tacitus[3] (AD 65: *Ann.* 16.61–4). Petronius' determination to control his own exit from life – to make a death forced on him seem natural and even willed – again forcefully recalls a scene from his novel in which the most memorable character, Trimalchio, reveals a prophecy of his own death and rehearses his own funeral in detail in the midst of a lavish banquet. He even composes a funerary epitaph for himself that concludes with a jab at philosophers. But while Trimalchio grows maudlin and absurd, Petronius does not. Even while joking and shunning heroic gestures he refuses to buckle under to the emperor and flatter him in his will, just as he refuses the consolations of philosophy. Instead his last act is one of satire, an explicit description of the emperor's novel vices including the names of his sexual partners, both male and female. Yet even at this moment Petronius does not neglect the details: he destroys his signet ring so that it cannot be used to implicate others. (According to another source, [Pliny the Elder, *N.H.* 37.20], he also broke a precious agate ladle so that the emperor's table could not inherit it, a gesture Trimalchio would have appreciated.) Petronius was clearly no less determined than was his creation Trimalchio to maintain the artist's control of experience up to the very end – and beyond it. Thanks to Tacitus' artistry he succeeds.[4]

Aside from Tacitus' telling portrait and the brief reference in Pliny, we know almost nothing of Petronius.[5] And Tacitus does not even mention the novel. We can add to these reports only a single comment found in an essay by Plutarch entitled 'How to Tell a Flatterer From a Friend': 'Next comes that dangerous practice so ruinous of foolish men when the flatterer accuses them of tendencies and weaknesses just the opposite of those they have ... [for example,] they will reproach profligate and lavish spenders for being stingy and mean, as Titus Petronius did with Nero' (60d–e). Plutarch's charge of flattery shows little appreciation of irony or of the context of Petronius' utterance. After all, Plutarch had little experience of megalomaniacal emperors.[6] In retrospect it is clear that Petronius was playing with fire in teasing the emperor about his notorious extravagance.

What conclusions can be drawn from this evidence relevant to a reading of the *Satyrica*? Probably very little that we could not have inferred from the novel itself given that literature was produced by and for a much smaller segment of society in antiquity than it is even in our own day. This fact and the evidence of the *Satyrica* itself would have led us to infer an author who was part of, or associated with, the Roman ruling classes, who was intimately familiar with their cultural and social frames of reference without necessarily sharing them. Yet, we still do not know such elementary facts as where and when Petronius was born or how he was educated. We can make plausible inferences about the latter in the light of Petronius' position in Roman society, but that is merely to ascribe typical experience to an author who interests us precisely because he is singular. We have no reports about Petronius as a writer, critic or social commentator, only as a courtier. We might well wonder what this talented operator thought of Nero, of Rome, of empire, but we do not know.

Still, Petronius' role as, in effect, overseer of arts for a volatile emperor who desperately wished to be seen as an artist[7] is precisely the kind of public role we might expect of an author endowed with the singular sophistication and brilliant eccentricity in evidence throughout the *Satyrica*. More specifically, Petronius' prominence at Nero's court means that we are justified in assuming that he was aware of the literary activities of his contemporaries such as Seneca, the philosopher, dramatist, and courtier, (AD 4–65); his nephew the epic poet Lucan (AD 39–65); and the satirist Persius (AD 34–62). But how does Petronius' work stand in relation to theirs or, more generally, to the practice of literature as it was then conceived? Who were his literary models? Who formed his audience? How can we make sense of the *Satyrica*'s unconventional aesthetics in the context of classical literary culture? Such questions lead us directly to the problem of the *Satyrica*'s genre, and away from biographical speculation and court intrigue.

Genre

It may seem odd that virtually the only type of literarure widely read today – prose fiction – should pose a problem of genre in a classical context. What could be easier to place generically or more accessible to contemporary readers than a work of prose fiction? What, in short, *is* the problem?

First, any reader of the *Satyrica* will notice that it is unlike most contemporary prose fiction in containing many passages of verse in various meters, some of them going on for pages. For while genres persist over very long periods of time, indeed for centuries, they are also subject to a continual process of change, as is the cultural context of their production and reception. Any given example of a genre is formally determined by a wide range of culturally specific engagements as well as by its ruling generic design. The practice of Athenian tragedy, for example, differs significantly from that of Elizabethan or modern forms of tragedy, but they have enough features in common for us to feel justified in grouping them together generically as 'tragedy'. Knowledge of the cultural context in which particular examples of a genre developed allows us to decipher conventions peculiar to them, and thus learn how to read them. Every genre of literature is in this sense also a form of experience for readers – 'a specific form of thinking, a way of visualizing the world' not otherwise available.[8] To locate any work within a given genre as it existed in a specific cultural context creates certain expectations and, hence, frames for interpreting what we read.

The problem posed by the genre of the *Satyrica* is complicated by the fact that it is the earliest extant work of prose fiction in Latin: we cannot compare Petronius' practice with that of his Roman predecessors to see how he shaped the genre for his own aesthetic purposes. Further, most ancient genres had long traditions behind them that served to define their constituent elements – their matter, manner, means, and specific effects. While writers were, of course, always free to innovate, the traditional conception of the genres determined the parameters within which experimentation could be recognized as such. None of this applies to prose fiction (as it does to classical verse genres), since it lacked an authoritative canon or acknowledged set of aesthetic norms – except for those implicit in popular but uncanonical examples of the genre. As the last major literary tradition to emerge in antiquity, prose fiction never received the critical attention or cultural prestige of the older classical kinds such as epic, lyric and drama.

Indeed, the singularity of the *Satyrica* may seem to be at odds with the very idea of genre as a set of repeatable rules and conventions; but, in fact, genre yields the only means of grasping that singularity and specifying its distinguishing features within the context of classical literary culture. While Petronius may have written the first full scale novel in Latin, there would of course have been many kinds of narrative already familiar to him and his audience: the mythological narratives found in classical epic, lyric and dramatic poetry in both Greek and Latin; popular prose genres in written form such as Greek romance, romanticized history and travel literature; popular dramatic genres such as New Comedy and the Mime in both Greek and Latin; and oral genres of many kinds including fables, jokes, ghost stories, apothegms and the other ingredients of folklore. And then there are works and traditions that seem to straddle or confound the dichotomy of oral versus written genres[9] such as *The Life of Aesop*, a collection of jokes and comic vignettes about the legendary dwarfish, ugly, and mute but clever slave, Aesop; or the

Milesian tales, a tradition of bawdy tales like the French fabliaux (referred to by Apuleius in the prologue to *The Golden Ass*) that do not survive outside of their appearance in the Roman novel. What distinguishes the *Satyrica* is not just that it responds to such a remarkable range of narrative forms (including even non-narrative genres of lyric poetry) but that it reshapes and combines them as only a novel can – by bringing them into a dialogue mediated by a narrating consciousness. What results is something without attested classical precedent.[10]

Latin literature as a whole can usefully be considered as an extended response to the literary culture of Greece, which dominated classical civilization from beginning to end. While it is obviously beyond the scope of an introduction – not to mention the patience of our readers – to delineate the relationship of Petronius to all the varieties of Greek and Latin literature to which he responds, his approach to two genres in particular can serve to exemplify his working methods. At this point many introductory accounts of Petronius will confidently assert his defining relationship to one of two genres, both Greek in origin, namely, Menippean satire and romance. While both traditions are of central importance to Petronius, to suggest that his work somehow bears the same relationship to these genres as, for example, Senecan tragedy does to Hellenistic or Republican tragedy, or the satires of Persius do to those of Horace, is to misconstrue the nature of the novel as a genre.

Neither Menippean satire nor romance is an ancient generic term but both genres are ancient and well documented. Menippean satire is usually identified as a form that mixes verse and prose – as if this feature alone could define a genre or could not be found in some form in other genres as different as Platonic dialogue or Greek romance! But the idea of mixtures and mis-alliances of all kinds is generically significant, and the impropriety by classical standards of embedding characters who speak verse in a prose narrative exemplifies this tendency.[11] Historically Menippean satire refers to a tradition of satiric parody that goes back to the Cynic parodist and polemicist Menippus of Gadara (third century BC), whose influence is remarkable but whose writings are lost. This tradition entered Latin literature through the free adaptations of the learned Varro (first century BC). The earliest extant example of Menippean satire, however, is the *Apocolocyntosis*, an exuberant parody of the deification of the emperor Claudius attributed to Petronius' contemporary Seneca. A glance at this work reveals the central ingredients of the genre: a fantastic journey from this world to that of myth that progresses by multiple forms of parody and mythological burlesque as told by a ridiculous narrator intent on answering some question that defies mortal knowledge. In Seneca the question is: 'what happened in heaven when the emperor Claudius, deified after death, arrived hoping to join the ranks of the immortals?' (Everyone knows what happened on earth, comments the narrator, since no one forgets his own good luck! [*Apoc.* 5]) The *Apocolocyntosis* therefore resembles not a novel, but the extant Greek examples of Menippean satire, the Menippus narratives of Lucian (second century AD), in which the quest of the Cynic hero, Menippus, makes mythological parody a vehicle for satirizing humanity in general, and philosophers in particular, in the course of attempting to answer a single urgent but overwhelming question – 'What is the best kind of life for human beings?'

If this all sounds distinctly odd, then we have managed to convey an accurate idea of this genre. As a current historian of the Menippean tradition has argued: 'Menippean satire is abnormal in all of its aspects. It is an anti-genre; insofar as it is a satire it is ultimately a satire on literature itself and all its pretensions to meaning.'[12] This sounds, in turn, suspiciously postmodern, and that may explain why Menippean satire has received so much attention in recent decades after being all but forgotten for generations.

It is highly significant that apart from Menippean satire the most important literary tradition for Petronius, namely, romance, comes from the opposite end of the literary spectrum. Menippean satire is a self-consciously written form, the product of a learned, chirographic culture, and as such it is a literary composite completely alien to the older oral traditions of mythical narrative that it appropriates for parody and satire. It is accordingly radically mixed in form, critical in intent, and satirically estranging in its effects. Its means and ends are thus deeply expressive of the literate, writerly culture that gave rise to it. This fact is most obvious when we consider the demands it makes on its audience's knowledge of previous literature and philosophy, without which much of its humor and, hence, its *raison d'être* is lost. Its sophisticated and irreverent play with inherited literary forms contrasts sharply with the conservative stance toward the classical canon assumed by romance, just as its recherché subject matter contrasts with the more popular themes of romance.

Greek romance emerges in the works of Chariton of Aphrodisias (first century BC/AD?) and Xenophon of Ephesus (second century BC?) as an idealizing and sentimental form of narrative that recounts in excited tones the love, separation and reunion of two beautiful young heterosexual Greeks, who embody much of what their culture admired. The separation – effected by pirates, storms, gods and rivals – delays the predictable dénouement, thereby creating much of the narrative's appeal, its suspense (what will happen?) and its mystery (why did it happen?).[13] The delay puts the heroine and the hero under stress and thus generates the 'sentiment', that is, 'the representations of feeling, anxieties and moral choices' that provide the real source of interest and value in 'sentimental romance'.[14] Thus, as David Lodge observes, structurally the love story consists of the delayed fulfilment of desire – of the heroine's desire for the man she wants and of the reader's desire for the answers to the questions raised by narrative suspense and mystery.[15]

The general shape of the plot, its use of a unified literary language, its quasi heroic characters and its wish-fulfilling ending that affirms society's future through marriage all align Greek romance with the Odyssean narrative paradigm,[16] which it translates into the contemporary prosaic world of its Hellenistic and Roman audiences. While Menippean satire appeals to our intellect and aims to demystify the great traditions of myth and philosophy while exposing the world's hocus pocus – such as the deification of emperors among other idols of the tribe – the ends of romance are just the opposite: to engage our imaginative sympathies as fully as possible in the improbably romantic adventures of star-crossed lovers – the perennial ingredients of popular fiction from Chariton to the Harlequin romances. In other words, if Menippean satire is a seriocomic critique of the inherited myths of classical culture, ancient romance is its generic antitype – a new myth, that of *eros* in the cosmopolitan Greek world that surrounded the ancient Mediterranean in the wake of Alexander's conquests and the Greek diaspora.[17] The radically differing aesthetics of the two genres may imply corresponding differences in the audiences addressed by each, although such distinctions cannot be easily made within the elite world of classical literary culture.[18]

While it has often been noted that Petronius is funnier than the other ancient writers of prose fiction, it is not often recognized how central the humor is to his novelistic aesthetic. The sophisticated humor and ironic tone of Petronius' narrative have their origin in his novelistic fusion of two genres that differ radically in form, tone, style, characteristic effects and, perhaps, even in the audiences addressed. Out of this hybridization, crossbreeding, or fusion of genres emerged what can fairly be called the first novel.[19] These metaphors for literary invention are not meant to suggest a homogeneous blending, or simple combination of known ingredients – like a vinaigrette salad dressing – but something so paradoxical and strange as to be suspect – like 'cold fusion'. Menippean satire is of crucial importance precisely because it is formally disruptive and intrusive, a satiric solvent that acts as a catalyst for generic mixture and mutation but in this case within a fictional narrative framework that originates in romance. Inside this framework the Menippean mode of writing permits movement up and down the literary scales (high and low, oral and literary, verse and prose) and between genres and forms of speech that would either not appear in literary discourse at all (e.g., the freedmen's speeches [37 ff.] or the report on Trimalchio's holdings [53][20]) or not in contiguity with one another (e.g., Eumolpus' epic recital follows a scene of scatalogical comedy [117–18]).

This account is of course still a fairly broad simplification. Petronius draws on a great variety of discourses, including works we no longer have, and he draws on different genres in fundamentally different ways depending on their place in the canon and their function in his narrative.[21] The traditions of Menippean satire and Greek romance should be conceived as important subtexts, as two of a series of shifting generic frames of reference, not as 'sources' for the *Satyrica*. It is of course what Petronius does with them that makes his work so obviously different from either. If romance remains his most conspicuous model it is because it is the only kind of prose fiction – as opposed to traditional storytelling – that he would have known. While recent papyrological discoveries suggest that Greek fiction may have been more varied than was once thought,[22] the tradition that runs from Chariton to Heliodorus (third to fourth century AD) makes it clear that the dominant strain was idealizing and sentimental and is in general much closer to what is suggested by the generic term 'romance' than by the more modern English term 'novel'. This distinction is a complicated one that does not hinge only on subject matter – such as the heroine-centered plot of romance – but also on the parodic manner in which the novel reflects the values, premises, and conventions of romance. The relationship of Fielding to Richardson, or of Cervantes to chivalric romance, provides a useful model for understanding Petronius' relationship to Greek romance. Just as reading Richardson will enhance our appreciation of the comedy of *Joseph Andrews*, so Petronius' many forms of parody will be far more accessible to those who have also read Chariton and the Greek romancers.[23]

This account of the genre of the *Satyrica* might be taken to suggest that the novel is a strictly literary phenomenon that bears little relation to the historical context of its origins. But this, once again, would be to misconstrue the nature of the novel as a genre and, hence, its relationship to the institution of literature – the inherited modes of writing, speaking, and thinking.

While narrative may be of antediluvian antiquity, novelistic narrative is not. As Plato points out in his classic analysis of narrative discourse in Book III of the *Republic*, epic, the most prestigious and influential form of narrative in antiquity, alternates exclusively between two distinct modes of discourse – that of the poet/narrator (*diegesis*) and that of the characters (*mimesis*). The poet is either speaking in the narrator's voice (*diegesis*) or 'imitating' the voices of characters in directly quoted speech (*mimesis*). There are only very limited forms of indirect speech in Homer.[24] The voice of the poet/narrator and that of his characters are therefore kept clearly distinct by the use of formulaic introductions, as if by quotation marks, precisely because they are so linguistically homogeneous as to be otherwise indistinguishable. Indeed, the characters and the narrator speak the very same language, so the kind of variety and individuality of speech we expect from a novel is not possible. Furthermore, our access to the consciousness of the characters is limited to the poet's narration of their actions (*diegesis*) and his direct quotation of their words (*mimesis*). The formal history of the novel is the story of how the relations between *mimesis* and *diegesis* were altered to permit more varied and subtle ways of representing the consciousness of others – of characters – through forms of indirect discourse, interior monologue and narrative focalized through a character's consciousness – what the great Russian critic Mikhail Bakhtin calls 'doubly-voiced' speech,[25] speech that refers to other speech, as, for example, parody does.

The difference between the traditional epic style of narrative and that of the novel is seen most clearly in Petronius' decision to make his authorial narrator a character in the story. This is very different from letting a character speak at length and thereby become a narrator in exactly the same style and language used by the poet himself, as Homer does with Odysseus. What Petronius has done would be the equivalent of replacing the authorial narrator, Homer, with a character/narrator; something not done in epic or in any example of fiction known to him. This was a radical innovation and produced 'a quantum leap'[26] in the realism and immediacy of the entire narrative. Even the *diegesis* (narrative) is now an act of *mimesis*, the speech of a character; consequently, the relations between the speech of the narrator and that of his characters has been profoundly altered. They are now in the same fictional world, unlike an authorial narrator who hovers godlike over his characters and their world or an epic singer who looks back to an heroic past.

Petronius pursues the implications of his innovation consistently.[27] As a character in this fictional world his narrator's speech will perforce differ from that of other characters, as it would in fact. Since the speech of the characters is not assimilated to the style of an authorial narrator, as it is in epic or romance, the variety and individuality of speech can be registered. The way is open for the novelist to represent speech that differs not only from his own but from that of the existing literary repertoires and, thereby, to confront the conventionally literary genres of speech, both popular and classical, with those appropriated from other extra-literary areas of culture.[28] This is a Bakhtinian conception of the genre that has been persuasively applied to the Renaissance and modern novel by Walter Reed.[29] History, in the form of contemporary, extra-literary genres of speech, is therefore always part of the novel's distinctive generic purview. It is what enables the dialogue between contemporary experience and the traditional modes of representing and interpreting that experience that constitutes the underlying structure of the genre and insures that it will never take the same shape for long.

Work

It is significant that Petronius' *Satyrica* is the only surviving example of ancient prose fiction (romances or novels) with a metaphorical title (with the possible exception of Apuleius' *Golden Ass*).[30] Greek romances were typically named (metonymically) after their hero and heroine (e.g., Chariton's *Chaireas and Callirhoe*) or after their exotic setting (e.g., Heliodorus' *An Ethiopian Story* [*Aethiopica*] or Iamblichus' *Babyloniaca*). Instead of naming his work after its heroes or setting, Petronius chose a title that evokes two closely related but distinguishable ideas. The first is that of the satyr, the hybrid of man and animal whose human form is typically augmented by a bushy tail and horse's ears. The satyr's degree of animality varies: on vases they can be represented as animals playing the role of men or as men playing the role of animals.[31] They also form Dionysus' male retinue, as maenads do the female. (Dionysus, the god of wine, theater and ecstasy, is, according to some traditions, the father of Priapus,[32] the ithyphallic fertility god who comes up several times in the *Satyrica*.) The second idea evoked by Petronius' title is that of the satyr-play, which was performed in classical Athens at the spring festival of Dionysus following the tragedies. The satyr-play, called 'tragedy at play' by an ancient critic, has traditionally been regarded as a comic antidote to the preceding tragedies. (The only example of the genre to survive largely intact is Euripides' *Cyclops*.) The satyrs were not the heroes of these plays but formed their choruses and are characteristically represented as shunning the burdens of civilized life – such as work or warfare – and as demons of nature who witness with astonishment the epochal starting points of civilization, such as the invention of fire, of wine, or of the lyre (from a tortoise shell.) In general, they are shameless hedonists preoccupied with the pursuit of pleasures – wine, dance, and music – under the auspices of Dionysus. The earliest reference to them (in Hesiod's *Catalogue of Women*) is as 'the race of lazy good-for-nothing satyrs'. On vases they are typically shown with enormous erections chasing maenads. In Euripides' *Cyclops* Odysseus saves the satyrs from enslavement by the Cyclops and restores them to the service of Dionysus – whose servitude is perfect liberty.[33]

Thus, as a title, *Satyrica* simultaneously evokes the mythical world of satyrs and a specific literary tradition of representing

that world.[34] The novel's heroes, however, are never called satyrs
or explicitly compared to them. *Satyrica* (the neuter plural of the
adjective 'satyric')[35] is rather a heuristic metaphor for the moral
ambiance of the fictional world Petronius has created. There are
several references in the *Satyrica* to Odysseus' escape from the
Cyclops' cave, and if we had the whole novel we might well find
satyric traditions drawn on in other ways as well. It is clear that
among the preoccupations of the satyr-play as a genre were the
origins and nature of civilized life, which the satyrs were ideally
suited to explore since they were partly human and civilized
(e.g., they speak Greek and drink wine) and partly animal and
incorrigibly wild.[36] As Nietzsche observes in *The Birth of
Tragedy*, 'in the presence of a chorus of satyrs the cultured Greek
felt his civilization dissolve.'[37] (On various festive occasions it
was customary to dress up like a satyr.) One of the recurring
topics of Petronius' *Satyrica* is the apparent decline of civilization
and culture. A little thought will suggest many other echoes and
reworkings of satyric topoi.[38]

The word *satyrica* is not related to the Latin word for satire
(*satura*), but the association is still suggested by the similar sound
of the words and the fact that some topoi of Roman verse satire
(that runs from Lucilius [second century BC] through Horace
[65–8 BC] to Persius and Juvenal [c. AD 67–127] crop up in the
Satyrica: e.g., fortune-hunting, luxury, and literature. But the
treatment they receive in the novel is categorically different from
that of Roman verse satire. The generic term *satura*, is generally
thought to derive from the phrase *lanx satura*, a platter of many
different kinds of first-fruits offered to the gods in ancient times
(Diomedes *GL* 1.45). While the idea of the genre of satire as a
kind of mixture is foregrounded by this etymology, formally
Roman verse satire had been written largely in hexameters since
Lucilius and its repertoire of typical themes is already established
by Horace. It has been argued that the *Satyrica* parodies the
moralizing tilt of Roman verse satire[39] but if so it is only as part
of a much more general hostility to the classicizing tendencies of
the established canon of genres, which would certainly include
verse satire. But in general the relationship of Roman verse satire
to the *Satyrica* is oblique and diffuse.[40]

Rhetoric, however, is as central a feature of the text as it was
of the literary culture that gave rise to the *Satyrica*. Classical
literary culture is unimaginable apart from the informing role

that the arts of rhetoric played in the education of the Greek and Roman elites, who produced almost all the literature that survives. Even before it was institutionalized at the school of Isocrates in classical Athens, rhetoric had begun to affect all forms of literary production and its influence only increased over time. In the *Satyrica* rhetoric appears both as a controversial cultural practice and as an aspect of the novel's prose style. In the opening scene of the novel (as we have it) Encolpius launches an eloquent and witty attack on the educational value of rhetoric as it was then taught, arguing that the practice of composing and delivering speeches on hypothetical themes (declamations) lacks practical value, while contrasting the artificiality of rhetoric with the natural, untutored eloquence of the classics. Thus, the debate about the educational role of rhetoric is part of the larger controversy over the current state of the arts and the causes of their modern decadence, which Eumolpus takes up later. The fact that Encolpius himself (and Ascyltos) are said to make their living by their knowledge of letters is clearly significant in this context (10). This description could mean that they merely teach reading and writing or that they offer more advanced instruction in composition and, hence, rhetoric. On either interpretation Petronius is setting up a dialogue among his characters (Encolpius, Ascyltos, Agamemnon, Trimalchio, Eumolpus) on the nature and value of specifically literary forms of knowledge that had long been culturally pre-eminent.

While rhetoric as the art of persuasion may be considered an aspect of any act of speech that seeks to affect an audience, the artifice of persuasion can also be foregrounded for parodic effect, as it is when Eumolpus tries to defend Encolpius and Giton against the charge of having tried to sneak aboard Lichas' ship (107). The comic lengths to which Eumolpus pushes his argument is an excellent example of the overly ingenious modes of argumentation that were characteristic of rhetorical declamations. Such ingenuity made the practice of declamation admired by many, even as it left it open to the charge of unreality, as much academic writing still is. More generally, rhetoric as the practical study of the art of speaking plays an incalculable role in the development of novelistic discourse. In composing declamations students learn to inhabit alien and often bizarre points of view and to articulate them as effectively as possible. In the process they learn how 'to work language while remaining outside of it',[41] to use Bakhtin's characterization of the novelist's forte. While the most overtly rhetorical element – characters who speechify – would ultimately come to seem unnovelistic in its artificiality, this should not lead us to underestimate the importance of the institution of rhetoric for the emergence of prose fiction.

Of course the fragmented state of the text should make us cautious in characterizing the *Satyrica*'s literary qualities. Since we do not know how long the original was, we do not know how much of it we possess. What we do have lacks the beginning and end of the story and is frequently interrupted by gaps or lacunae in the manuscripts. Our sources indicate that what we have comes from books 14–16 of the original. In this translation we have followed the usual order of the narrative fragments but arranged them into chapters named after significant characters that first appear in them (rather than into the original books [14–15–16], whose extent is editorial guess-work).[42]

What we call the *Satyrica* is a series of substantial fragments from a long first-person account narrated by Encolpius about his escapades with his boyfriend, Giton, and two travelling companions – Ascyltos, an itinerant teacher like Encolpius, and Eumolpus, a poet and con man. Part of the narrative is concerned with the sexual rivalry between Encolpius and his travelling companions over Giton, while the rest is devoted to the characters encountered by Encolpius on his journey: Agamemnon, a professor of rhetoric; Quartilla, a priestess of Priapus; Trimalchio, a millionaire, and his fellow ex-slaves; Lichas and Tryphaena, friends in search of Encolpius for reasons of love and revenge; Circe, a mythically beautiful woman who wants to be Encolpius' mistress; and Oenothea, another priestess of Priapus.

It is often unclear precisely how one episode relates to another. Indeed, it is surprising how strong the narrative pull of the *Satyrica* still is in spite of the fact that we do not know what set our hero into motion or what his destination is. Most scenes are motivated by the needs of the moment – to escape, to eat, to argue, to love, to survive until the next day or the next page. One recurring motif is the role of Priapus. That there are at least two priestesses of Priapus[43] in the episodes we possess is striking and probably significant given how few priestesses of Priapus appear elsewhere in classical literature in any genre or period. Encolpius also produces a poem on heroes who suffer the wrath of gods

(139) that compares him as an object of Priapus' wrath to heroes of myth, such as Hercules and Ulysses, who were persecuted by Juno and Neptune. This has led some scholars to see Encolpius' travels as motivated primarily by divine anger, as Odysseus' are after he blinds the Cyclops, son of Poseidon.[44] The parodic treatment of the epic motif of divine anger dovetails perfectly with the view taken here that the *Satyrica* is a novelistic experiment that grew out of the parodic reworking of classical narrative forms.[45] The gods are often invoked in Greek romance as the ultimate causes of events, as they are in epic.[46] Just as the lowly fertility god, Priapus – a comic figure with enormous genitals – is substituted for such Olympians as the Poseidon of the *Odyssey* or the Aphrodite who presides over Chariton's romance, so the culturally paradigmatic heroes of Greek romance and myth are replaced by cultured outlaws:[47] our narrator Encolpius admits to having committed murder and sacrilege (130) and is in love with a boy whom he describes at one point as a male whore (81). The inversion and deformation of the idealizing tendencies of classical romance and myth could not be more emphatic and thoroughgoing.[48] The effect of this process is richly comic; its purpose is exploratory and experimental – to investigate those areas of experience denied representation in the inherited forms of literary narrative and to fashion them into novel contexts in which to interrogate the traditional literary versions of experience.

Verse

Petronius' verse is remarkably varied in meter and style,[49] though all marked by sure technical competence; its most noteworthy feature is at least arguably its sheer variety, furnishing as it does an inclusive parodic synopsis both of metrical genres and several genre-linked cultural modes. Three of Petronius' meters (elegiac couplets, hendecasyllables, choliambs) coincide with those used in the *Carmina priapea* – a bawdy, subversive collection of poems to Priapus occasionally ascribed to the likes of Vergil, Ovid, and Martial – but in each case Petronius avoids any fixed or predictable linkage between scabrous content and this or that form. On the other hand, he does resort to the still more licentious Sotadean meter for a pair of poems closely connected (as that meter frequently is) with the scandalous antics of *galli* ('castrated males') or *cinaedi* ('catamites'). Elsewhere Petronius is equally ready to exploit, for much subtler parodic effects, more old-fashioned and dignified measures like standard dramatic-recit-ative *senarii* (55, 89) or the hexameters common to epic and formal verse satire, sometimes transposing them and their content in order to see what results. The quite various ways in which verse serves or offsets the drift of the prose have been well inventoried in the more general study of Pabst.[50] Four long poems found in Chapters 5, 55, 89, and 119–24 are all specimens of their speakers' self-ironizing pretension as well as the novelist's parodic-mimetic adroitness. Other poems more directly expose a given characters' faults or proclivities, while at least Encolpius' hymn to Priapus in Chapter 133 serves a ritual end in a form which it seems is prescribed by the context itself. A few verses estrange actual dialogue of which they form part (Chapters 14, 18, 108) and most others if reliably placed in the prose compose more or less maudlin mock-epic or melodramatic asides on some squalid new twist in Encolpius' epic of impotence. In Pabst's view both the first long poems' salient concern with the 'placing' of stylistic norms and the whole fiction's constant recourse to bathetic verse amplifications for comic effect are distinctive expressions of this text's Menippean affinities. We would ascribe these more generally still to Petronius' project of novelizing the classical literary tradition by transposing canonical genres into jarringly contemporary contexts.

Text, Translation and Commentary

The text of Petronius' novel has known almost as many unlucky and lucky adventures as its roguish heroes.[51] It may be that whatever we know of the text is derived from a single perhaps incomplete manuscript partly transcribed in France sometime in the ninth century; a descendant of this partial transcript empha-sizing sententious verse excerpts and shunning obscenity came to furnish the basis for the first faulty printed editions beginning in 1482. A very different collection of excerpts chosen mainly to abstract prose narrative, no matter how bawdy, was on hand by the high Middle Ages for another French scribe to conflate with the former, and a pair of descendants of this compound text (the so-called longer excerpts), complete with a battery of asterisks signalizing chief gaps and omissions, formed the principal basis for less threadbare editions beginning with Pierre Pithou's first edition of 1577. Even here Pithou took drastic measures to splice certain narrative gaps, as in interpolating the spurious *Carm.* 63 in Encolpius' misadventures with Circe, and even these much-extended editions lacked the bulk of Trimalchio's banquet, the *Cena* (Chapters 26–78). Tantalizingly, another French scribe working after the so-called longer excerpts were gathered was somehow still able to cite words from these mislaid chapters, and the *Cena* text he used may well have indeed been the same one the humanist Poggio Bracciolini transcribed from Cologne (*ex Colonia XV liber Petronii*) in 1423. Poggio's transcript of 'Petronius' Book XV' was then seemingly lost altogether until 1650 and first published in 1664. Thus, apart from a handful of fragments and poetic excerpts from other late-classical and medieval authors, the whole text of Petronius as we now possess it consists of a somewhat precarious and haphazard sampling of two or, more likely, three books from a total of at least sixteen. The poetic fragments at the end of this volume probably all belong to the same extended manuscript tradition, and may well all be part of the *Satyrica*, but cannot reliably be placed in the narrative. In translating the text we ourselves have used mainly the third, revised modern edition of Müller and Ehlers (Munich, 1983) but without hesitating to favor alternative readings where this seemed in order;[52] lacking other, more primitive texts to compare, the best critics' decrees on the text's precise shape are – as they doubtless should be – discretionary.

In translating Petronius we have tried for a racy and funny modernity that avoids stultifying anachronism; though Petronius' parodic-satiric romance fairly clearly takes up his whole culture's incoherence as one of its principal themes, we have not taken that as a license to deepen the muddle while angling for laughs at particular speakers' or narrative agents' expense. Even these thwarted, partial alternative doers and tellers are left free to make sense of themselves and their lives in a manner of speaking, at least; doing something like justice to that manner of speaking in a plausible near-equivalent modern idiom is the difference between an authentic translation and a time-serving topical gloss that at best gets us by. Only one earlier rendering, the much-altered and supplemented one[53] falsely ascribed to Oscar Wilde, has done anything like this sort of justice to the content and style of Petronius' verse in particular (even though the medieval texts featured Petronius' poems as distinctively authoritative distillations of normative judgments artistic and cultural alike). *We* may like our verse parody broad, but the novelized comedy of styles that Petronius serves up involves far more respect for specific inflections than we find in the stock para-Poundian rant of the long poems in recent English renderings.[54] 'Wilde' shows more tact in treating the poems as a gallery or palette of half-achieved manners or styles; the most interesting poetic failures are rarely mere frauds, and like 'Wilde', although varying his palette, we have rendered the poems line-for-line as a nuanced array of ironically placed half-successes, seriocomic essays (or assays) all by way of the novel's mimetic inclusiveness.

Our main end in preparing this text as a team was to complement each other's strengths and deficiencies; in the process, perhaps, we have furthermore had some success reckoning with the shortcomings of previous versions, not least in their shortage of notes where the lay reader needs them the most.[55] This is a thoroughgoing collaboration and we are jointly responsible for its strengths and failings. Last, but clearly not least, you the reader are chiefly responsible for your discreet share in the pleasures of this, the most peccant and piquant of texts, offering, as *Carm.* 31 memorably puts it,

> Something for one and all, for not all lines
> converge; one plucks a flower, another spines.

R. BRACHT BRANHAM
DANIEL KINNEY

References

1. The only other ancient references to Petronius refer to him as Titus Petronius [Pliny (*N.H.* 37.20); Plutarch (*Mor.* 60e)], which is why the C. at 16.18 is bracketed in most texts. This has led most scholars to identify Petronius Arbiter, the author, with Titus Petronius Niger, consul suffectus in AD 62, who met the end described by Tacitus (*Ann.* 16.18), but is wrongly identified by him as Gaius Petronius. Cf. M. S. Smith, ed., *Petronii Arbitri 'Cena Trimalchionis'* (Oxford, 1975) Appendix I; K. F. C. Rose, 'The Date and Author of the Satiricon', *Mnemosyne*, Suppl. 16 (1971).

2. According to H. Furneaux's note on this passage *profligator* ('spendthrift') is a Tacitean neologism.

3. The contrast with Seneca, who spends his last moments dictating eloquent utterances to his scribes (*Ann.* 15.62), is instructive. Seneca's last words were later published. All this emphasizes the public, theatrical nature of the deaths so recorded.

4. See C. Connors, 'Famous Last Words: Authorship and Death in the *Satiricon* and Neronian Rome', in *Reflections of Nero: Culture, History and Representation*, eds. J. Elsner and J. Masters (London, 1994) 225–35.

5. There is one other passing reference in Macrobius (*In Somnium Scipionis* 1.2.7) who dismisses the novels of Petronius and Apuleius as 'plots full of lovers' fictional adventures' only fit for children's nurseries. See Petronius and His Critics, p. 172.

6. Cf. Dio Cassius' observation (61.14) that Nero did not hear a word of truth from anybody.

7. When it dawned on Nero that his [i.e. Nero's] time was up he exclaimed: 'Dead! and so great an artist!' (Suetonius, *Nero* 49, tr. Graves).

8. G. S. Morson, C. Emerson, *Mikhail Bakhtin: Creation of a Prosaics* (Stanford, 1990) 306.

9. For this fundamental distinction, see W. J. Ong, *Orality and Literacy: The Technologizing of the Word* (London, 1982).

10. For an interesting attempt to locate the origins of classical fiction in the pre-classical narrative forms of Egypt and the Near East, see G. Anderson, *Ancient Fiction: The Novel in the Graeco-Roman World* (London, 1984). It is the genre of the novel, not the individual plot motifs, that is without classical precedent.

11. While the use of verse is probably the most demonstrably 'Menippean' feature of the *Satyrica*, it is important to note that the extent and originality of the verse in Petronius transcends its more limited use – as comic quotation and parody – in Menippean satire. We should think of Petronius as 'novelizing' the more circumscribed genre of Menippean satire rather than as working within its generic constraints. See also note 40 below.

12. J. Relihan, *Ancient Menippean Satire* (Baltimore, 1993) 28.

13. See David Lodge, *After Bakhtin: Essays on Fiction and Criticism* (London, 1990) Chapter 8.

14. See Lodge, 117.

15. See Lodge, 118. While Lodge's characterization of eighteenth-century fiction forcefully recalls classical romance, a recent study of

Greek romance (David Konstan, *Sexual Symmetry: Love in the Ancient Novel and Related Genres* [Princeton, 1994]) reveals basic generic differences in the representation of love and desire. Cf. nn. 17 and 46 below.

16. For important differences from the Odyssean paradigm, see Konstan, 170–5.

17. Konstan argues persuasively that Greek romance is distinguished 'as a genre from all other amatory literature in the classical world' and from the emerging modern novel by 'a pattern of symmetrical or reciprocal love, in which the attraction is both mutual and between social equals' (7), which provides the underlying structure and raison d'être of the genre. This is the new myth of *eros* invented in its literary form by the authors of Greek romance. As Konstan shows, it differs fundamentally from the prevailing conceptions of *eros* as represented in other genres or as seen in social practice. For another discussion of ancient Greek romance as a form of post-classical myth see B. P. Reardon, *Courants littéraires grecs des II. et III. siècles après J.-C.* (Paris, 1971) 309–405. See note 46.

18. See W. V. Harris, *Ancient Literacy* (Cambridge, Massachusetts, 1989) Chapter 7. Harris argues plausibly that no ancient genre sought a mass audience; yet some genres were undoubtedly more 'popular' – more accessible, more widely read – than others: 'We should rather see the romances as the light reading of a limited public possessing a real degree of education' (228). What makes them 'light reading' is exactly what makes them 'popular' and hence 'likely to attract a readership among the educated bourgeoisie', as E. L. Bowie puts it ('The Readership of Greek Novels in the Ancient World', in *In Search of the Ancient Novel*, ed. J. Tatum [Baltimore, 1993] 440). Cf. Susan A. Stephens' discussion, found in the same volume, 'Who Read Ancient Novels?'

19. Compare the characterization of *Don Quixote* (by M. Bell, 'How Primordial is Narrative', *Narrative in Culture: The Uses of Story-telling in the Sciences, Philosophy, and Literature*, ed. C. Nash [London]) as uniting 'two powerful, internally coherent, and yet incommensurable traditions: the exemplary idealism of chivalric romances and the incipient realism of the picaresque' (180); (cited by Konstan, 73.)

20. References to the text of Petronius are to chapters.

21. See N. W. Slater, *Reading Petronius* (Baltimore, 1990).

22. For a lucid account, see Relihan, Appendix A.

23. For translations, see B. P. Reardon, ed., *Collected Ancient Greek Novels* (Berkeley, 1989).

24. See S. Richardson, *The Homeric Narrator* (Nashville, 1990) Chapter 3.

25. For the concept, see Morson, Emerson, *Mikhail Bakhtin: Creation of a Prosaics*, 142–70.

26. See Lodge, 30 (speaking of the eighteenth-century English novel).

27. In the second century AD Apuleius and Achilles Tatius attempt long homodiegetic narratives with very different results.

28. For examples, see Introduction xix and the Trimalchio chapter generally.

29. See W. L. Reed, *An Exemplary History of the Novel: The Quixotic versus the Picaresque* (Chicago, 1981). Petronius pursues both the novelistic strategies persuasively analyzed by Reed: that of the picaresque that works by 'the exclusion of literature as a cultural institution' and that of the Quixotic that works by 'ironic inclusion' of alternative literary versions of experience (75). The freedmen exemplify the former as Eumolpus does the latter. Encolpius himself alternates between the 'basic situation of the picaresque hero – the marginal man's career of deception' (71) and an ironic version of a romantic hero.

30. See J. J. Winkler, *Auctor & Actor: A Narratological Reading of Apuleius' 'Golden Ass'* (Berkeley, 1985), 298–321.

31. F. Lissarague, 'On the Wildness of Satyrs', *Masks of Dionysus*, eds. T. H. Carpenter, C. A. Farone (Ithaca, 1993) 208–9.

32. Several accounts make Aphrodite the mother.

33. For satyrs and satyr-plays, see R. Seaford, *Euripides' 'Cyclops'* (Oxford, 1984) 1–59.

34. Cf. however, the phrase *satyrica signa* in Pliny (*N.H.* 19.50), which evidently refers to apotropaic effigies of satyrs. See also Chapter 138, note 1.

35. The common but incorrect title *Satyricon* is an abbreviation of the Latin *Satyricon libri* or 'Books of Satyrica'.

36. See Lissarague, 220: 'The function of satyrs in images is to invert or deform the rules of culture, a process that not only creates a comic effect but also has an exploratory value.'

37. Cited by Seaford, 32.

38. E.g., the word *satyrion* from satyr (often translated as 'aphrodisiac') occurs twice in what we have of Petronius and suggests the connection between the idea of satyrs and that of potency, fertility, etc. See Chapter 8, note 10. Cf. the comment attributed to Ion of Chios by

Plutarch (*Pericles* 5; cited by Seaford, 7) that virtue, like a performance of tragedies, should not be without a satyric element.

39. Relihan, 98.

40. The satires of Petronius' contemporary Persius show how fundamentally the two genres differ and why verse satire is too small a target to tell us much about the aesthetics of Petronius. Unlike Horace or Lucilius, Varro (1st c. BC) is not referred to in what we have of Petronius, and the badly fragmented state of the 150 books of his *Saturae menippeae* make it difficult to assess their specific relation to Petronius or to Seneca's *Apocolocyntosis*. See Relihan, Chapter 4, for a valuable account.

41. M. M. Bakhtin, 'The Problem of the Text in Linguistics, Philology, and the Human Sciences: An Experiment in Philosophical Analysis' in *Speech Genres and Other Late Essays*, trans. V. W. McGee (Austin, 1986) 110; cited by Lodge, 10.

42. K. Müller's division is the most plausible: book 14: sections 1–26.6; book 15: sections 26.7–78; book 16: sections 79–141. Book 15 therefore coincides with the Trimalchio episode.

43. In addition to Quartilla and Oenothea, Proselenus is also associated with Priapus.

44. Cf. E. Klebs, 'Zur Komposition von Petronius Satirae' *Philologus* 47 (1889) 623–35; J. P. Sullivan, *The Satyricon of Petronius: A Literary Study* (London, 1968); P. G. Walsh, *The Roman Novel: The 'Satyricon' of Petronius and the 'Metamorphoses' of Apuleius* (Cambridge, 1970); H. D. Rankin, *Petronius the Artist: Essays on the Satyricon and Its Author* (The Hague, 1971); M. Coffey, *Roman Satire* (London, 1976). Contrast B. Baldwin, 'Ira Priapi' *CP* 68 (1973) 294–6; T. K. Hubbard, 'The Narrative Architecture of Petronius' *Satyricon*' *AC* 55 (1986) 190–212.

45. For the *Satyrica* as a form of parody: see R. Heinze, 'Petron und der Griechische Roman', *Hermes* 34 (1889) 494–519; E. Courtney, 'Parody and Literary Allusion in Menippean Satire', *Philologus* 106 (1962) 86–100; Walsh; R. Astbury, 'Petronius, P. Oxy. 3010, and Menippean Satire' *CP* 72 (1977) 22–31; A. Scobie, *Aspects of the Ancient Romance and Its Heritage* (Meisenheim am Glan 1969); G. Anderson, *Eros Sophistes: Ancient Novelists at Play* (Chico, 1982); Slater, especially Chapters 7–8.

46. One of the important senses in which the romances are 'idealizing' narratives is that they consistently imagine the constancy of eros as the agent of happiness (and salvation) in a providentially ordered world. As Konstan observes, 'though chance or Tyche, may seem to

rule mortal destinies, it is Providence, we learn, that has presided over the action from the beginning' (56).

47. Cf. J. F. Nagy, *The Wisdom of the Outlaw: The Boyhood Deeds of Finn in Gaelic Narrative Tradition* (Berkeley, 1985). To use an outlaw as narrator in a written narrative is to reintroduce and refunction a folkloric type.

48. The 'desublimation' of romance in the *Satyrica* – its subversion of the myth of romance – works not only by way of a pointedly homoerotic inflection that inverts the norms of Greek romance (see Konstan, esp. 113–25) but also by transposing the quasi-heroic trials of classical romance into parodically debased sexual and social contexts (what A. Richlin calls 'sleazy surroundings'; see the useful addendum in Richlin's *The Garden of Priapus*, 2nd ed. [New York, 1992] 287). We have argued elsewhere (e.g., *Unruly Eloquence*, Chapter 1) that humor is a means of perception (as well as aggression) and therefore rewards an approach that emphasizes rhetorical analysis and context. Accordingly, we favour a view of the *Priapea* in Petronius that does justice to what Bakhtin has taught us about the ambivalence of folk humor, particularly as it is represented in sophisticated literary texts. On our view, males, perhaps even more than females, in Petronius' text are the farcically hapless prisoners of Priapus' dominion. See our comments on sexual spellbinding in Chapter 131, note 1.

49. Here is a slightly revised version of the 'Index Metrorum' supplied in Ernout, 211–13: choliambs, 5.1–8; dactylic hexameters, 5.9–22, 58, 83, 108, 112, 119–24, 127, 128, 131, 132, 133, 134, 135, 136, 139, *Carmm.* 27, 28, 30, 32, 35, 37, 39, 41, [63]; two dactylic hexameters and a pentameter, 34, 55; elegiac distichs, 14, 18, 80 (bis), 82, 109, 126, 132, 137, *Carmm.* 26, 31, 33, 34, 36, 38, 40, 42, 43, 44, 45, 46, 47, 48, 49, 50, [52], [53], [55], [57], [58], [59], [60], [61], [64]; Sotadeans, 23, 132; hendecasyllables, 15, 79, 93, 109, *Frag.* 25, *Carmm.* 29, [54], [56], [62]; *senarii*, 55, 89; trochaic septenarius, 58; anacreontics: catalectic iambic dimeter, *Frag.* 19, 21; with anapestic substitution, *Frag.* 20. We here follow convention in numbering Petronius' more or less intact poems '*Carmina* 26, 27,' and so on, following on the standard 25 fragments; numbers given in square brackets are for poems probably *not* by Petronius in their present form.

50. B. Pabst, *Prosimetrum: Tradition und Wandel einer Literaturform zwischen Spätantike und Spätmittelalter*, 2 vols. (Cologne and Vienna, 1994) 1: 65–73. For other useful accounts of Petronius' verse, see

P. Dronke, *Verse with Prose from Petronius to Dante* (Cambridge, Massachusetts, and London, 1994), and Slater.

51. For the two new rescensions of Müller, which appeared too late to be the basis of this translation, see *The Petronian Society Newsletter* vol. 16 nos. 1–2 (May 1996) 3. For a useful discussion in English, see M. D. Reeve in Reynolds and, more recently, W. Richardson.

52. Thus our verse readings differ from Müller's at the following points: 119.9 Ephyreiacum *Heinsius*; 11 crustas *Scaliger*; 14 auro *MSS*; 16 fames *MSS*; 17 aurata *MSS*; 112–16 *traditional order of verses retained*; 212 rumoris *Helm*; 220–37 *traditional order of verses retained*; 131.8 furta *Buecheler*; 133.3 semper ovans *Buecheler*; 135.13–15 *traditional order retained*; 17 Battiadae vatis *Pius*; Mirandam *anon.*; *Carm.* 30.16 *brackets deleted*. For simplicity's sake we have here cited line-numbers from Petronius' *Bellum civile* (Chapters 119–24) as if it were all part of one chapter, i.e., 119.

53. Like many early-modern renderings the 'Wilde' text relies heavily on the Renaissance reworkings still featured in Burman's edition of 1709, many of which are based on the spurious interpolations in F. Nodot's *Satyricon cum fragmentis Albae Graecae repertis* (Cologne, 1691).

54. Cf. Arrowsmith and Sullivan's notes with our comments on Chapters 89, 119.

55. Though diffuse and occasionally misleading or simply mistaken, the notes in P. Burman's variorum edition of 1709 (faultier new ed. 1743) are still often the best notes available.

SATYRICA

AGAMEMNON

As told by Encolpius[1]

1. 'I have to wonder,' I said, 'is there some tribe of Furies that makes you professors of rhetoric blather on like this: '*These the wounds I received for our common liberty. This the eye I lost for you. Please, will someone lead me to my children? I can scarcely walk on these battle-scarred legs.*'[2] Even this patriotic pap might be bearable if it cleared the path to real eloquence. Hardly – the bloated content and empty posturing have only one result: when the students actually go to court, they think they've landed on another planet. Why are young minds so completely stultified in college? Because they neither hear nor see anything they can use: instead they study pirates wielding chains on a beach, tyrants ordering sons to decapitate their own fathers, oracles that require the sacrifice of at least three virgins to fend off a plague – sticky gobs of speech, every word and deed slathered with poppy and sesame seeds.

2. 'Whoever grows up on this stuff will be about as tasteful as someone who lives in a kitchen is fragrant. With all due respect, Agamemnon, the decay of eloquence started with you rhetoricians. Your cult of euphony has made speech into a pointless game, while the body of eloquence has shrivelled up and died. Young men weren't confined to rhetorical exercises when Sophocles or Euripides were shaping the language. No gloomy grammarians had annihilated our native wit when Pindar and the nine lyric poets shrank from singing Homer's songs. But the poets were not alone. I'm not aware of Plato or Demos-

---

[1] Our story begins with Encolpius in mid-utterance, supposedly somewhere in the fourteenth book of the *Satyrica*. See Introduction, xxv.

[2] Standard speakers' emotional appeals; see for instance Quintilian 6.1.28–

thenes ever having enrolled in The Fundamentals of Rhetoric.'[1]
Great oratory is, if you will, modest, not flashy or artificial;
it flourishes on natural elegance. But that flatulent, inflated
magniloquence later imported from Asia to Athens has infected
every aspiring writer like a pestilential breeze.[2] When standards
fall, eloquence falls silent. Who has even approached the greatness of Thucydides, the glory of Hyperides? Nor does poetry
look any healthier; no, everything as if fed on the same
unwholesome diet wilts before it matures. Not even painting
resisted the general rot after the Egyptians had the brass to
come up with their short-cut to "great art." "[3]

[2.1] The philosopher Plato (427–343 BC) and the orator Demosthenes (284–
322 BC), like the historian Thucydides (c. 460–399 BC) and the orator Hyperides
(389–22 BC) mentioned below, were considered the great masters of Greek prose
style in their genres and as such were idolized by 'Atticists' – classicizing prose
writers of the late Republic and empire – as having established once and for all
the standards of artistic prose. On 'Atticism' versus 'Asianism', see note 3, below.
For an hilarious satire on Atticism, see Lucian's *Lexiphanes*.

[2.2] Hyperbole? 'Asianism' is a polemical concept developed by first century BC
'Atticists' – admirers of Attic, i.e., Athenian prose writers of the classical period
(5th–4th centuries BC) – to denounce later, Hellenistic departures from classical
Attic style that first appeared in Asia Minor. 'Asianism' is, therefore, not a recent
phenomenon, but the controversy it excited (classical versus postclassical, ancients
versus moderns) has persisted throughout the history of rhetoric. Cf. Cicero,
Brutus, 51; Dionysius of Halicarnassus, *On the Ancient Orators*, preface; Quintillian 12.10.16–19; Tacitus, *Dialogue on Orators*.

[2.3] Encolpius' main target is specifically Roman rhetorical training, the focus
of education in Petronius' day, with its emphasis on practice orations
('declamations') on often bizarrely hypothetical premises; the more advanced
exercises were fictitious trials (*controversiae*: see, e.g. Chapter 48), while *sua-
soriae*, speeches purporting to offer advice on legendary decisions of the past
(e.g. should Agamemnon sacrifice his daughter?) were assigned to boys. See the
Introduction, xxiv–xxv.

While it is true, as commentators have often pointed out, that Encolpius' own
complaints, for all their verve, echo some rhetorical commonplaces, it is not
always noticed that Petronius is putting a parodic spin on a debate still taken
seriously a generation later by Tacitus, Quintillian, et al. Moreover, Encolpius'
philhellenism – all his examples are Greek – clearly set him apart from the more
conventional traditionalism of his addressee, the rhetorician Agamemnon. For
philhellenism as a cultural practice, see Morford, 'Nero's Patronage and Participation in Literature and the Arts'. For the decline of rhetoric as a topos, see
Seneca the Elder, *Controversiae*, 1, preface 6–10; Quintillian 2.10.1–15; Tacitus,
Dialogue on Orators, especially 1, 28–9, 31, 35. Contrast the diagnosis of
Dionysius of Halicarnassus, *On the Ancient Orators*, preface.

3. Agamemnon was not about to let me sound off in the portico any longer than he had spent sweating inside the college: 'Young man,' he said, 'since your speech shows unusual taste and, even more remarkably, a measure of good sense, I won't try to deceive you about the tricks of the trade. But is it really surprising that the professors engage in these admittedly preposterous performances given the lunatics they work for? As the great Cicero once observed, if teachers don't cater to their students, 'they'll be the only ones left in school.'[1] Like the parasites in comedy wangling dinner from rich hosts, who think only of what will appeal to their patrons (for they won't get what they want if they don't lay some traps for the ear),[2] the professor of rhetoric is like a fisherman: if he doesn't bait his hook with something he knows the little fish like, he'll sit on his rock all day without a nibble.

4. 'What can we do? It's the parents who deserve your outrage. They don't want their children to get a serious education. First of all they sacrifice their hopes, like everything else, to their ambition. They're in such a hurry, they push the neophytes into court and thrust rhetoric – which they claim to admire enormously, of course – into students still wet behind the ears. If only they would let the students proceed gradually! Then eager students could cultivate their taste for serious reading and form their souls on the precepts of wisdom. Then they might learn how to rummage for just the right word and to listen for hours to the masters they would emulate. They might even discover that to please a puerile palate is no great accomplishment. Then the noble art of oratory could regain the authority conferred by greatness. Instead, boys play through school and as young men get laughed out of court. But, worst of all, even in old age, they won't admit what a shoddy education they received. Not that I have anything against a little

---

[1] Cicero, *Pro Cael.* 41.
[2] On the comic parasite's flattery as bait, see especially Terence, *Eun.* 247–53.

down-home improvisation in the style of old Lucilius.[1] In fact,
I will show you what I mean in verse:

5. 'Wanted: to learn a serious art—
    to nurture greatness in the heart—
    smooth first the soul with rectitude;
    forget the court's hauteur, the rude
    dull host's repast, no fitting place
    for One to brew One's own disgrace
    in borrowed wine; no worthy cause
    to sell the clown One's canned applause!

   Whether the citadel of Athens be his home
   or where the Spartan farmer dwells,
   or the Sirens' haunt, let him devote his first years to the muses
   and drink his happy fill at the Maeonian fount.
   Once he's stuffed with Socrates and his kind,
   give him free rein; let him brandish the weapons of
       GIANT DEMOSTHENES.
   After that, let a cohort of Romans surround him,
   and let them free his taste from Greek mastery.
   Next let his writing cast off the forum's constraints,
   and in its swift career let his fortune sound notes all its own;

[4.1] Lucilius (2nd c. BC), the ferocious first master of Roman verse satire, was
renowned and notorious as a rough-and-ready poetic improviser (cf. Horace, *Sat.*
1.4); on the other hand, *this* poem succeeds at its speaker's expense, being a
comically stilted effusion of stock good advice which is also at odds with the
speaker's own practice in Chapters 4, 48. Naïve satire from a still earlier era
might not have avoided a medley of meters like the present conflation of dramatic
senarii (or iambic trimeters) and epic-satiric hexameters; here it hints at the
speaker's prosodic ineptness, and an aesthetic which is alien to his chosen classical
models.

[5.1] 'The Sirens' haunt': traditionally in the vicinity of Naples. 'Maeonian':
Homeric. 'Socrates and the like': the Socratic philosophers, e.g., Plato; cf. here
Horace, *Ars poetica* 310. Agamemnon's advice is a bizarre combination of
careerism and lofty poetic idealism, and unclear as to whether it mainly suits
pleaders or poets; symptomatically, then, Agamemnon appears to make Cicero a
model for epic composition even though he was famously weak as a poet though
strong as a forensic speaker. The professional poet Eumolpus later assails lawyers'
dabbling in epic-composition as if it were merely a way to relax after work
('having cast off the forum's constraints'); see Chapter 118 below.

let his words serve up banquets and battles in a savage chant
and in threatening echoes of MIGHTY CICERO;
charged with these arts, as if from a bottomless hole
you will spill speech sublime from the depths of your soul.'[1]

6. I was listening so intently to Agamemnon I didn't notice that Ascyltos was already gone. As I walked along, absorbed in our heated conversation, a vast throng of students had burst into the portico. Apparently they'd just heard the speaker after Agamemnon give an extemporaneous performance. While the students laughed at his sententious style and ridiculed his entire presentation, I managed to sneak away and took off at a trot after Ascyltos. But I lost my way somehow and had no idea where our lodgings were.[1] Every turn I took led me back to the same spot until, out of breath and soaked with sweat, I approached an old woman selling fresh vegetables.

7. 'Excuse me, Ma'am,' I said, 'you wouldn't happen to know where I'm staying, would you?'

Charmed by the polite delivery of my foolish query, she replied 'Of course,' and promptly got up and led the way. I thought she must be divine...[1]

Suddenly, just as we entered an unfamiliar part of town, this street-wise woman threw back a motley curtain and announced: 'You ought to live here!' I was just about to say I'd never laid eyes on the place, when I glimpsed a line of naked whores with some customers prowling around them. I began to grasp – all too slowly – that I'd been led right into a cathouse. I cursed the woman's tricks, tried to hide my face and dashed across the room. But when I reached the doorway, I ran smack into Ascyltos, as dead tired as I was; you'd have thought he

---

[6.1] The precise scene of much of the novel is uncertain; since these first chapters take place not far from Trimalchio's villa, which itself seems remotely contiguous with both Terracina and Cumae (cf. Chapters 48, 77), the most probable setting is a town on the Bay of Naples, renowned both for its luxury and its mythical links with the infernal regions (Chapters 47, 119.67–75). Sullivan's Puteoli/Pozzuoli is one possible venue among several.

[7.1] Cf. Vergil, *Aen.* 1.330 ff.

had the same guide. I greeted him with a laugh and asked how he ended up in this dive.

8. Wiping away the sweat with both hands, he said: 'If you only knew what I've been through!'

'What now?' I asked.

'Well,' he sighed, as if too tired to speak, 'I was wandering all over town and couldn't even find our lodgings, until a fatherly old man came up and kindly offered to lead the way. He brought me here by some roundabout route and then offered to pay me for a quickie. A madam had already collected for the room and this guy had his arm around me. If I hadn't been stronger than he was, I would have had to pay the price...'

* 1

Everyone there looked to me as if they'd drunk *satyrion.*[2] We joined forces and defied the troublemaker.

*

9. As if in a haze, I spotted Giton standing at the edge of a path and rushed toward him ... When I asked what my lover[1] had gotten us for lunch, the boy sat down on the bed and brushed away a stream of tears with his thumb. Troubled at my lover's state, I asked what was wrong. He didn't want to tell me at first, but when I started to get angry he opened up: 'That lover of yours,' he said, 'your buddy, just came into our room a minute ago and wanted to have me then and there. When I started to scream, he pulled a knife on me and said, "If you want to play Lucretia, you've found your Tarquin."'[2]

When I heard this, I shook my fist in Ascyltos' face: 'What

[8.1] Asterisks mark a gap (or lacuna) as indicated in the manuscripts.

[8.2] *Satyrion,* 'satyr-plant', usually translated as 'aphrodisiac', was probably an orchid (= 'testicle') thought to perk up libido by natural sympathy (cf. Chapters 20–21); Pliny the Elder, *N.H.* 26.96–8. For satyrs and the title *Satyrica* see Introduction, xxii–xxiii.

[9.1] The word here (and elsewhere) translated as 'lover' is *frater* or 'brother'. The use of *frater* to mean 'same-sex lover' is not otherwise attested.

[9.2] A proverbial Roman mismatch; Tarquin's rape of the conjugal paragon Lucrece (Livy 1) was the outrage that brought down Rome's monarchy.

about it, you male slut, you – with foul breath to match!'

Ascyltos pretended to be shocked at first but a moment later was shaking his fists and shouting even more loudly than I had. 'Just shut up,' he said, 'you filthy gladiator— no, even the arena didn't want you! Just shut up, you sneaking cutthroat! Why, you couldn't even make it with a decent woman when you had the strength! Didn't I play your lover in the garden just as this boy does now in the inn!'[3]

I shot back, 'You slunk off while I was talking to the professor.'

10. 'What am I supposed to do, stupid, starve to death? Or listen to those pompous epigrams – I'd rather hear bottles broken and dreams interpreted!'[1] For god's sake, you're far more shameless than I am. The way you kissed that poet's ass to cop a free dinner – ' So our ugly quarrel ended in gales of laughter, and we turned calmly to the business at hand ...

*

But I couldn't forget what he had done. 'Ascyltos,' I said, 'it's obvious that we can't get along. Let's split up our things and try to fight off poverty on our own. You're a scholar and so am I; but to stay out of your way I'll try something else. Otherwise we'll quarrel a thousand times a day and scandalize the whole town.'

Ascyltos had to admit I was right. 'Since we're invited out as scholars tonight, let's not ruin the evening. But tomorrow I'll be more than happy to find my own place – and another lover.'

'Gratification delayed is gratification denied,' I quipped ...

*

Lust was the cause of this hurried separation. I'd been

9.3 Perhaps three or four references to lost episodes, none of which it would seem reflected well on Encolpius' manliness; but if the whole text was actually concerned with the 'wrath of Priapus' (cf. Chapter 139) it perforce yields us something quite like an inclusive exposé of standard manliness and its vicissitudes.

10.1 The first mockery of meanings imputed to dreams (cf. Chapters 17, 104, and Carm. 30).

wanting to get rid of that obnoxious chaperone so Giton and
I could live as before...

*

11. I looked the whole town over for myself before returning
to our little room. At last, I could ask for kisses without looking
over my shoulder. I held Giton snug in my arms and was just
on the verge of enjoying the most enviable of pleasures. The
party was just beginning, when Ascyltos slunk up to the room,
forced the bar from the door, and caught us in the act. He filled
the little room with his laughter and mock-applause as he
pulled off the cloak that covered me. 'Well, well, what have we
here, my right honourable friend? Isn't this tent a bit small for
two, soldier?' He didn't stop there either, but grabbed a strap
from his bag and proceeded to give me a good, thorough
thrashing while tossing out taunts like salt on a wound. 'Aren't
friends supposed to hold all things in common?'

*

12. It was just beginning to get dark when we entered the
market. There were lots of things for sale – junk for the most
part – but the failing light helped to obscure their dubious
origins. Since we had the stolen cloak with us, we took advantage of this opportunity to display its border in a corner of the
market in the hope that the splendid material might attract a
buyer. Almost immediately, a peasant, who looked strangely
familiar, walked up with a young woman and began to eye our
cloak very carefully. Ascyltos looked him up and down and
then suddenly paled and fell silent. Even I couldn't look at him
without rubbing my eyes! Of course! This had to be the guy
who found our tunic in the middle of nowhere! Yes, this was

the guy. But Ascyltos couldn't believe his eyes and, before doing anything rash, walked over like a prospective buyer, lifted the tunic off the man's shoulders and fingered it carefully.

13. What a marvellous piece of luck! So far the hick's meddle-some paws hadn't touched the seam. Indeed, he proffered it with some distaste – like a beggar's leavings. When Ascyltos saw that our money had not been touched and what a rube the seller was, he pulled me aside. 'Brother, do you realize the treasure I was grumbling about has come home again? That little tunic still looks chock full of gold! What are we going to do? How can we reclaim our property legally?'

I was elated – not just because of the treasure, but because I was now relieved of an ugly suspicion.[1] I was against doing anything devious. I thought we should sue him openly, then, if he refused to restore our property, he would find himself facing a court injunction.

14. But Ascyltos feared the law. 'Who in the world knows us here?' he asked. 'Who will believe our story? We're much better off if we simply buy it – even if it is ours – and get back our treasure for a few coins instead of risking it in a lawsuit.

> 'Where cash alone is king, what good are laws,
> where no poor man can ever win his cause?
> The Cynics, though they put the times to shame,
> will now and then, for pennies, throw the game,
> while law's official guardians sell her dear,
> the judge presiding as the auctioneer.'[1]

The problem was, that except for a single coin – which we would have spent on beans – we were empty-handed. We couldn't let the booty escape, so we decided to undersell our cloak and accept a little loss for a greater gain. As soon as we unfurled our wares the woman with her head uncovered [who

---

13.1 Encolpius implies that he had suspected Ascyltos of stealing the treasure.

14.1 Bona fide Cynic sages were known for outspoken social criticism as well as disdain for conventional 'property', cash included (cf. also Chapter 11, n.1). But Cynic beggars are often denounced as hypocrites in the empire, as in Lucian's *The Runaways*.

had been standing with the peasant] inspected some marks on the cloak very carefully before grabbing it firmly in both hands and screaming at the top of her lungs: 'Stop the thieves!' We were caught completely off guard, but instead of standing there looking stupid, we grabbed that rag of a tunic and shouted back with equal fervour that *they* were thieves. The argument was absurd. Street dealers attracted by the uproar naturally ridiculed our perverse insistence: while we were laying claim to a rag not worth patching, our rivals were after an obviously costly piece of clothing.

15. At this point, Ascyltos managed to quell the laughter saying, 'Look, everyone likes his own things best: let them return our tunic and they may have their cloak.'

A trade was fine all round; but there were already some shady lawyers on hand who wanted to profit from our cloak. They pressed us to deposit both articles with them so that a judge could settle the dispute the next day. There was not, after all, only the issue of ownership at stake, they insisted, but the fact that we were all under suspicion of theft. They were already appointing 'trustees' – some street dealer, bald on top, with a forehead positively bristling with warts. He had pled some cases, he said, as he seized our cloak as exhibit A for the coming trial. The aim of all this was clear enough: to let a pack of thieves get a stranglehold on our cloak in the belief that we would not appear at the appointed time for fear of being charged with a crime...

We were obviously after the same thing and chance helped us both get what we wanted. When we demanded that the old tunic also be treated as evidence, the peasant flew off the handle and threw it in Ascyltos' face. He wanted us to forget the whole thing and for us to return the cloak which had started all the trouble...

With the treasure retrieved, as we thought then, we raced back to our room, shut the door, and had a good laugh at the wiles of those street dealers and con men who so shrewdly recovered our money for us:

I like succeeding by degrees;
'too easy' spoils the victories.

*

16. We were just filling up on dinner, thanks to Giton, when someone banged noisily on the door...

Frightened, we asked who was there, and a voice replied, 'Open up and find out!'

Before we could answer, the bar fell from the door, admitting the intruder. It was a woman with her head covered. 'Did you think you'd have the last laugh?' she said. 'I am the maid of Quartilla whose holy rite you disrupted in front of the grotto.[1] Yes, she herself is coming to your humble lodgings and wishes to have a word with you. Don't worry: her desire is not to blame you for your blunder, nor to punish you. No, in fact, she only wonders what god brought such elegant young men in her direction.'

17. So far we were silent and had agreed to nothing, when the mistress herself entered, accompanied by a young girl. She promptly plopped down on my bed and proceeded to cry for some time. Even then we didn't say a word but sat in astonishment waiting for her tearjerker to end. When this showy storm of tears finally subsided, she unveiled an aristocratic profile, stretched both hands out in front of her, and cracked her knuckles: 'Just who do you think you are? And where did you learn to rival the robbers of romance?[1] God

---

[1] 16.1 The disruption of this rite (or orgy) appears to have been one main cause (but by no means the only one) of the 'wrath of Priapus' (Chapter 139) expressed in Encolpius' impotence; evidently the sexual ordeals that follow represent an atonement-in-kind. For Encolpius' (other) affronts to Priapus see Chapters 133, 137, 139, and *Frag.* 4.

[1] 17.1 The term translated as 'romance' (*fabula*) is quite general and this sentence could refer to the bandits common in Greek romance or to the banditry of such legendary heroes as Ulysses, Achilles, or Hercules. Cf. Encolpius' poem (Chapter 139) which compares his labors to those of legendary heroes.

knows, I pity you. No one looks with impunity on what it is forbidden to see. Especially since this part of the world is so full of spirits, it's easier to find a god than a man. But don't think I've come here for revenge. I am moved more by compassion for your youth than by the wrong you have done me. You have, quite innocently, I think, committed an irremissible crime. Indeed, on that very night I shook so frightfully with chills that I feared the onset of a fever. So I sought a cure in my dreams.[2] I have been instructed to seek you out and to assuage the onslaught of illness by the secret method revealed to me. But working a cure is not my only worry; another far greater sorrow drives me to distraction and may mean my death: if in your youthful recklessness you divulge what you saw in the shrine of Priapus and profane the mysteries of the gods, I beg and pray by all that's holy that you not mock our nocturnal rites nor betray those ancient secrets that scarcely three mortals have ever known.'

18. She punctuated this prayer with another burst of tears before rolling over face down on my bed, her whole body shaking with sobs. I was torn between pity and fear. I told her to take heart, that she had nothing to fear on either count: no one would profane her rites and, if a god had revealed a remedy to her, we would fill the divine prescription even at our own peril. Almost instantly her mood changed: she leaned over and gave me a wet kiss; laughing through her tears, she gently stroked the hair over my ears. 'I will make peace with you and drop the charges I had filed,' she announced matter-of-factly. 'But if you hadn't agreed to my 'cure', tomorrow a lynch-mob would have been on hand to avenge the wrong done me and defend my honor.

> Neglect is scorn; to rule, a thing of awe;
> what *I* love is to lay down my own law!
> Neglected, even a sage can turn to mayhem;
> to beat a man in style, girls, never slay him!

[17.2] For Priapic oracular dreaming, see also Chapter 104.

Then she clapped her hands and suddenly sang out in a loud, frightening cackle. Both her maid and young attendant joined in from opposite sides of the room.

19. The whole place echoed with their stagy laughter,[1] while we stood there wondering what had happened – why this sudden change of mood? – and stared in stupefaction first at each other, then at the women...

*

'I have forbidden any mortal from setting foot in this inn today in order that you may apply the remedy for my fever without interruption.' Thus spoke Quartilla. Ascyltos was momentarily stunned and I felt an alpine chill go up my spine that left me speechless. I would have been even more frightened without my reinforcements. After all, if push came to shove, we were only facing three girls – all three weaklings, presumably. On the other side, we were, if nothing else, physically male. And we were better dressed for a scuffle. I had even matched us up mentally in case of a fight: I would take on Quartilla, Ascyltos the maid, and Giton the girl...

*

We lost our nerve in a flash, and an unavoidable death loomed before our eyes...

*

20. 'Please Ma'am,' I said, 'if there's anything worse in store for us, get it over with; we didn't commit a crime so great that we deserve to be tortured to death...'

[19.1] The Latin here, *mimico risu*, compares this scene to a mime – a popular, bawdy, unmasked form of stage farce, acted by both men and women, and associated particularly with the names Decimus Laberius and Publilius Syrus (first century BC). (Publilius is a favorite of Trimalchio [Chapter 58].) Events in the *Satyrica* are repeatedly compared to a mime (cf. Chapters 80, 94, 106, 117), pantomime (Chapter 31), or a tragedy (Chapters 70, 108, 110, 140). For the pantomime, see Chapter 31, n.1; C. Panayotakis, *Theatrum Arbitri: Theatrical Elements in the 'Satyrica' of Petronius* (London, 1995).

A maid, who was called Psyche, very carefully spread a little blanket on the floor...

*

She diligently applied herself to my groin, which was now as cold as if it had died a thousand deaths...

Ascyltos covered his head; presumably he had learned how dangerous it was to meddle in other men's secrets...

*

A maid pulled two scarves from inside her blouse and proceeded to bind our feet with one and our hands with the other...

*

As our conversation began to run dry, Ascyltos said, 'Hey, don't I deserve a drink?'

Responding to my laughter, the maid clapped her hands and said, 'I put one right there, young man. Did you drink up the whole dose yourself?'

'What's that?' piped up Quartilla, 'Did Encolpius guzzle down all our *satyrion*?...'

*

A pleasing laugh shook her sides...

*

Finally Giton couldn't help laughing, especially when the little girl hugged him around the neck and gave him countless kisses without meeting any resistance.

*

21. We wanted to cry out in desperation, but there was no one to help. Besides, Psyche stood by with a sharp hairpin, and whenever I was about to call on my fellow citizens for help, she would prick my cheeks while the girl bore down on Ascyltos from the other side with a painter's brush soaked in *satyrion*.

*

Finally, a drag queen appeared on the scene decked out in dark green linen, which he had hiked up under his belt ... He laid into us with his haunches grinding, then besmeared us with his stinking kisses. At last, Quartilla, with her skirt tucked up, called for an intermission with a wave of her whalebone staff ...

*

Both of us swore by all the religion in us that so dreadful a secret would die with us ...

*

Several masseurs came in and restored us with a rub-down with the usual oil. When we had shaken off our fatigue, we dressed for dinner again and were led into the next room where we found three couches set up amid all the accoutrements of a sumptuous banquet. We were invited to take our places and, after tasting some marvellous antipasto, were inundated with the finest Falernian wine. After several courses, we began to feel drowsy. 'What is this?' cried Quartilla, 'do you intend to sleep when you know this whole night is consecrated to the beneficent powers of Priapus?'

*

22. When Ascyltos fell asleep wrung out by so many trials, the maid whom he had earlier spurned with a blow rubbed a handful of ashes all over his face. Then, while he was still unconscious, she painted his shoulders and sides with phallic symbols.

I was equally exhausted by our Priapic labors and had just gotten my first taste of sleep; the whole household was doing the same thing, inside and out. Some of the servants lay scattered at the feet of sleeping guests, others were propped up against a wall, a couple even slouched head to head in the doorway. As a thin flicker of light shone from the last oil in the lamps, two Syrians in search of plunder stepped into the dining room. While fighting greedily over the silver, they tore a large decanter in two; the table set with silver promptly collapsed and a huge goblet, pitched high in the air, came down with a thud on the head of a servant girl draped across a nearby couch. Her screams succeeded in both betraying the thieves and waking some of the revellers from their drunken sleep. The Syrians had come for profit, but realizing they were caught *in flagrante*, they instantly collapsed side by side behind a couch – you'd have thought they planned it that way – and started snoring as if they'd been asleep there for hours....

By now a steward had gotten up and begun pouring oil into empty lamps while slaves returned to their posts, still rubbing the sleep from their eyes. Then a cymbal-player appeared waking everyone up with her clashing of brass.

23. The party was reborn: Quartilla exhorted us all to begin drinking again and the festive songs of the cymbal-player added to the merriment...

*

An old queen came in – a man as thoroughly distasteful as he was clearly worthy of the Villa Quartilla. He was snapping his fingers while he spouted verses like this:

> Come and get it! Come quickly, you bum-boys outrageous!
> Get it on! Giddyup! Try to follow!
> All you ace organ-grinders, dude-buggies, glad-handers
> old and fey, caponized by Apollo![1]

After serving up these verses, he befouled me with a slobbery kiss. Then he got up on my bed and in spite of my resistance forced the covers off me. He labored long and hard over my groin – in vain! The make-up caked on his face melted and streamed off in rivulets; there was so much rouge in his wrinkles you'd have thought of an old wall battered by a rainstorm.

24. I was at the end of my rope, on the verge of tears, when I managed to say, 'Ma'am, didn't I hear you order us an appetizer?'

---

[1] The joke consists of the comparison of *cinaedi* ('catamites') to capons; Ernout refers to the skilled poulterers of Delos, the isle of Apollo. This poem is one of two in the scabrous Sotadean meter (cf. Chapter 132).

Quartilla clapped her hands gently and said, 'Oh, aren't you a sly one! A fountain of native wit! You mean, you didn't know "Appetizer" is what we call this queen?'

So my compadre wouldn't get off the hook too easily, I said, 'Damn it, is Ascyltos the only one here on vacation?'

'Not at all,' replied Quartilla taking my cue, 'Ascyltos shall also get his taste of Appetizer.' At the sound of her voice the queen changed his mount and rolled over to batter Ascyltos with his buns and lips. Giton stood there in the midst of all this and was about to split a seam, he was laughing so hard. This got Quartilla's attention. She asked very deliberately whose boy he was. When I said that he was my boyfriend, she said, 'Then why hasn't he kissed me?' No sooner had she uttered the words than she was leaning into Giton with a kiss. She slipped her hand into his lap and carefully fingered his tender vessel, saying, 'This will serve to whet our appetites tomorrow. I don't think I'd enjoy a sardine after today's sword-fish!'

25. With that, Psyche lit up with a broad grin and came over to whisper something to Quartilla. 'Yes, yes!' she exclaimed, 'What an excellent suggestion! Why not – since this is the perfect occasion – let our girl, Toute-la-nuit, be deflowered?'

A rather pretty girl was produced on the spot. She couldn't have been more than seven. I stood there in amazement as everyone around me applauded the idea and egged on the marriage. I insisted that Giton was a very modest boy and not up to this kind of kinkiness; nor was the girl of an age to take on the woman's role.

Quartilla objected: 'Is she any younger than I was when I had my first man? May Juno desert me if I can even remember when I was a virgin! Even when I was little, I was very naughty with my playmates. Later I applied myself to older boys until I came of age. I guess that's where the old saying comes from: "Whoever's carried a calf can bear a bull."' [1]

For fear that something still worse might happen to dear

[25.1] Cf. Quintilian 1.9.5 on the training of Milo the wrestler. In Petronius this training is mockingly sexualized and transferred to a girl from a strongman.

Giton in my absence, I rose to play my part in the marriage
ceremony.

26. Psyche had already dressed the girl in a flame-colored
wedding veil. Appetizer led the procession with a torch;
drunken women stood clapping in a line after decking the bridal
chamber with erotic hangings. These bawdy antics aroused
Quartilla who got up, grabbed Giton, and dragged him into
the bedroom.

To be sure, Giton was not exactly reluctant; nor, I must say,
was the poor girl frightened by the idea of her 'wedding night'.
Once they were ensconced in bed, we all perched on the
threshold of the bridal chamber. Quartilla was the first to put
an inquisitive eye to an all-too-well-placed crack in the door
and spy on their childish sport with all the concentration of a
true lecher. Eventually, she pulled me over to take a look.
Because we were cheek to cheek in front of the crack, whenever
the peeping proved dull, she would move her lips to the side
and pepper me with furtive kisses . . .

*

Spread on the bed, we spent the rest of the night without
fear . . .

*

The third day had already arrived,[1] and that meant the prospect of a free meal.[2] But we were so tattered and bruised we felt more like running away than resting. While we morosely pondered how to avoid the coming storm, one of Agamemnon's slaves interrupted us: 'What's wrong? Don't you know who your host is today? It's Trimalchio, a most elegant man ... He has a waterclock[3] in his dining room and a trumpeter on call to announce the time, so that he knows at any moment how much of life he's already lost.'[4]

We promptly forgot all our troubles, dressed up, and asked Giton, who so willingly played the servant's role, to accompany us to the baths ...

27. While we wandered the grounds in our evening clothes – or rather joked around and mingled with groups of guests playing games – we suddenly encountered a bald old man in a blood-red tunic playing ball with some long-haired boys. It was not so much the boys who caught our attention – although they were well worth it – as the paterfamilias himself. He stood there in his slippers playing intently with a leek-green ball. If the ball hit the ground, he didn't chase it, but had a slave with

[1] A gap in the manuscripts just before the Trimalchio episode means that we lack a context for these opening remarks in Chapter 26.

[2] *Liberae cenae*, a phrase also referring to a gladiator's or a prisoner's sometimes sumptuous last meal (Müller and Ehlers), and thus used metaphorically here. For more explicit statements of 'rogues' fatalism', see Chapters 99, 125.

[3] Compare the *horologium*, presumably a sundial, on Trimalchio's tomb (Chapter 71). Clocks were no more common than they were accurate (cf. Seneca, *Apocolocyntosis* 2.2).

[4] Falstaff makes a similarly uneasy game of time's passing in Shakespeare's *1 Henry 4* I.ii. Cf. also Schopenhauer's maxim ('On the Vanity of Existence', tr. Hollingdale): 'Every evening we are poorer by a day.'

a bag full of balls give the players a new one. We noticed some other novelties: there were two eunuchs stationed at different points in a circle; one was holding a silver chamber pot, the other was counting the balls – not those batted back and forth by the players, but only those that fell on the ground![1]

While we wondered at the extravagance of all this, Menelaus ran up and said, '*This* is the guy who's throwing the party! What you see is only the prelude to dinner.' As Menelaus spoke, Trimalchio snapped his fingers as a signal to the eunuch to hold out the chamber pot for him as he continued to play. After emptying his bladder, he called for water for his hands, sprinkled it lightly on his fingers and then wiped them dry on the head of a young slave . . .

28. There wasn't time to take it all in, so we entered the baths, and the minute we began to sweat moved on to the cold pool. Trimalchio was already drenched in perfume and being towelled down, not with linen, but with Greek comforters of the softest wool. Right in front of him three masseurs were guzzling a fine Falernian wine. When they proceeded to spill most of it in a scuffle, he blithely observed that this was 'a libation in his honor'.

He was then wrapped in a scarlet cloak and placed upon a litter. Four runners bristling with decorations pranced before him along with a little wagon on which his darling was riding – a boy past his prime, puffy eyed, and even uglier than his master. As Trimalchio was being carried out, a musician holding a tiny flute ran up to his side and – just as if he were whispering a secret in his ear – played for him the whole way!

Utterly astonished, we made our way to the door with Agamemnon. By the entrance we saw a notice posted:

[27.1] Trimalchio's game hasn't been identified (Smith, 55) but clearly the joke depends on his eccentric manner of keeping score: instead of counting the number of successful throws (or returns), Trimalchio has a slave count the number of balls dropped!

Smith presents this appearance of eunuchs as a gesture at 'regal magnificence'; rather similar imperial themes in Trimalchio's own antic recasting have been noted in Chapters 29–30, 47, 49, 53, 54, 60, 64, 77 and 78.

ANY SLAVE WHO LEAVES THE PREMISES
WITHOUT PERMISSION OF THE MASTER WILL RECEIVE
ONE HUNDRED LASHES

Just inside stood a doorman dressed entirely in green except for a cherry-red belt around his waist. He was shucking peas into a silver dish. Over the doorsill hung a golden cage from which a motley-colored magpie called salutations to the guests.

29. While I stared in stupefaction at all this, I almost fell over backwards and broke a leg. For just to the left of the entrance (not far from the porter's lodge), was the most enormous dog tethered by a chain – painted on the wall under some large block letters that said:

BEWARE OF DOG[1]

My companions laughed at my fright, but I pulled myself together to look at the rest of the wall.[2] It depicted a slave market complete with price tags. Trimalchio himself was in the picture; his hair is long and in his hand he grips the wand of Mercury. Minerva leads the way as our hero enters Rome. A painstaking artist had carefully portrayed the whole course of his career, complete with captions: how he first learned to keep the books and then was put in charge of the cash. In the last scene of the fresco Mercury lifts him by the chin up to a lofty dais. Fortuna is at his side carrying her burgeoning cornucopia, as the three Fates spin the golden threads.

I also noticed a team of runners in the nearby colonnade exercising with their trainer. In the corner stood an imposing cabinet: inside I saw a little shrine containing the household

29.1 Such illusionist dogs were a visual joke also found in rich villas in (for instance) Pompeii.

29.2 The large mural in an unsubtle way claims a near-epic status for its self-made hero's ascent. Compare the Trojan War mural so transporting *its* own central figure, Aeneas, in Vergil's *Aen.* 1.450 ff. In Trimalchio's mural, Mercury, god of trade, and Minerva, the goddess of craft, co-preside with the Fates and the goddess Fortuna over this ex-slave's startling success-story. Only funerary art from antiquity is known to feature such autobiographical narrative; see J. Bodel, 'Trimalchio's Underworld', *In Search of the Ancient Novel*, ed. J. Tatum (Baltimore, 1993) 242.

gods sculpted in silver, a marble statuette of Venus, and a none-too-small golden casket, which, they said, preserved the master's first beard[3] ...

I started to ask the steward what they had painted in the atrium. 'The *Iliad* and the *Odyssey*, he said, 'and the gladiator show put on by Laenas.' It was too much to contemplate ...

30. We had already reached the dining room. In the entryway a bookkeeper was poring over the accounts. But what caught my eye were the rods and axes fixed on the doorposts. They were mounted on top of what looked like the bronze prow of a ship that bore the inscription:

PRESENTED TO C. POMPEIUS TRIMALCHIO
PRIEST OF THE COLLEGE OF AUGUSTUS[1]
BY CINNAMUS THE STEWARD

Beneath this inscription was a double lamp suspended from the ceiling and two wooden tablets, one on each doorpost. I seem to remember that one of them read:

OUR GAIUS IS DINING OUT
ON THE 30TH AND 31ST OF DECEMBER[2]

29.3 The first beard was often preserved as a solemn memento, but there may be a more personal reference in these lines, to the gold box in which Nero kept *his* first beard (Suetonius, *Nero* 12.4).

30.1 The six members (*seviri*) of municipal cults of the deified Augustus were fairly minor ceremonial dignitaries, not infrequently freedmen (cf. Bodel, 248 in Tatum); nonetheless the *seviri* did have a qualified second-hand claim while in office to the first of the symbols of power mentioned here, rods and axes, the *fasces* of rule. The bronze prow takes the *seviri*'s claim comically over the edge, though it may hint in one sense at shipping successes as well as (in this case pretended) naval victories.

30.2 Trimalchio's *praenomen*, 'Gaius', is obtrusively used as a mark of his new freedman status (see Chapter 74 and Smith, 62, n. 3). This unseasonable public memorandum (for it is not actually December *or* the Saturnalia unless the speaker errs here in Chapter 58) may be meant to suggest that Trimalchio has no compelling incentive for dining away except (puzzlingly) these two last days of the year. Given the topsy-turvy holiday-logic that characterizes Saturnalian revels in other respects, there may also be here some suggestion that Trimalchio gives others their turn at playing carnival-host for just two nights a year, keeping that role himself for the rest (cf. Chapters 45, 70). The other placard sketched here is Trimalchio's astrological calendar, one of many reminders of Trimalchio's pronounced superstitiousness. For the Saturnalia, see Chapters 44, n.1 and 47, n.1.

On the other were painted the phases of the moon and images of the seven planets, and lucky and unlucky days were marked with studs of different colors.

When we had had enough of these diversions and were ready to enter the dining room, a slave – evidently assigned this job – shouted, 'Right foot first!' We were momentarily taken aback, for fear one of us should commit some faux pas as he entered the room. But just as we moved our right feet forward in unison, a slave stripped for flogging threw himself at our feet and begged us to save him! He was only guilty of a minor offense, it seemed: the bookkeeper's clothes had been stolen from him at the baths. They were only worth a pittance. We drew back our right feet and begged a pardon from the bookkeeper as he sat there counting gold pieces in the hallway. He looked up like royalty and said, 'It is not the financial loss that irks me, but the sheer negligence of this worthless slave! He lost *my* dress clothes, a birthday present from a client, dyed of course in the finest Tyrian purple. Admittedly they had been washed once.[3] Well, what can I say? You can have him!'

31. Grateful for the bookkeeper's munificence, we now entered the dining room. Then the slave we had just saved ran up and, before we knew what had hit us, smothered us in kisses and thanked us effusively for our kindness. 'Listen,' he whispered, 'you'll see in a minute who it is you've befriended: the master's wine, courtesy of your waiter!'

At last we took our places. Some Alexandrian slave-boys poured melted snow over our hands, while others tended our feet, meticulously paring our hangnails. Not even this distasteful task was done in silence: they kept singing as they worked. I wanted to find out whether the entire household sang, so I ordered a drink. A most attentive slave promptly responded in a grating soprano. In fact, every request was answered in song. You would have thought you were in a

---

30.3 Even Trimalchio's slaves boast luxurious Tyrian purple; spurning once-laundered clothes was another affectation of Nero (Suetonius, *Nero* 30).

pantomime, not a formal dining room.[1] Nonetheless, they served great antipasto. Everyone was now in their place except for Trimalchio, who, following the current fashion, had reserved the most prominent seat for himself.[2]

On the hors d'oeuvres tray stood a donkey of Corinthian bronze bearing saddlebags stuffed with olives, white in one side, black in the other. Two platters flanked the animal; their weight in silver and Trimalchio's name were engraved along their edges. Little bridges welded to the plate supported dormice sprinkled with honey and poppyseeds. There were even sausages sizzling on a silver gridiron, which arched over some Syrian plums and pomegranate seeds.

32. We were in the midst of these delicacies when Trimalchio was carried in to a fanfare of trumpets and placed amid a veritable fortress of cushions – a sight that elicited some indiscreet laughter from the guests. For his shaven head poked out of a scarlet shawl, and round his muffled neck he had tucked a napkin bearing a stripe of senatorial purple and a fringe of tassels that dangled here and there. On the smallest finger of his left hand he wore a huge gilded ring. On the very last joint of the next finger he wore a smaller ring that appeared to be pure gold, but actually was studded with little iron stars.[1] But

---

[31.1] The *pantomimus* was an interpretive dancer who silently mimed a myth to the accompaniment of a chorus and instrumental music. The pantomime became one of the most popular forms of entertainment in the empire, much to the consternation of moralists. (For a defense, see Lucian, *On the Dance*.) Petronius' contemporary Lucan is said to have written libretti for pantomimes. Operatic effects of this sort emphasize the rehearsed and performative character of Trimalchio's lavishness, as well as the sensuous heightening favored by both Petronius and Trimalchio (cf. *Carm.* 44).

[31.2] For the seating arrangements see the detailed account in Smith's notes p. 66, with a picture of three sets of three couches facing three sides of a large central table, the fourth side being left open for servers. According to Smith, counter-clockwise from left, the nine couches are taken respectively by Trimalchio, Agamemnon, Hermeros, Encolpius, Ascyltus, Habinnas, Scintilla and Fortunata, Proculus, and Diogenes.

[32.1] The purple napkin Trimalchio flaunts falsely signals senatorial status, and his rings of near-gold verge on claiming equestrian status as well. While Trimalchio's shaven head is especially appropriate to his status as a freedman (cf. here Chapter 103 and n.1), it also suggests his role as a *stupidus*, the mime-comedian. According to J. J. Winkler, *Auctor & Actor: A Narratological Reading*

his display of wealth didn't stop there; he exposed his right biceps, which was adorned with a golden armlet and a bangle of ivory fastened by a bright metal clasp.

33. After picking his teeth with a silver toothpick, he began: 'Friends, I really wasn't in the mood to come to dinner yet; but rather than keep you waiting, I have denied myself every pleasure. At least allow me to finish my game.'

A slave followed with a board of terebinth and a pair of crystal dice. Then I noticed the most extravagant touch yet: instead of the usual white and black counting-stones, he had substituted coins of gold and silver. While he chattered away over his game and we tasted the hors d'oeuvres, a tray was served with a basket on it. There sat a wooden hen with her wings spread out in a circle, just as they do when they're hatching eggs. Two slaves immediately came up and, as the music blared on, began to search through the straw. Peahens' eggs were found and promptly distributed to the guests.

Trimalchio looked over at this scene and said, 'Friends, I had peahens' eggs placed under the chicken. But to tell the truth, I'm afraid they may have already been fertilized! Let's try them and see if they can still be sucked.'

We picked up our spoons – weighing no less than half a pound each – and poked at the eggs, which were encased in fine pastry. I was about to throw mine away, because it already seemed to have a chick inside it. Then I overheard a more experienced guest remark, 'I'll bet there's something good in here!' So I pushed my finger through the shell and found the fattest little fig-pecker marinated in peppered egg yolk.

34. Since his game was now interrupted, Trimalchio had ordered all the same dishes for himself and announced in a loud voice that whoever wanted a second glass of aperitif could have one. Then, suddenly, a musical cue was given and all at

of Apuleius' 'Golden Ass' (Berkeley, 1985), 226, mime-comedians were the second easily recognized class of shaved persons besides priests of Isis; he goes on to cite Arnobius, 7.33, on what pagans enjoyed most in mimes: 'They love the morons with their shaved heads, the resonant sound of heads being boxed, the applause, the shameful jokes and gestures, the huge red phalluses.'

once our hors d'oeuvres were whisked away by a chorus of
singing slaves. Amid all the commotion one of the dishes was
accidentally dropped and a slave retrieved it from the floor.
Trimalchio noticed this, had the servant's ears boxed, and
ordered him to throw the dish back on the floor. A house slave
appeared and began to sweep up the silverware along with the
rest of the mess. Then two long-haired Ethiopians came in
holding little wineskins – like those used to dampen the sand
at the amphitheatre – and they poured wine over our hands.
No one even offered water.

When complimented on his elegant service, Trimalchio
replied, 'Mars loves a level playing field.¹ So I've had each guest
assigned his own table. And that way the bustle of these smelly
slaves won't bother us so.'

Carefully sealed wine bottles were promptly served; attached
to their necks were labels:

FALERNIAN WINE
BOTTLED IN THE CONSULSHIP OF OPIMIUS
ONE HUNDRED YEARS OLD²

While we were studying the labels, Trimalchio clapped his
hands together and cried, 'How sad! Even a bottle of wine
outlives a mere man. So, let's wet our whistles, friends. Wine
is life – and *this* wine's real Opimian! I didn't serve anything
this good yesterday, and the guests were much classier.'

We were drinking the wine and thoroughly relishing all the
luxuries of the feast when a slave brought in a silver skeleton
so loosely jointed that its limbs swivelled in every direction.
He promptly threw it down on the table several times. Each
time its floppy limbs fell in a different pattern. Trimalchio
responded in verse:

34.1 War or strife no respecter of persons: see Homer *Il.* 18.309.
34.2 A distinctly suspicious label, since Opimius was consul in 121 BC, and the
label at best would have held true for only one year somewhere back in the reign
of Augustus. This would be like serving a wine labeled 'Bottled in the Jacksonian
Era: One Hundred Years Old.' Falernian wine, a fine wine from a region near
Naples, would not bear such long keeping in any case.

'Alas! Poor us! We all add up to squat;
once Hades gets his hooks in, that's the lot;
so live while it's your turn, 'cause then it's not.'[3]

35. Our applause was followed by a dish that was disappointingly small, but so odd it had everyone staring at it. On a round serving tray the twelve signs of the zodiac were arranged in a circle. Over each sign the specialty chef had placed the kind of food that fit its character: over Aries the ram, a ramifying pea; on Taurus the bull, a slice of rump roast; over Gemini the twins, testicles and kidneys; on the Crab, a crown of flowers; over the Lion, a virile African fig; on Virgo, the womb of a barren sow; over Libra, a set of scales with a cheesetart on one side, balanced by a pancake on the other; on Scorpio, [the scorpion fish]; on Sagittarius, a seahorse; on Capricorn, a lobster; on Aquarius, a goose; on Pisces, a pair of snapper. In the middle of all this was a piece of turf, torn out roots and all, with a honeycomb sitting on it. An Egyptian slave boy was bringing bread around in a silver chafing dish ... while the master himself belted out a tune from the mime, *The North African Quack*, in a hideous voice.

36. We were looking gloomily at this vile fare when Trimalchio piped up, 'Please let's eat! This is just the preamble to our dinner!'

As he spoke, four male dancers bounced up in time to the music and snatched the lid off the next dish. Inside we saw some fowl and sows' udders and a hare adorned with wings to look like Pegasus. At the corners of the dish we noticed four little statues of Marsyas the satyr; from their wineskins a pepper sauce poured over fish that looked as if they were swimming in a little canal. We all joined in the applause started by the slaves, and, grinning broadly, proceeded to attack the choicest items.

[34.3] There is a crude hedonist pun in Trimalchio's last clause, *dum licet esse bene*, lit., 'while we are free to be (or eat) well'. The combination of two hexameters with an elegiac pentameter here and in 55 smacks of metrical muddle on Trimalchio's part: standard elegiac couplets comprise one hexameter line followed by a pentameter.

And Trimalchio, no less amused by such tricks, called out,
'Carver!' A butcher instantly appeared and, waving his arms
to the beat of the music, sliced up the meat. You would have
thought of a charioteer fighting to the sound of a water organ.
Trimalchio kept egging him on, muttering under his breath,
'Carv-er! Carv-er!' Suspecting that some joke was being played,
I wasn't embarrassed to ask the man next to me what he
thought. An old hand at these games, he said, 'You see that
guy who's carving the fish up? His name is "Carver". So every
time Trimalchio says the word "carver," he's both calling his
name and giving him orders!'

37. I couldn't eat another bite. So I turned to my table companion to find out as much as I could. I started to pump him
for stories, and began by asking who that woman was bustling
up and down the dining room.

'Trimalchio's wife,' he said. 'Her name's Fortunata, and she
counts her money by the ton![1] And what was she the day before
yesterday? Well, if I may be frank, you wouldn't have touched
bread from her hand. But now – god knows how or why –
she's in hog heaven and Trimalchio revolves around her. Listen,
if she said day was night, he'd believe it. Trimalchio himself is
so filthy rich he doesn't even know what he owns. But this
bitch knows it all in advance, gets there first every time. She's
a dry one, sober and savvy – you see all the gold, don't you?
But she has a vicious tongue – a real household hellcat. If she
likes you, she likes you; if she doesn't, well, she doesn't. And
Trimalchio? His estates run as far as the crow flies – money
makes money! He has more silver lying around his porter's
lodge than other guys have in their entire fortunes. And slaves?
Holy shit, I don't think even one in ten knows who owns him.
Listen, he could buy and sell one of these young hot shots here
without even noticing it.

38. 'Not that he buys anything. Everything is home grown:

[1] Fortunata seems as good at retaining as her spouse at spending, and what
better name might be devised for the frugal keeper-consort of an omen-struck
man like Trimalchio? See Glossary of Important Names, p. 170.

wool, lemons, pepper – you name it. You want hen's milk? You
got it. For example, his wool wasn't good enough for him. He
bought some rams from south Italy and turned them loose on
his flock. He wanted home-grown Attic honey, so he had some
bees brought over from Athens; that way even the native bees
get better. Why, just the other day he placed an order for
mushroom spores – from India! He won't even own a mule
unless it was sired by a wild ass! See all these cushions? – even
the stuffing is dyed purple or scarlet! Now that's what I call
happy!

'But don't look down your nose at these other ex-slaves
here. They're loaded. You see that guy at the end of the last
table? He's got eight hundred grand. He started with nothing.
In fact, he used to schlep wood around on his back. Anyway,
they say – I don't know, what I *heard* was – that he snatched
the cap off a gnome and found his treasure! I don't begrudge
anyone a godsend. But now that he's been slapped into
freedom, he wants a good time. He put a sign on his old
place saying:

> GARRET OF C. POMPEIUS DIOGENES
> AVAILABLE TO LET FROM THE FIRST OF JULY:
> HE OWNS HIS OWN HOUSE NOW

For that matter the guy in the freedman's seat there had it laid
in the shade – not that I blame him. He had his hands on a
million and dropped the ball. Now I don't think he owns his
own hair! It's not his fault, god knows. You'll never meet a
nicer guy. Some damned freedmen made a killing at his expense.
You know how it goes: you have partners, so your pot never
boils, and when the business craters out, your friends vanish.
What a righteous business he had, and look at him now! He
was an undertaker.

'He used to eat like a king too – boars roasted whole, fancy
pastry, poultry – his own cooks and bakers. He spilled more
wine on his floor than other guys keep in their cellars. A legend
in his own mind. When his business went bust and he was
afraid his creditors would catch on to the mess he was in, he
put up an auction notice like this:

FOR SALE:
SOME UNNEEDED ASSETS,
CONTACT C. IULIUS PROCULUS

39. Trimalchio interrupted his charming story; for the second
course had now been removed, and the guests were buoyed up
by the wine and engrossed in conversation. Leaning on his
elbow, our host began, 'I hope you're doing justice to this wine.
Fish gotta swim! Tell me, did you really think I'd be satisfied
with those signs of the zodiac you saw served on that covered
serving-dish? 'Is that the Ulysses you know?'[1] What's that? You
mustn't forget your classics, even at dinner! May the bones of
my old master rest in peace; he wanted me to be a man among
men. So nobody can teach me anything new; the clear proof is
this *fête accomplie*.

Heaven here, where the twelve gods dwell, turns into the
same number of signs. First, there is Aries, the Ram. Whoever
is born under the Ram has many flocks, lots of wool, a shameless mug, a hard head, and a horny noggin. Under this sign are
born many scholars and other boneheads.'

We commended our astrologer's wit, and so he continued:
'Then the whole sky changes into Taurus, the Bull. So bull-
headed types are born, and cattlemen, and people who look
out for number one. Now under Gemini pairs are born, horses
and oxen, ballsy fellows, and people who like it both ways. I
was born under Cancer. So I have many legs to stand on, and
I have many possessions on land and sea. Either way fits a
crab! That's why I didn't put anything on top of the crab – so
I wouldn't weigh down my sign! Under the Lion piggy eaters
and bossy people are born. Under Virgo come sissies, runaway
slaves, and candidates for a chain gang. Under the Scales come
butchers, perfumers, and whoever weighs things up for a living.
Under Scorpio, you get poisoners and assassins. Under Sagittarius are the shifty-eyed types who squint at the vegetables
and pocket the bacon. Under Capricorn are people in trouble
who worry so much they sprout little horns. Under Aquarius,
the Water-Bearer, come bartenders and people with water on

[1] Vergil, *Aen.* 2.44.

the brain. Under Pisces are fishmongers and rhetoricians.

'So the whole world whirls around just like a millstone, and it's always up to no good, what with people getting born or dying. And that dirt clod you saw in the middle – with the honeycomb on top? That was no accident. Everything I do has a reason: mother earth is in the middle of all, round as an egg, and she has all good things inside her, like a honeycomb.'

40. 'Brilliant!' we cry in a single voice, and with our hands raised toward the ceiling, we swear that the great astronomers Hipparchus and Aratus[1] were nothing compared to him. Meanwhile servants came in and in front of our couches spread out embroidered coverlets depicting men with nets and spears poised in their hands, and the whole drama of the hunt. We still didn't know what to expect when we heard an awful racket in the next room, and lo and behold, a pack of Spartan hunting dogs started to charge around our table! They were followed by a serving tray carrying a wild boar of the most enormous proportions with a little cap of freedom perched on its head. From its tusks dangled baskets woven from palm leaves – one full of fresh Syrian dates, the other of dried Egyptian dates. Little piglets made of cake were placed around the boar as if they were hanging on its teats, so we would think we had a sow before us.[2] These were actually gifts to take home.

The boar was not carved by the inimitable Carver – who had massacred the fowl – but by a huge bearded man decked out in leggings and a fancy striped hunting jacket. He proceeded to draw a hunting knife and plunge it into the boar's side as if his life depended on it; out of the gash he made exploded a covey of quail. Fowlers were ready with their reeds and quickly caught the birds as they flew about the dining room. Trimalchio gave orders that everyone should be served his own bird and then remarked facetiously, 'Would you take a look at the acorns that boar's been dining on in the forest!' Two young slaves

[1] Both renowned Greek astronomers of the second and third centuries BC.

[2] Pork served up with a twist, like so many of Trimalchio's specialties, not to mention Petronius' own. It seems this is a male boar tricked out as a sow giving suck; for as Smith notes, despite its supposed brood of piglets, Encolpius and partner continue to speak of the porker as a male.

instantly stepped up to the baskets hanging from the boar's
tusks and distributed the Theban and Syrian dates equally
among the guests.

41. Meanwhile I was wondering to myself why on earth that
boar had come in with a freedom cap on its head. After
imagining all kinds of nonsense, I ventured to tell my 'guide'
what was puzzling me. He replied, 'Even your humble servant
could figure that one out. It's no puzzle – it's plain as day. The
boar was ordered for the main course yesterday, but the guests
chose to let it go, so it comes back to the banquet today just
like a "freedman"!' I cursed my stupidity and asked no more
questions: I didn't want them to think I'd never dined in good
company!

While we were talking, a beautiful boy wearing a wreath of
vine leaves and ivy brought around a little basket of grapes
and pretended to be Dionysus in his various guises: first, he
was Bromius the Roarer, then Lyaeus the Liberator, and Euhius
the Reveler. He also served up his master's lyrics in a piercing
soprano. Trimalchio turned around at the sound and said,
'Dionysus, be Liberated.' The boy promptly took the cap of
freedom off the boar's head and put it on his own. Then
Trimalchio quipped, 'You can't deny that I have a Free Father!'[1]
We applauded Trimalchio's bon mot and gave the boy a wet
kiss when he came by.

After this course Trimalchio got up to go to the toilet.
Free of our imperious host we began to incite the guests to
conversation. Dama was the first to talk after calling for
another round of wine: 'A day's nothin'. Before ya can turn
around it's night. So nothin's better than goin' straight from
bed to dinner. An' it's been downright frigid lately. A bath
hardly thaws me out. But a hot drink's as good as a warm coat!
I've been drinking by the jug, and I'm sloshed. The wine's gone
right to my brain.'

42. Seleucus then joined in the conversation: 'Now, I don't take

---

[41.1] Trimalchio puns here on the standard Latin title for the god Dionysus,
Liber Pater or 'Free Father,' to claim facetiously that his own father was free –
an impossibility for a freedman.

a bath everyday, the water's got a bite to it and melts your insides – it's like gettin' launder'd everyday! But when I've just downed a jug of spiced wine, I tell Mr Cold to "fuck off, please." Couldn't even take a bath anyway – had to go to a funeral today. A swell guy, good old Chrysanthus has blown his last bubble. I ran into him just the other day, ya know. I can almost see myself talking to him ... Goddamn pitiful, ain't it? We're just walking windbags. Worse'n flies; even flies got somethin' to 'em, but we're not worth a goddamn bubble!

'And what if Chrysanthus hadn't tried that strict starvation diet? Not a crumb of bread or drop of water touched his lips for five days! Now he's joined the silent majority. His doctors killed him – no, it was just plain bad luck. The doctors are just there to cheer us up on the way out. Anyway, it was a nice funeral – first-rate casket, nice lining and all. And what a loud crowd of mourners – except for his wife (he'd obviously freed some slaves to swell the crowd). And what if he wasn't the greatest husband in the world? Women and vultures: the same animal, ain't it? Don't do a woman no favors. Might as well chuck it down a well. Yeah, an old love is an old sore.'

43. This guy was getting to be a bore. Phileros interjected loudly, 'Let us remember the living! Your friend has balanced his books: he lived a decent life and died the same way. What's there to complain about? He started with a nickel in his pocket and was always ready to pluck a dime out of the dung with his teeth. So whatever he touched grew like a honeycomb. By god, I'll bet he left a hundred thousand "free and clear", all in hard cash. To tell the truth – since I've got a bit of the Cynic in me – he had a big mouth and a vicious tongue – a walking quarrel, not a man. His brother, on the other hand, was brave, loyal, open-handed and hospitable. But Chrysanthus got started on the wrong foot, until his first vintage set him right. He could name his price for that wine.[1] What kept his head above water was that he came into an inheritance – and stole more than

---

43.1 Either the speaker here is being ungrammatical in Latin, which would be consistent with his freedman status, or the Latin means simply that Chrysanthus sold as much wine as he wanted to.

was left him. Then, the jerk left the money to some nobody
because he was mad at his own brother! Whoever runs out on
his family has to run a long way. Then he trusted those slaves
who ruined him. Businessmen can't afford to be gullible. But
he enjoyed what he had while he had it ... You only get what's
given, not what you aim for. He was a lucky dog; lead turned
to gold in his hands. It's easy when everything runs along, fair
and square. How old do you think he was? Over seventy.
He was hard as nails, carried his age well, and his hair was
black as a crow. I knew the guy for years and years, and he
was still horny. By god, I don't think a dog was safe in his house!
What's more, he still went in for boys too – a real jack-
of-all-trades. Not that I blame him – that's all he took with
him.'

44. This was Phileros, and Ganymede followed: 'What on earth
are you goin' on about? Don't you care how the price of corn
is pinching us? Goddamn it, I couldn't even find a bite of bread
this morning! And how this drought drags on. We've already
been starvin' a whole year. Damn those bureaucrats! They're
makin' deals with the bakers: "You scratch my back and I'll
scratch yours." So the little guy slaves away and the fat cats
live like every day's the Saturnalia.[1] If we only had some real
men around, like the kind I found here when I arrived from
Asia.

'Now those were the days ... they used to knock the holy
tar out of corrupt officials, put the fear of god in 'em. I still
remember Safinius. He used to live down by the old arch when
I was a boy. A hot pepper, not a man: Yeah, he used to singe
the ground with his feet. But he was honest, reliable, a loyal
friend – you could play how-many-fingers with him in the dark.
And how he used to lay into some of them on the town council –
he didn't beat around the bush, he attacked head-on. When he
was pleading a case in court, his voice boomed like a tuba. He

[44.1] The festival of Saturn, originally confined to one day only, December 17,
was expanded to a five-day holiday by Claudius (Dio. 60.25.8). It was associated
with all sorts of carnival license and playful role-reversal, especially between
masters and slaves. Horace invokes the *libertas Decembri* in *Sat.* 2.7.4 to introduce
a diatribe addressed to him by his slave.

didn't sweat or spit much either – I guess he was just blessed by the gods. He always had a friendly word for you, knew everybody's name, was just like one of us. So, food was cheap as dirt then. You could buy more bread for a penny than you and your buddy could choke down. I've seen bull's-eyes bigger than the loaves they sell now.

'Shit, it's getting worse every day. This town's got it all ass backwards. Why do we have this mayor who's not worth a fig? He'd sell us down the river for small change. He sits there at home, happy as a clam; pockets more money in a day than most of us have in the bank. (I happen to know where he got a grand in cash.) If we had any balls, we'd wipe that smile off his face. Nowadays, everyone's a lion at home, a fox on the street.

'Take me, I've already eaten my rags; if food prices stay up, I'll have to sell my little cottage. What's gonna happen to us if neither gods nor men take pity on this town? And I'll be damn'd if it's not all the gods' doin'. No one believes heaven is heaven these days. No one fasts. No one gives a fig for Jove. Instead, they bow their heads to count their profits. In the old days mothers used to climb the hill to pray for rain in long robes and bare feet with their hair down and their minds pure – and it poured buckets! It was now or never. And everyone used to come home looking like drowned rats. If the gods are angry, it's because we're not religious any more. Our fields just lie there—'

45. 'Hey!' blurted out Echion, the ragman, 'watch what you say – it's bad luck. If it ain't one thing, it's another – like the yokel said when he lost his spotted pig. What today isn't, tomorrow will be. And so it goes. By god, you couldn't name a better town than this, if we only had the men. Sure, times are hard – and not just here. We shouldn't be too pers-nickety though – we all live under the same sky. If you were anywhere else, you'd say the pigs walk around here already roasted!'[1]

[45.1] A stock feature of visions of festive abundance (cf. our own 'pie-in-the-sky'), and a strangely apt image for a scene of preposterous bounty like Trimalchio's.

'And listen, in a couple of days we're gonna have a swell fight at the festival, and not just an old troupe of gladiators either but lots of freedmen too. Our Titus has a big heart and likes to go whole hog. This will be the real thing, whatever he does: I'm one of his people, ya know, and he doesn't do anything halfway. He'll put on a great fight with no mercy: a regular butcher's shop right in the middle, where everybody can really see it. After all, he's got the dough; he came into a bundle when his old man died. Tough luck! He could spend half a million and not even miss it. And his name'll go down in history. He's already got some dwarfs, a woman charioteer and Glyco's steward – who was caught in the act of givin' the missus a good time. You'll see the crowd split – the jealous husbands versus the back-door men. Hell, Glyco's not worth a red penny and he's feedin' his own man to the bears! Guess who's been cuckolded? Now, whose fault's that? A slave's just followin' orders. Now that latrine of a wife ought to get the bull's horns! But whoever can't beat his donkey, slaughters his saddle. Why did Glyco think that weedy daughter of Hermogenes would ever be worth a damn? Hermogenes himself could steal the feathers off a bird in flight! You can't make a snake into rope. And Glyco? He's doin' in his own people! As long as he lives he'll be branded, till Orcus blots it out. But we all have to make our own mistakes.

'I can almost taste what Mammaea's gonna give us to eat – two bits apiece for me and mine. And if he does, he'll sure steal the show from Norbanus. Lemme tell ya, we're gonna win hands down. After all, what has Norbanus ever done for us? He put on some two-bit gladiators so decrepit they'd fall over if you blew on 'em. I've seen better bear-bait. He killed some horsemen that looked like lamp decorations – you'd have thought 'em a bunch of barnyard roosters! One looked like the stick you'd use to beat a mule, another had a club-foot and the third-stringer – who was crippled – looked already dead! There was one Thracian with some guts, but even he fought by the rules. Of course, they were all flogged afterwards. All they heard from the crowd was, "Let 'em have it!" What a bunch of cowards.

' "Still, I put on a show for you," says Norbanus. And for

that I give him a hand, which is more than he gave us. Add it up. One hand washes another.

46. 'Agamemnon, I'll bet you're thinkin': "What is this clown yammerin' on about?" You're the one who knows how to talk, but you ain't talkin'. You're not like us – you think the way us poor men talk is funny. We know you're just crazy about words, Mr Professor – so what? Can't I still get you to come down to my house someday and see my little place? We'll find something to eat – a chicken, some eggs. It'll be swell, even if the weather has dried up damn near everything! We'll find a way to get full.

'Ya know, my boy is already growin' into one of your pupils. He even knows his fractions! If he survives, you'll have a little slave at your side. His head's over that writing tablet every time he's got a chance. He's clever; there's something to him – even if he is half crazy over birds. I just killed his three finches and told him a weasel ate them. He's already discovered some other foolery: he likes to paint plenty. Still, he's got a toehold in Greek and is beginning to take to Latin, even if his teacher is a show-off and won't stick to the subject. He knows his stuff, just don't like to work. Now the boy's other tutor isn't exactly educated, but he's thorough – teaches more than he knows! He even keeps coming on holidays, and he's happy with whatever you give him!

'Now I've bought the boy some law books. I wanted him to get a taste of law for home use: there's bread in it. He's spoiled enough by literature. But if he doesn't take to it, I'm gonna teach him a trade, as a barber, or an auctioneer, or a lawyer at least – something they can't take away from ya till the day ya die. Every day I drum it into him: "Primigenius, believe me, whatever ya learn, ya learn for yourself. Ya see Phileros, the lawyer? If he hadn't studied, he'd be starvin'. It was just the other day when he used to lug a flea-market around on his back! Now he can even sue Norbanus!" Yessir, learnin's a treasure, and a trade never starves.'

47. The air was buzzing with talk like this when Trimalchio waltzed in, mopped his brow, washed his hands in some scented

water, and, after pausing a moment, said: 'My friends, forgive me, but my stomach has been unresponsive for many days. The doctors are lost. Nonetheless, a concoction of pomegranate rind mixed with pine sap boiled in vinegar has loosened things up a bit. I hope my stomach remembers its manners now; otherwise it's as noisy as a bull. And if anyone of you wants to relieve himself, there's nothing to be ashamed about. None of us was ever born solid inside. I don't think there's any greater torment than holding yourself in. This is the one thing Jove himself cannot deny us. Are you smiling, Fortunata, when your stomach keeps me awake all night?[1]

'I don't object to your doing anything here in the dining room if it makes you feel better. Even doctors forbid holding it in. And if more comes out than you expected, well, there are facilities just outside – water, chamber pots, and little sponges. Believe me, those vapors go right into your brain and upset the whole body. I personally know many, many men who've died because they wouldn't admit the truth to themselves.'

We complimented him on his enlightened attitude, and drowned our laughter in our glasses. We didn't know yet that we were only 'halfway up the hill', as the saying goes. The tables were cleared to the sound of music and three white pigs were led in wearing halters and little bells. The headwaiter said one was two years old, another three, and the third almost six. I thought some acrobats had arrived and the pigs would perform some amazing stunts, as they do in street shows. This expectation was dispelled when Trimalchio asked:

'Which one do you want for dinner right now? Any slob can turn out a roast chicken, some minestrone, or other trifles; my chefs are used to cooking up whole calves!'

He had a cook summoned immediately and, without waiting for us, ordered him to slaughter the oldest pig. Then in a loud

[47.1] Trimalchio's bathroom-talk here helps distinguish him as both a boor (cf. Theophrastus, *Characters*, on 'Offensiveness') and a carnival Lord of Misrule (cf. Seneca's *Apocolocyntosis* 8.2, on the emperor Claudius as a *Saturnalicius princeps*; on Saturnalian impertinence and Saturnalian festivities more generally, see Chapter 44, n.). In presenting his guests with a license to fart in this chapter (47) Trimalchio once more takes after the emperor Claudius (Suetonius, *Claudius* 32).

voice he said: 'Boy, which division are you in?'

When the cook replied that he was in 'the fortieth', Trimalchio asked, 'Were you bought, or were you born on my estates?'

'Neither,' said the cook, 'I was left to you in Pansa's will.'

'Better do a careful job,' replied Trimalchio, 'or I'll demote you to the messenger brigade!' The cook took the next course back to the kitchen, reminded of his master's power.

48. Trimalchio then gave us a friendly look and said, 'If you don't like the wine, I'll change it. It's up to you to do it justice. Thank god I don't buy it. Whatever makes your mouth water here is grown on some estate, which I haven't seen yet. It's supposed to be a spread in between Terracina and Tarentum.[1] What I want to do is to add Sicily to my little holdings; that way if I want to go to Africa, I won't have to leave my own property!

'Now tell me, Agamemnon, what theme did you speak on today?[2] Even if I don't plead in court myself, I did learn to read and write for home use. I'm no anti-intellectual. I own two libraries: one in Greek and one in Latin. So tell me, please, what was the theme of your speech?'

When Agamemnon had begun, 'A poor and rich man were enemies—' Trimalchio retorted, 'A poor man? What's that?' 'Clever!' replied Agamemnon, as he proceeded to explain some hypothetical case. Again, Trimalchio shot back a response, 'If this happened, it isn't hypothetical; if it didn't happen, it's nothing!'

We accorded these and other responses the most extravagant praise.

'My dear Agamemnon,' said Trimalchio, 'what do you know of the twelve labors of Hercules or the story of Ulysses and

---

[1] Approximately 150 miles apart, and therefore quite a spread!

[2] On such practice-orations with fictitious themes, often verging on those of a far-fetched romance, see especially Chapter 2, n. 3 above, and the Introduction, xxiv–xxv.

how the Cyclops got his thumb pinched in the tongs?[3] As a
boy, I used to read these stories in Homer. Yes, and at Cumae
I saw the Sibyl with my own eyes hanging there in a bottle,
and when some little boys asked her in Greek, "Sibyl, what do
you want?" she replied, "I want to die!" '[4]

49. Trimalchio was still chattering on like this when our table
was covered by a tray with a huge pig on it. We were astonished
by how speedily it had been prepared and swore you couldn't
cook a run-of-the-mill rooster that fast, especially since the pig
seemed much bigger than the boar that had been served a bit
earlier.[1] Then, looking intently at the pig, Trimalchio exclaimed, 'What is this? Has this pig been gutted? No, it hasn't, by
god! Get that cook in here now!'

A contrite looking cook appeared in front of our table and
admitted that he'd forgotten to gut the pig. 'What? Forgotten!'
shouted Trimalchio. 'You'd think he'd forgotten to add the salt
and pepper, the way he says it; off with his shirt!' In no time
the poor man was stripped and flanked by two executioners.[2]
Everyone tried to get him off the hook saying: 'This happens
all the time. Please, let him go. If it happens again, no one will
speak up for him.'

Given my natural severity I couldn't resist turning to Agamemnon and whispering in his ear: 'This slave must be a perfect
idiot: how could anyone forget to gut a pig? God knows, I
wouldn't forgive him if he'd forgotten to clean a fish!'

Not so Trimalchio: his face relaxed into an hilarious grin as

---

[48.3] Scrambled cultural literacy, Trimalchio-style (cf. Chapters 50–2, 59, and
the opening of Walter Sellars' *1066 and All That* [London, 1931], on the modern
vulgarian equivalent: 'History is not what happened; it is what you can
remember.') The Cumaean sibyl is presumably Trimalchio's close-to-home answer
to Odysseus' own dealings with numinous beings; the Bay of Naples' Cumae was
traditionally the point where, with help from a Sibyl, Aeneas descended to the
underworld.

[48.4] Both the question and answer are given in Greek, the sole Greek sentences
in the *Satyrica*. (Cf. Chapter 58, n.3 and *monoknemon*, Chapter 83.)

[49.1] A so-called 'Trojan pig,' because served as if pregnant with other beasts
sealed up inside (Macrobius, *Saturnalia* 3.13.13); thus, as Smith notes, *not* a
novel idea to sophisticates.

[49.2] Another quasi-imperial touch – Trimalchio has his own executioners.

he said, 'O.K., since you've got such a bad memory, gut him right here in front of us.' The cook donned his tunic, again, grabbed his butcher knife, and sliced the pig's belly every which way with a quivering hand. The slits immediately gave way to the pressure from inside and roasted sausages and giblets gushed out of the wounds!

50. The slaves broke into applause for the trick and cheered in unison, 'Bravo Gaius!' The cook was honored with a drink and silver crown, and also received a drinking bowl served on a plate of Corinthian bronze. As Agamemnon eyed the plate rather closely, Trimalchio observed: 'I alone own genuine Corinthian.' I was waiting for him to boast as usual that his vases were imported directly from Corinth, but he did better than that: 'Perhaps you're wondering why I am unique in owning Corinthian plates? Because, of course, the dealer I buy it from is named "Corinthus". How could it be Corinthian unless you get it from Corinthus? I'm no ignoramus, ya know; I know very well how Corinthian bronze originated. When Troy was sacked, Hannibal – a clever fellow and a real snake in the grass – piled all the bronze, gold and silver statues into a single heap and set them on fire; They melted into a single bronze alloy. From this amalgam craftsmen made little bowls, side dishes, and statuettes. Thus was Corinthian bronze born – neither this nor that, but one from all. If you don't mind my saying so, I actually prefer glass – it doesn't smell. If it didn't break, I'd prefer it to gold; as it is, the price is right.

51. 'But there once was a craftsman who made an unbreakable glass bowl.[1] When he was given an audience with the emperor to present his invention ... he had Caesar hand it back and then tossed it on the pavement.[2] The emperor couldn't have been more alarmed! But this fellow picked the bowl up off the floor – it was dented like a bronze vase – pulled a hammer from his pocket, and smoothed it out very nicely. He thought

[51.1] In Pliny the Elder, *N. H.* 36.195, the same story is placed in the reign of Tiberius.
[51.2] The text here is uncertain (see Smith, 136–7, n. 2).

he had Jupiter by the balls then, especially when the emperor asked, "Does anyone else know how to make glass like this?"

'But look what happened: he said "no" and the emperor had him beheaded! And no wonder! If an idea like that got out, our gold wouldn't be worth potter's clay!'

52. Of course, silver is my favorite. I have some enormous wine cups ... showing how Cassandra killed her sons. The way the dead boys lie there – you'd think they were alive![1] I have a sacrificial bowl, which King Minos left my patron, that shows Daedalus shutting Niobe up in the Trojan horse. I even have the fights of the gladiators Hermeros and Petraites[2] on my drinking cups – and, boy, are they heavy. You just can't put a price on that kind of thing.'

As he was talking, a slave dropped a drinking cup. Trimalchio glared at him and said, 'Quickly, off with your head, since you're good-for-nothing.' Instantly, the boy's face fell and he begged Trimalchio's pardon. 'Why do you ask me, as if I were your problem? I suggest you beg yourself not to be a good-for-nothing.' Finally, we prevailed on him to pardon the boy. As soon as he was off the hook, he danced about the table ...

'Water for the outside, wine for the insides,' shouted Trimalchio, and we laughed approvingly at his jest, especially Agamemnon, who certainly knew how to get invited back to dinner. Feeling appreciated, Trimalchio drank happily and, when he was virtually drunk, said, 'Won't any of you ask my Fortunata to dance? Believe me, no one does the bump and grind better!'[3]

He then held his hands up in front of his forehead and impersonated the actor Syrus,[4] while the whole household

---

[1] A joke mocking naive notions of artistic realism; cf. the joke mocking the taste for illusionistic art – and the naivety of our narrator? – in Chapter 29. Cf. also Nero's Homeric drinking cups (Suetonius, *Nero*, 47) and Pliny the Elder, *N. H.* 35.66.

[2] Evidently two gladiators famous in the mid-first century AD (Smith, 139–40, n. 3). For the guest also named Hermeros, see Chapters 37–8, 57–8 and the Glossary of Important Names.

[3] The dance specified here, i.e., the *cordax*, was long associated with Old Comedy and its exuberant obscenity.

[4] Otherwise unknown.

chanted, 'Do it! Do it!' He would have taken the floor, if Fortunata hadn't whispered something in his ear. I imagine she told him that such clownery didn't become him. But nothing was so unpredictable: one moment he would cower before Fortunata, and the next, revert to his natural self.

53. The impulse to dance was checked by a clerk who read aloud as if from a government document:[1]

'July 26th: on the estate at Cumae, which belongs to Trimalchio, there were born thirty male slaves, forty females; 500,000 pecks of wheat were transferred from the threshing floor to the barn; 500 oxen were broken in.

'On the same day, the slave Mithridates was crucified for speaking disrespectfully of the guardian spirit of our Gaius.'

'On the same day, 10,000,000 in coin that could not be invested was returned to the strong-box.

'On the same day, there was a fire in the gardens at Pompeii that started in the house of Nasta the caretaker.

'What's that? When did I buy gardens in Pompeii?' asked Trimalchio.

'Last year,' said the clerk. 'So they are not yet on the books.'

Trimalchio was incensed: 'I forbid any property bought for me to be entered on the books unless I know of it within six months!'

Even the police reports were being read and the wills of some game-keepers, in which Trimalchio was disinherited in a codicil. The names of some caretakers followed and a divorce was announced – of a night watchman from a freedwoman: she had been caught *in flagrante* with a bath attendant. A porter had been exiled to Baiae;[2] a steward was being prosecuted; and a law suit between some valets had been decided.

But finally, the acrobats arrived: some big lug stood there with a ladder and had a boy jump from rung to rung and dance

53.1 Another quasi-imperial touch. Note the summary treatment of one slave insulting Trimalchio, the implied presence of a personal court and enforcers, and the casual acceptance of an honorable mention with no legacy (Chapter 53.9; emperors generally thought it *their* due to be named in a rich person's will, as in Chapter 76).

53.2 A luxury resort on the Bay of Naples, i.e., not an arduous exile.

a jig at the top. Then he made the boy jump through burning hoops, and pick up a large wine bottle with his teeth! All this impressed Trimalchio alone, who kept saying, 'the arts are unappreciated.' But the two things he most enjoyed watching in all the world were acrobats and trumpeters; the other shows he thought were 'lightweight'. 'I even bought a troupe of professional actors,' he said, 'but I had them do Atellan farces and told my chorister to sing in Latin.'[3]

54. Just as he was speaking, the acrobat ... slipped and fell smack into our Trimalchio.[1] The guests cried out as did the slaves, not on account of this pathetic creature whose neck they would happily have seen broken, but because it would spoil the dinner to end with a lament over a perfect stranger. Trimalchio himself groaned aloud and bent over his arm as if he'd been wounded. Doctors ran up, and leading the way was Fortunata with her hair down and a goblet in hand crying out what a poor, unhappy creature she was. The boy who had fallen was already crawling around our feet begging for mercy. What was worse, as far as I was concerned, was that these pleadings might be the set-up for some kind of joke: I still remembered the cook who'd forgotten to gut the pig. So I was looking all over the dining room to see what kind of jack-in-the-box was about to spring out at us, especially after a slave was beaten for dressing Trimalchio's bruised arm in white instead of purple wool! My suspicion wasn't misplaced: instead of punishing the acrobat, Trimalchio gave him his freedom!

[53.3] Trimalchio buys a Greek troupe, then has them perform crass Roman skits, a bit like forcing Royal Shakespeare Company actors to do in-the-buff pie-in-the-face routines (see the similar mongrel conflation of Vergil and Atellan farce in Chapter 68, below). The Atellan farce (from Atella near Naples) was the oldest form of native Italian comedy. The characters were broad comic types, as their names suggest: Bucco, Maccus, Pappus. Atellan farce was cultivated particularly in the first century BC. It could draw on Greek New Comedy and was also used, like a satyr play, to follow a tragedy. Otherwise, we know little about it, for like other low, popular forms – e.g., mime and pantomime – it has left few clear traces.

[54.1] Nero was similarly bespattered by an acrobat-Icarus (see Suetonius, Nero 12).

That way no one could say that a man of his stature had been wounded by a lowly slave.

55. We applauded his clemency and chatted about the mutability of fortune. 'We mustn't let this event pass without a trace,' said Trimalchio; he immediately called for writing paper and, with scarcely a moment's thought, composed these verses:

> 'Things always spin the way no one expects;
> Fortune on High all our affairs directs;
> more good wine, boy, to counter these effects!'

This epigram excited talk of poets, and it was maintained that the summit of poetry was held by Mopsus of Thrace,[1] until Trimalchio said, 'Professor, how would you compare Cicero and Publilius the mime?[2] In my opinion, the orator has more eloquence, the mime more nobility. What could be more ennobling than this?

> "Wanton jaws eat away at Mars' walls from within;
> peacocks fatten in cages for your palate's sin,
> sporting their gilded Babylon-plumes in the pen;
> with the capon ex-rooster, you cram Guinea's hen.
> Even storks, even those cherished guests from afar,
> family values' friends, shapely *chanteuses* that they are,
> runaways from cold weather and warrants of warm,
> take up nests in your fleshpots to their mortal harm.
> Why so value that fruit of the Indies, the pearl?
> So your wife tarted up like some crass glitter-girl
> can spread lecherous legs in another man's bed?
> What good that precious glass, those green emeralds, that red,

---

[55.1] As Ehlers notes, 'Mopsus of Thrace' seems to be a vulgar confusion of the legendary Orpheus of Thrace with the minor seer Mopsus of Asia Minor.

[55.2] Though this question has the shape of a serious literary query, the comparison at hand is as fatuous as one might expect. Though Publilius enjoyed quite high prestige for a writer of mimes, pairing Cicero with him is like pairing Thomas Jefferson with Will Rogers. The sixteen lines cited here from 'Publilius' may in fact be Petronius' invention. Certainly they leaven old-fashioned sententious rhetoric with grotesque touches verging on parody. The last two lines are especially close to a hostile remark on silk garments in Pliny the Elder, *N.H.* 6.54.

that chalcedony gleaming like fire caught in stone,
unless what lends them luster is virtue alone?
Is it *right* when a bride flaunts a dress of thin air,
all decked out in sheer see-through, to strut her stuff bare?"

56. 'Who do you think has the hardest job after writers?'
Trimalchio asked. 'I think doctors and moneychangers do.
Your doctor has to know what folks have in their insides and
when a fever comes on. I hate them though, because they're
always putting me on a diet. Your moneychanger's job is hard
because he has to spot the copper beneath the silver. Now
among dumb animals your hardest workers are sheep and
oxen: thanks to the ox, we eat bread; thanks to sheep, we are
clothed in glorious wool – it's a real crime to eat lamb and
wear shirts! But I think bees are divine creatures – they vomit
honey – even if some say it comes from Jove. And that's why
they have stings – because wherever there is something sweet
you'll also find something bitter!'[1]

He was already putting the philosophers out of work when
little tickets were brought around in a bowl and the slave in
charge read out what the guests were given to take home.[2] *Pig
in a Poke*: a ham was brought in under some vinegar bowls.
Headrest: a turkey neck was served up. *Hindsight and Insults*:
black-eyed peas and a plate of tongue were the presents. *Something lean, something mean*: the guest got a whip and a knife.
Sparrows and a fly-catcher: spare-ribs and Attic honey were
served. *Something for dinner and something for business*: a
pork chop and writing tablets were brought in. *Something
canine and something pedestrian*: a rabbit and a slipper were
presented. *A catfish and a letter*: a cat was brought in with a
fish tied to its back; beside it lay a dead bee. We laughed for
ages at jokes like these, and there were scads more like them
that I can't remember.

[56.1] Trimalchio's menagerie of platitudes is in fact not so different from what
passed for serious reflection on our fellow-creatures the beasts (cf. Pliny the
Elder).

[56.2] This practice of bestowing whimsical gifts matched with misleading descrip-
tions was evidently a custom associated particularly with the Saturnalia. Suetonius
reports that Augustus enjoyed such practical joking (*Augustus* 75).

57. But when Ascyltos, unruly as ever, threw up his hands joking and laughing at everything until tears came to his eyes, he enraged one of Trimalchio's cronies (who was sitting right next to me): 'What are you laughing at, muttonhead? Isn't my master's entertainment good enough for you? I'm sure you're richer and used to better parties! So help me god, if he was sittin' next to me, I'd teach him how to bleat. A real wise guy, laughing at other people! Some fly-by-night bum who isn't worth his own piss! Listen, if I pissed around him, he wouldn't know which way to turn. By god, I don't have a temper, but maggots grow in rotten meat! He laughs: what does he have to laugh about? Did his daddy pay cash for him, is that it? So you're a Roman knight?[1] Yeah, like I'm a prince!

'*Then why were you a slave?*' ''Cause I wanted to be. I decided to be a Roman citizen, so I wouldn't have to pay tribute.[2] And I hope the way I live now makes me nobody's fool. I'm a man among men, and I walk with my head up. I don't owe anyone a red cent. No, and I've never been sued. No one in the forum has ever told me, "Pay up!"

'Yeah, I bought some dirt and I've got my own dough now. I feed twenty bellies and a dog. I even bought my wife, so no one could wipe his hands on her hair. And I bought my own freedom for a thousand, and I was made a priest of Augustus free of charge. And when I die, I hope I won't have anything to blush about in the grave.

'Are you so busy you just can't see yourself? That's right, you see the lice on the other guy, but miss the flies on you. Only you think we're some kind of bad joke. Look, your professor here is older and wiser; he likes us. But you're still on the tit. You don't know your a's from your z's. You're a crock, no, a soggy shoelace – limper not better.

'Go ahead and live it up; have lunch and dinner twice a day. I wouldn't trade my good name for a million. Listen, did anyone ever have to dun me for a debt? I slaved away for

---

[1] This suggests Ascyltos wears a gold ring (cf. Chapter 32, n. 1 and the disparaging reference to Giton's light-colored boxwood rings in Chapter 58, below).

[2] Under special circumstances a non-citizen might actually be enslaved to a Roman so that he could be freed as a citizen.

twenty years, but no one could even tell if I was a slave or not! I came here a curly-haired kid. There wasn't even a town hall then. I just tried to please my master, a real gentleman whose little finger was worth more than all of you put together. Sure, I had some enemies at home who wanted to trip me up here and there. But I kept my head above water, thanks to my master. Now, these are real accomplishments. Hell, bein' born free is as easy as saying "I'll take one." Now, why are you staring at me like a goat caught in the garden?'

58. At this remark Giton, who was standing at my feet, erupted into a raucous cackle that he'd been trying desperately to stifle for some time. When Ascyltos' critic realized this, he turned in rage at the boy: 'You too?' he said, 'you're laughing, you onion head? Well, whoopee! What is this, the Saturnalia?[1] When did you pay your freedom tax?[2] Ya know, you'll look good on the cross feasting crows. By god, I ought to give you hell, and that master of yours who won't keep you at heel! As sure as I get my belly full, I'd give you what for right here, if it wasn't for my friend Trimalchio, a fellow freedman. We're all just having a good time, but you freeloaders, well—. Like master like slave, right?

'I'm really pissed off – I don't have a bad temper, but once I get started I don't give a plug nickel for my own mother! Damn right, I'm gonna find you on the street – you rat, you fungus! I won't budge till I've knocked your master upside down and inside out, an' I won't let you off if you scream bloody murder. I'll make sure your cheap curls and two-bit master won't save you then. Damn right, when I get my teeth into you, if I know me, you won't be laughin'. I don't care if you've got a beard of solid gold. I'm gonna give you hell – and that jerk who made you his step-and-fetch-it.

'No, I haven't learned your geometries, criticisms, or non-sense like "Sing the wrath",[3] – but I can write in capitals n' do

[58.1] See Chapter 44, n.1.

[58.2] 'When were *you* bought out of slavery?' On being freed a slave or sometimes the ex-owner had to pay five per cent of the slave's market price as a 'freedom tax'.

[58.3] Seemingly a half-literate reference to Homer, *Il.* 1.1.

percentages in copper, weights, or cash. Listen, you and I can make a little bet, if ya want. Come on, I'll put down money. I'll show you your father wasted his dough teaching you rhetoric. Try this:

Of us I am, and *long* and *broad* involve me; solve me![4]

'Here's a hint: what part of us runs and never leaves its place; what grows out of us and becomes smaller? You look as scared n' confused as a mouse caught in a piss pot. So shut it up and don't bother your betters – who don't even know you were born! And don't think I'm taken in by those boxwood rings you swiped from your girlfriend. Heaven help us! Let's go into town and borrow some money, then you'll see what credit this iron ring of mine has.

'Shit! Ain't he a pretty sight – like a fox caught in the rain? I sure hope I don't get rich and die so happy that folks swear by my grave, if I don't hunt you down like an executioner. That master of yours sure is a pretty sight! What a teacher! Should a been a clown, not a professor. When we went to school the teacher used to say, "Your things in order?" "Go straight home!" "Mind your own business!" "Don't talk back!" But now, schools've gone to hell. Nothin' worth a damn comes out of 'em. Thank god for my trade; it made me what you see.'

59. Ascyltos was about to answer this abuse when Trimalchio, delighted with the eloquence of his fellow freedman, said, 'Come now, let's stop this bickering! Let's enjoy ourselves, and you, Hermeros, forgive the boy. His blood's boiling – you should know better. The real winner is always the one who loses this kind of argument. Besides, you were a real cock-of-the-walk once and didn't have a grain of sense. So, it's better to start the party again and watch these rhapsodes perform.'

In trooped the actors at once amid a clatter of spears and shields. Trimalchio was perched on his pillow, and, while the

---

[58.4] Variously 'solved' as a shadow, a foot, or a penis, the same way the next two may be 'solved' as the nose and one's hair; but whatever the real meanings are, the speakers pride in knowing the answers to such riddles is comically out of proportion to their difficulty.

rhapsodes chattered to one another in Greek verse, as is their impudent habit, he read the Latin text aloud in a sonorous voice. Soon there was a pause, and Trimalchio said, 'Do you know what they're performing? Diomedes and Ganymede were two brothers. Helen was their sister. Agamemnon stole her and then gave Diana a stag instead. So now Homer tells how the Trojans went to war with the Parisians. Of course, Agamemnon won and made his daughter, Iphigeneia, Achilles' wife. That's why Ajax went crazy, as he'll explain in a minute!'[1]

As Trimalchio spoke, the rhapsodes raised a shout and a throng of slaves carried in a boiled calf on a two-hundred pound platter. It was wearing a helmet. Ajax followed and, with his sword drawn as if in a fit of madness, he attacked the calf. Waving his sword up and down, he collected slices on its tip and then served them up to the astonished guests.

60. We didn't have long to admire this elegant performance: all of a sudden the paneled ceiling began to creak and the whole dining room trembled. I leapt to my feet in panic for fear that some acrobat was about to tumble down through the roof. The other guests also looked up in amazement wondering what novel portent was descending from heaven. And suddenly the ceiling *did* part, and an enormous hoop was lowered toward us. From its rim hung golden crowns and alabaster casks of perfume. We were being invited to take these as gifts when I looked back at the table...

[59.1] See Chapter 48, above, and the real-life description in Seneca (*Epist.* 27.5–8) of the rich rube Calvisius Sabinus who, to compensate for his own ignorance, bought expensive slaves who had Homer, Hesiod et. al. memorized. Trimalchio's recombinant version of what happened at Troy represents a hilarious garbling of standard accounts. Diomedes and Ganymede[s] had no more than rhymed endings in common; Helen's actual brothers in myth were named Castor and Pollux/Polydeuces, and Agamemnon was actually her husband's brother, not her abductor; the stag given Diana was actually a proxy supplied by Diana when Agamemnon was ready to placate the goddess by killing his daughter in lieu of a previously slain stag; though this daughter, named Iphigeneia, was told she would marry Achilles, *that* story was merely a ruse; and what drove Ajax mad was not being denied Iphigeneia, but rather, not winning the armor of Achilles when Achilles himself had been slain. Trimalchio's 'Parisians' were not doubt Foreign-Legion adherents of the Paris who was Helen's real ravisher.

A dessert tray loaded with little cakes had already been served. In the middle the baker had made a Priapus with all kinds of apples and grapes heaped in his ample lap in the popular fashion. We were greedily helping ourselves to this splendid offering, when a new game promptly rekindled our hilarity. As soon as any of the cakes or fruit was even touched, a saffron perfume spurted out – some of the damned juice squirted right in our faces. Thinking a dish so suffused with a religious aura must be a sacred offering, we leapt to our feet and shouted: 'God save Augustus, father of our country!'

Even after this ritual some guests were grabbing the apples. In fact, we filled our napkins with them, especially me, since I thought no gift too ample for me to stuff in Giton's pockets.

In the meantime three boys entered in short white tunics: two of them placed household gods adorned with lockets on the table in front of us; the third carried around a bowl of wine shouting, 'May the gods be gracious...'

Trimalchio said one of the gods was called Gain, the second Luck, and the third Profit.[1] There was also a life-like portrait of Trimalchio himself, and since everyone else kissed it, we were too embarrassed not to do the same.[2]

61. As soon as everyone had prayed for good sense and good health,[1] Trimalchio looked at Niceros and said, 'You used to be livelier company. I don't know why you're so quiet. You haven't made a peep. Please, you won't see me happy until you tell us about that adventure of yours.'

Delighted with this attention from his friend, Niceros replied, 'May I never make another penny of profit if I'm not jumping for joy to see you in this mood. Let's have a real giggle – but I'm afraid your scholars here may laugh at me. Well, let them laugh. I will tell my story. What does it matter to me who laughs? As long as I'm laughed at, not laughed down.'

60.1 Mercenary recastings of the traditional household gods, the *lares*. Smith notes (p. 169) that all three appear elsewhere as the names of slaves.

60.2 Hence Trimalchio's image gets kissed as the guests pledge the health of Augustus, the deified Emperor.

61.1 A conventional prayer (cf. Chapter 88, below, and esp. Juvenal 10.356).

With these winged words,[2] Niceros began his story:

'When I was still a slave we used to live in a narrow little street, where Gavilla's house is now. There, as the gods would have it, I fell in love with the wife of Terentius, the innkeeper. You remember Melissa of Tarentum – what a luscious tomato! But I swear it wasn't her body or the sex that got to me but her good nature. Whatever I asked for, she never said "no". If she had two bits, I had one. Whatever I had I kept in her pocket, and she never cheated me. Now one day her husband died out at his master's estate. So I plotted and planned by hook or by crook to get to her: ya know how a friend in need is a friend indeed.

62. 'Luckily my master went off to Capua to sell some nice junk. I grabbed the chance to get a house guest to come with me to the fifth milestone. He was a soldier and brave as hell. We push off around cockcrow; the moon was bright as daylight. When we get to a cemetery, my buddy takes off for some tombstones to do his business. I keep goin' just hummin' and countin' the stars. When I look for my buddy I see he'd stripped and piled his clothes by the roadside. My heart was in my mouth – I just stood there like a corpse. He pees in a circle round his clothes and then, just like that, turns into a wolf! I'm not kiddin' either; I wouldn't lie to you for anything. But, what I'd started to say, is that after he turned into a wolf he started howling and then ran off in the woods.

'At first, I didn't know where I was, but then I go to pick up his clothes – they'd turned to stone! Was I scared, or what? I drew my sword and stabbed at shadows along the road til I got to my girlfriend's house. I walked in like a zombie and almost gave up the ghost then and there! The sweat ran down my crotch, my eyes felt dead. I could barely pull myself out of it.

'Melissa was surprised that I came so late: "If you'd come earlier, you could have helped us. A wolf got into the farm and attacked our flocks; he bled them like a butcher. He may have gotten away, but he didn't get the last laugh; one of our slaves speared him through the neck."

[61.2] A formulaic hexameter half-line transition (cf. e.g., Vergil, *Aen.* 2.790, and Chapter 121, line 100, below).

'I couldn't sleep a wink after I heard this, but at daybreak I hurried home like the defrauded innkeeper. When I came to the place where the clothes had turned to stone, I found nothin' but blood. But when I got home, my friend, the soldier, was lying in bed like an ox, and a doctor was treating his neck. I realized of course that he was a werewolf. After that I couldn't bring myself to eat with him, not on my life! Now I don't care whether you buy this or not, but I'll be damned if I'm lyin'!'

63. The entire room was struck dumb with astonishment. 'With all respect for your story,' said Trimalchio, 'you can take my word for it – my hair stood on end, cause I know Niceros doesn't tell tall tales. No, he's real reliable, not a blabbermouth.

'Now I'll tell you something really scary – a regular ass-on-the-roof story. When I was still a long-haired boy – I lived like a Greek in those days – my master's favorite died. By god, he was a gem of a catamite, one in a million. Well, when his poor old mother was mourning him and several of us were grieving with her, some witches suddenly started to screech like owls[1] – you'd think it was a dog chasing down a hare.

'At that time, we had a man from Cappadocia: tall, real brave, and was he strong! He could lift an angry bull off the ground. This guy rushed outside with his sword drawn and his left hand carefully covered and ran a woman through right about here – may this spot I touch be safe! We heard her groan, but – see how truthful I am! – we didn't see the witches themselves. Our big lug came back in and threw himself on the bed; his whole body was black and blue as if he'd been flogged. Of course this was because the evil hand had touched him. We shut the door and returned to the funeral. But when the mother tried to hug her son's body, she reached out and found only a handful of straw! It had no heart, no innards, nothing. Of course the witches had already whisked the boy away and left a straw doll. Oh! you'd better believe it too: there really are witches, there are night riders, and what is high, they can make low. And that big lug never did look the same again. In fact, he died a raving lunatic just a few days later!'

[1] Cf. Ovid, *Fasti* 5. 139–40, and here, Chapter 134.

64. We were as amazed as we were gullible. We kissed the table and prayed that these night riders stay at home – til we could get back from dinner...

To tell the truth, by this time the lamps seemed to multiply before my eyes and the whole dining room began to blur. Then Trimalchio said, 'Say, Plocamus, aren't you going to tell us a story? Won't you entertain us? You used to be a live wire, reciting dialogue and even an occasional poem. How sad it is! The ripe figs have fallen!'

'Yes,' he said, 'my life in the fast lane ended when I got the gout. But when I was younger, I almost wore myself out with singing. You name it: dance, dialogue, barber shop gossip! I had no peer except Apelles himself.'[1] He then put his hand to his mouth and whistled some god-awful tune he later claimed was 'Greek'.

Not to be outdone, Trimalchio gave an imitation of trumpeters, and looked round for his favorite, whom he called Croesus.[2] The boy with his bleary eyes and filthy teeth was in the process of wrapping a green handkerchief around an obscenely fat, black puppy. He then put a piece of half-eaten bread on the couch and proceeded to stuff it down the little dog's throat until it gagged. This inspired Trimalchio to call for his own dog, Puppy, 'guardian of the home and family'.

A hound of enormous size was promptly led in on a chain, and, when ordered to lie down – with a swift kick from the steward – he sprawled right in front of the table. Trimalchio tossed him a piece of white bread and said, 'No one in my household loves me more!'

The boy was peeved to hear such praise lavished on Puppy, and so he put his pup on the ground and tried to get her to start a fight. True to his nature, Puppy promptly filled the room with his cacophonous barking and almost tore the head off

---

[1] Smith (p. 179, n. 4) suggests that 'Apelles' at this point refers to a tragic actor of Asian origin prominent in the time of Caligula (cf. Suetonius, *Caligula* 33).

[2] The name readily suggests both legendary wealth and hard-won wisdom; Croesus, overthrown monarch of Lydia, ends up as an attendant of Cyrus the Great (Herodotus 1.88 ff.). He had previously been warned by Solon in one of the most famous passages in Herodotus not to mistake mere wealth for happiness.

Croesus' Pearl. The uproar didn't stop with the dogfight either: a candelabrum toppled over one of the tables shattering all the crystal and spattering some guests with hot oil.

Trimalchio tried to make light of the mess, kissed the boy, and told him to climb on his back. Croesus promptly mounted him like a horse, and kept slapping him on his back giggling and shouting, 'Bucca, bucca, guess how many fingers I'm holding up?'

After Trimalchio calmed down a bit, he ordered a great bowl of wine to be mixed and drinks served to all the slaves, who were sitting at our feet. 'And if anyone turns his drink down,' he added, 'pour it over his head: daytime is serious, now is for fun!'

65. This display of good nature was followed by a Greek dessert, the very thought of which, frankly, is revolting. Instead of the usual thrush each guest was served a fat hen and garnished goose eggs, which Trimalchio kept urging us to eat calling them 'deboned chickens'.

Meanwhile, an official's attendant knocked on the dining room doors and a reveller dressed in white came in trailing a large crowd of followers.[1] His grand manner made me fear he was an important official. I started to get up and take off on my bare feet, when Agamemnon laughed at my panic saying, 'Calm down, you fool! Habinnas is an honorary priest and a mason best known for his tombstones.'

I sat down reassured by this news and greatly enjoyed watching Habinnas make his entrance. He was already drunk and ploughed along after his wife with his hands propped on her shoulders. A bunch of wreaths were piled on his head and scented oil streamed down his forehead into his eyes. He sat

---

[65.1] Possibly a reminder of Alcibiades' late, drunken arrival in Plato's *Symposium*, which had become a convention of sympotic literature. Habinnas is guest of honor less because of any private or public eminence than because as a mason he is charged with constructing Trimalchio's tomb (cf. Chapter 71). With a (Punic?) Semitic name (Sedgwick, 146) that is virtually an anagram of Hannibal or its Greek spelling *Annibas*, his attendance helps cap off Trimalchio's Greek-Asian conquest of Roman terrain, a theme generally best known by its far darker treatment in Juvenal's third satire.

down in the seat of honor and immediately called for wine and hot water. Charmed by his high spirits, Trimalchio ordered a larger bowl of wine for himself, and asked how his friend had been entertained at another party.

'We had it all – except for you,' he said. 'My thoughts were here. But it was damn nice. Scissa was having a funeral feast for some poor slave she'd freed on his deathbed. That'll make a nice bundle for the taxman: they say the guy was worth fifty thousand. But it was swell, even if we did have to pour half our drinks over his little bones.'

66. 'But what did you have for dinner?' asked Trimalchio.

'I'll tell you, if I can. My memory's a real marvel: constantly forget my own name. Well, for a first course we had a pig crowned with sausages and smothered in black puddings and gizzards roasted just right. And, of course, we had beets and pure whole wheat bread, which I like better than white: it gives you strength, and when nature calls, it doesn't hurt. The second course was a cold cheese tart and an excellent Spanish wine with warm honey in it. I didn't take a bite of the cheese tart but I soaked myself in the honey! There were chickpeas, lupines, a choice of nuts and an apple apiece. I took two myself and, look, here they are in my napkin. Ya see, if I don't have a present for my pet slave, there'll be trouble.

'Oh yeah, the boss reminds me: there was a hunk of bear set out, but when Scintilla tried it, she almost threw up her large intestine! But I ate almost a pound of it myself – it tasted just like wild boar. Yeah, I say if bears eat us men, why shouldn't men eat bears? We finished with cheese marinated in new wine, a round of snails, a bit of tripe, a little dish of liver, garnished eggs, some radish and mustard greens, a ragout, and dessert à la Palamedes. They even brought round a tub of pickled olives, which some folks were greedy enough to grab hand over fist. We had to pass up the ham.

'But tell me, Gaius, why isn't Fortunata here?'

67. 'You know how she is,' replied Trimalchio, 'she won't let water touch her lips until she's gathered up the silver and divided the leftovers among the slaves.'

Habinnas responded, 'If she doesn't join us, I'm gonna push off.' He started to stand up when all the slaves chimed in on cue calling, 'Fortunata! Fortunata!' over and over again. She then made her appearance with her skirt hitched up by a yellow sash to reveal a cherry-red slip, ankle bracelets and gilded Greek slippers. She wiped her hands on a handkerchief tied around her neck, and then took her place on the couch, where Scintilla, Habinnas' wife, was reclining. Scintilla was clapping her hands as Fortunata kissed her and asked, as if in disbelief, 'Is it really you?'

Fortunata then went so far as to take the jewelry off her beefy biceps and show them to a duly impressed Scintilla. Finally, she even took off her ankle bracelets and golden hair net, which she said was solid gold.

Trimalchio observed these goings on and had the jewelry brought to him. 'You see these? A woman's chains!' he said. 'This is how we fools get plundered. She must be wearing six-and-a-half pounds of gold! I've even got an arm band myself that weighs almost ten pounds – all made out of what I owe Mercury!' Then, to show he wasn't lying, he had a set of scales brought in and passed around to test the weight.

Scintilla was no better. From her neck she took a golden locket, which she called 'Lucky'. From the locket she produced two earrings shaped like castanets, which she in turn handed to Fortunata for inspection. Then she remarked, 'Thanks to my husband's generosity, no one else has better ones.'

'What?' exclaimed Habinnas. 'You cleaned me out to buy a glass bean? You know if I had a daughter, I'd cut her ears off! If it weren't for women, we'd think this stuff was just a bunch of rocks. Hell, now we've got to piss hot and drink cold!'

Meanwhile the wives were getting sloshed, laughing together and exchanging drunken kisses. One chatted on about her virtues as mistress of the house, the other of the boyfriends and vices of her husband. While they gossiped, Habinnas quietly got up, grabbed Fortunata by the ankles, and swung her legs up on the couch. 'Oh no!' she shrieked, as her dress flew up over her knees. She then rolled over into Scintilla's lap and buried a hot blush in her handkerchief.

68. After a brief intermission Trimalchio ordered a dessert course served. The slaves took out the old tables and brought in the new, and they scattered sawdust tinted with saffron and vermillion, and – something I'd never seen before – a glittering powder made of mica. Immediately Trimalchio quipped, 'I just might be satisfied with these dessert tables alone – you all have your just desserts now! – but if you have something sweet, bring it on!'

Meanwhile an Alexandrian boy, who was serving the hot water, started imitating a nightingale, while Trimalchio kept shouting, 'Do something else!'

Then there was another gag: a slave who sat at Habinnas' feet suddenly began to chant the *Aeneid*, evidently at his master's request:

Meanwhile Aeneas' fleet traversed the main . . .[1]

A more disgusting sound has never assaulted my ears. Not only did he barbarize the pitch and rhythm of the verse, he also interlarded lines from the Atellan farces. For the first time in my life I actually found Vergil revolting. When he finally got tired and quit, Habinnas boasted, 'Can you believe he never went to school? I took care of his education by putting him out with the street people. He has no peer when it comes to mimicking mule-drivers or street musicians. He's damn clever: a cobbler, a cook, a baker, a real "slave of every muse". There are just two things that keep him from bein' one in a million: he's circumcised and he snores. Now I don't mind that he's cross-eyed. So's Venus. That's why he's never quiet: one eye is always on the move. I only paid three hundred for him.'

69. Scintilla interrupted this paean. 'You forgot to mention one of your slaves "muses": he's a pimp. And if I have anything to say about it, he'll be branded.'

Trimalchio laughed and said, 'Oh, I see. A Cappadocian, huh? He doesn't cheat himself out of anything, and I can't blame him for that: no one gives you a good time when you're dead.

[1] Vergil, *Aen.* 5.1.

'Now don't be jealous, Scintilla. Believe me, we know what you women are like. So help me god, I used to bang my mistress (and how!) until even the master got suspicious. That's why he banished me to the farm. But be quiet, tongue, I will feed you.'

As if he'd just been praised to the skies, that worthless slave took a clay lamp out of his pocket and mimicked a trumpeter for more than half an hour, while Habinnas hummed along pressing his lower lip down with his hand. Finally, the slave strode into the middle of the room and did a flute-player with a handful of broken reeds. Then he donned a cloak and whip and did the *Life of a Mule-Driver* until Habinnas called him over, gave him a kiss, and handed him a drink. 'Bravo, Massa! I'm gonna give you a pair of boots!'

Our suffering would not have ended if a second dessert course hadn't been served: thrushes made of pastry and stuffed with raisins and nuts. Next were quinces bristling with thorns to look like sea urchins. All this would have been bearable if a more monstrous dish had not made us prefer death by starvation: what looked like a fat goose surrounded by fish and all kinds of birds was served. And Trimalchio said, 'Friends, all you see here is made of the same thing.'

Naturally wary, I immediately saw through the gag and, turning to Agamemnon, said, 'I'd be surprised if all this wasn't made from wax or clay. I saw this kind of fake dinner once at the Saturnalia in Rome.'[1]

70. I hadn't finished speaking when Trimalchio said, 'As sure as I hope to grow – in wealth not in bulk – my cook made this whole course out of a pig! He's a rare talent: if you want it, he'll make a fish out of a sow's womb, a pigeon out of bacon, a turtledove out of ham, a chicken out of pork knuckles! And so I had the bright idea of giving him an artistic name: we call him Daedalus.[1] And because he has good sense, I brought him a gift from Rome: knives made of Noric iron.'

[69.1] On this antic festivity see Chapter 44, n. 1.

[70.1] Daedalus, whose name recalls the legendary master-artist who designed the labyrinth of Crete, is predictably cast as Trimalchio's slave-master of special effects, even if he presides in a kitchen or palace of kitsch (note once more Petronius' own arch complicity).

He promptly had them brought in and marveled at them.
He even invited us to test the blades on our cheeks!

Two slaves stumbled abruptly into the room. They had evidently been fighting at the well. Anyway, they still carried large
water jars on their shoulders. Trimalchio tried to adjudicate
their quarrel, but they wouldn't listen to him. Instead, they
smashed each other's jars with their sticks. Shocked by their
drunken insolence, we couldn't take our eyes off the fight and
noticed scallops and oysters pouring out of their broken jars,
which a slave collected and brought around on a platter! The
talented cook was equal to the occasion: he served us snails on
a silver gridiron serenading us in a most repulsive, squeaky
voice.

I'm ashamed to say what happened next. Following some
unheard of custom, several long-haired boys presented us with
ointment in a silver basin and rubbed it on our feet as we lay
there, after tying little garlands around our ankles and calves![1]
Then some of the ointment was poured into the wine bowl and
the lamp!

Fortunata was beginning to feel like dancing. Scintilla was
already doing more clapping than talking, when Trimalchio
said, 'Philargyrus, even though you're a notorious fan of the
Greens,[2] you may sit down now, and invite your companion,
Menophila, to join you.'

Need I say more? We were almost thrown off our couches,
so completely did the entire room fill with slaves. Right next
to me I noticed the cook who had made the goose out of pork –
he reeked of pickles and sauces! Not content with having a
place at the table, he immediately launched into an imper-
sonation of the tragedian Ephesus,[3] and then offered his master
a bet that 'the Greens would win first prize at the games'!

71. Roused by this challenge Trimalchio said, 'Friends, slaves
are human beings too and sucked the same milk as everyone

[70.1] Cf. Pliny the Elder (*N.H.* 13.22), who says Nero learned this practice from
Otho.
[70.2] i.e. a supporter of the green 'team' at the Circus (Smith, 194, n. 10).
[70.3] Otherwise unknown.

else, even if bad luck has battered 'em down.¹ But if I live, they'll soon get a taste of freedom. In fact, I'm setting them all free in my will! To Philargyrus I'm giving his farm and his bedmate; to Carion, I'm leaving an apartment house, his freedom tax, and a bed with blankets. I'm making Fortunata my heir and commending her to all my friends. And I'm doing it all up front – so my whole household can love me now just as if I were already dead!'

Everyone had started to thank their master for his generosity, when he turned serious and had a copy of his will brought in. He then read it aloud from beginning to end, while the slaves groaned as if in grief.

Then turning to Habinnas he said, 'Tell me, old friend, are you building my tomb just as I told you to? Please be sure that you put my lap-dog at the foot of my statue along with plenty of wreaths and jars of perfume, and all the fights of Petraites² so that, thanks to you, I may live on after my death. And please make my plot a hundred feet wide and two hundred feet deep. For I want every kind of fruit tree growing around my ashes and lots of vines. It makes no sense to decorate the house you live in now but not the one where you'll spend so much longer. That's why over everything else, I want this inscribed:

> This Tomb Does NOT Go To My Heir!

But I'll make sure in my will that no one can wrong me when I'm dead: I'll appoint one of my freedmen to guard my tomb so that folks won't run up and take a crap on it!³

'And please put ships in full sail on the front and put me high on a ceremonial dais wearing my purple-striped toga and five golden rings as I pour money out of a sack in front of the

---

⁷¹·¹ Trimalchio's attitude toward slaves is much like that of Seneca, *Epist.* 47.10 (transl. Grummere): 'Kindly remember that he whom you call your slave sprang from the same seed, is smiled on by the same sky, breathes equally, lives equally, dies equally.' But Trimalchio of course speaks from experience.

⁷¹·² See Chapter 52, n. 2.

⁷¹·³ Cf. Horace, *Sat.* 1.8.38, Persius 1.113–14, Juvenal 1.131; ancient monuments were handier than fire-hydrants. 'This monument does not go to my heir,' or a paraphrase to that effect, is according to Smith quite a common inscription on monuments.

whole town! – For you know, I once put on a public banquet
that cost two-bits a head – and if it's all right with you, put
some banqueting tables up there and show the whole town
having a good time. On my right, put a statue of Fortunata
holding a dove, and let the puppy follow tied to her sash, and
include my favorite boy, and some giant jars of wine properly
sealed against leaks, and you can carve one urn broken and a
boy weeping over it. And put a sundial[4] in the middle so
whoever checks the time will read my name, like it or not!
Now listen to this epitaph and tell me if it sounds right:

> Here Lies C. Pompeius Trimalchio
> Freedman of Maecenas,[5]
> Elected Priest of Augustus
> *In Absentia:*
> He Could Have Had Any Job in Rome[6] –
> But Didn't.
> Loyal, Brave, and True,
> He Started With A Nickel in His Pocket,
> And Left His Heirs Thirty Million;
> AND HE NEVER ONCE LISTENED TO A
> PHILOSOPHER![7]
> Farewell, Trimalchio
> And You, Too, Traveller.

71.4 Cf. the monumental sundial in the Augustan complex in the Compus
Martius.

71.5 Possibly a reference to the renowned poets' patron and henchman of
Augustus Caesar, though this tie is not stressed; even if it is barely implied, it is
an additional hint of parodic connections between Trimalchio's own opulence
and that of the imperial regime. The name 'Pompeius' also signals that Trimalchio
once slaved for a family of that name, once again a great name from Roman
history of whom T. is, bizarrely enough, a prime heir.

71.6 i.e., he could have joined a *decuria* and been a lower civil servant. The
boast of having been voted a priest of Augustus *in absentia* is essentially no less
bathetic.

71.7 Such hostility to philosophy was not confined to Roman freedmen. See
Suetonius, *Nero*, 52, where Nero is said to have studied the usual subjects except
for philosophy, because Agrippina thought it an inappropriate pursuit for a future
ruler. After the Pisonian conspiracy Nero banished many philosophers from
Rome, presumably because Cynics (and Stoics) were vociferous critics of her-
editary monarchy in general and Nero in particular.

72. As he finished his epitaph, Trimalchio started to weep uncontrollably. And Fortunata wept. And Habinnas wept. And then all the slaves wept, as if invited to a funeral, filling the room with sobs.[1] Even I had started to cry, when Trimalchio said, 'Well then, since we know we're going to die, why don't we try living? And since I want to see you happy, let's take a bath together! I swear you won't regret it: that water's hot as an oven!'

'That's right!' chimed in Habinnas. 'I like nothing better than making one day into two!' He then jumped up on his bare feet and took off after Trimalchio who was already cheery.

So I turned to Ascyltos: 'What do you say? I'll faint on the spot, if I even have to look at another bath.'

'Let's play along,' he said, 'and while they're making their way to the bath, let's sneak out.'

We agreed to this plan, and Giton was leading us through the colonnade to the foyer, when that dog on a chain greeted us with such ferocious barking that Ascyltos backed into a fish pond![2] And I, who was no less drunk and had taken fright at a mere painted dog, was dragged into the same pool while trying to help Ascyltos paddle out. But we were saved by a porter whose intervention placated the hound even as he dragged us, shivering, onto terra firma. Meanwhile Giton had proceeded to buy off the watchdog with a clever trick: he had tossed the barker everything we'd passed along at dinner. The food had distracted him and muzzled his wrath.

But when, shivering wet, we asked the porter to show us out, he replied, 'You are mistaken if you think you can leave the same way you came in; no guest has ever left the way he came in: they come in one way and go out another.'

73. What were we poor mortals to do trapped in this new-

[1] Cf. Plato, *Phaedo*, esp. 117–18, along with the introduction to this volume, pp. ix–xiii, for Trimalchio's rehearsals of death as a parody of Socrates'.

[2] A live dog, but as if the first (*painted*) watchdog had come to life. Cerebus-like, this dog does more to keep *in* than *out*; there is no backing out of Trimalchio's Underworld.

fangled labyrinth?[1] Well, now we actually did want to bathe.
So we asked the porter to lead the way, threw off our clothes,
which Giton spread out to dry in the entry hall, and entered
the bath. It was narrow, you see, and shaped like a cold-water
cistern, with Trimalchio standing upright in it. We couldn't
escape his mindless prattle even there. He was saying that
nothing's better than bathing without a crowd, and that there
used to be a bakery located on that very spot. Then, he got
tired and sat down. Inspired by the echoing sound of the
bath, he threw his head back, opened his drunken mouth, and
massacred the songs of Menecrates.[2] At least, that's what those
who understood him said they were.

The rest of the guests joined hands and ran around the bath.
The hall resounded with shrieks and giggles. Others tried to
pick up rings off the floor with their hands tied behind their
backs, or got down on their knees and tried to bend so far
backward they could touch the tips of their big toes. While
they played these games, we stepped down into a private tub
that was being warmed up for Trimalchio.

So after we'd sobered up a bit we were led into another
dining room, where Fortunata had set out every luxury ... we
noticed bronze statues of fishermen on the lamps as well as
tables of solid silver decked with gilded chalices and wine
decanted through a cloth filter right before our eyes.

Then Trimalchio said, 'Friends, a slave of mine is celebrating
his first shave today. He's a good little crumb-saver, if I may
say so, so let's drink deep and dine until dawn.'

74. While he was still speaking, a rooster crowed. Startled by
the sound Trimalchio ordered that wine be poured under the
table and that the lamp be sprinkled with unmixed wine.

[73.1] Is Trimalchio's funhouse more like Hades or like Daedalus' labyrinth? If
the latter is the Minotaur-resident Trimalchio himself? Cf. Bodel (253, n. 68 in
Tatum) on a maze-drawing found on a pillar in an opulent villa of Pompeii with
the cryptic inscription, 'Labyrinth: Here lives the Minotaur'. Daedalus' labyrinth
is associated with Aeneas' Cumaean descent to the Underworld in Vergil's *Aen.*
6.23–30.

[73.2] Probably the musician (i.e., citharoedus) lavishly endowed by Nero (see
Suetonius, *Nero* 30).

And he even switched a ring to his right finger. 'This is no coincidence,' he said. 'That rooster's giving us a sign. This either means there'll be a fire, or someone in the neighborhood is about to breathe his last. Spare us! Whoever brings me this prophet will get a tip.'[1]

This was no sooner said than the rooster was brought in and Trimalchio gave orders for him to be cooked in wine. So he was butchered by that learned cook, who had earlier made fish and birds out of pork, and thrown in a cauldron. While Daedalus drank down the steaming broth, Fortunata ground up some pepper in a wooden mill.

When these savories were dispatched, Trimalchio looked at his slaves and said, 'Why haven't you eaten yet? Be off then, and let some others come to work.' So another team walked in, and, as their predecessors shouted 'Good-bye, Gaius,' they shouted, 'Hello, Gaius!'[2]

It was then that the party began to go sour.[3] A handsome young boy turned up among our new waiters, and Trimalchio cornered him and proceeded to lavish kisses on him. To assert her wifely rights, Fortunata responded by bad-mouthing Trimalchio, calling him 'scum' and 'a disgrace' for not controlling his lust. Finally, she called him a 'dog'. Provoked by her abuse, Trimalchio threw his cup in her face. She screamed as if she had lost an eye and held her trembling hands to her face. Scintilla was also upset and sheltered her shuddering friend on her breast. A dutiful slave held an icy jar to Fortunata's cheek, which she leaned on as she moaned and wept.

But Trimalchio said, 'What's all this about? Has this whore forgotten where she was bought? I took her out of the gutter and made her fit for human society. But she puffs herself up

74.1 Water under the table was more often used for averting a fire (cf. Pliny the Elder, N.H. 28.26). Trimalchio actually *gets* his fire, in a manner of speaking, in Chapter 78.

74.2 For the familiarity with which Trimalchio treats his slaves, and vice versa, cf. Seneca's praise of old egalitarian manners in *Epist*. 47.14. Seneca notes that the old ways persist in the mime. For additional reminiscences of mime in the *Satyrica* see Chapter 19, n. 1.

74.3 Is this inconsequential marital brawl an Olympian parody of some sort? (Cf. Homer, *Il*. 15.14-33, and the wrangling of Titania and Oberon over her Indian boy in Shakespeare's *A Midsummer Night's Dream*).

like the proverbial bullfrog. She doesn't even spit in her bosom:[5]
a blockhead, not a woman! If you're born in a hovel, don't
dream of palaces. I'll be damned if I'm going to give in to this
"Cassandra in army boots".

'And I could have married for millions, penniless as I was.
You know I'm not lying. Agatho, the perfumer, took me aside
just the other day. "I beg you," he said, "don't let your family
die out." But good-natured fool that I am, I didn't want to
seem fickle, so I stuck the axe in my own leg.

'Damn right, I'll make you want to dig me up with your own
fingernails! And to show you here and now what you've done
to yourself – now hear this: Habinnas, I forbid you to erect a
statue of her on my tomb, so at least I won't hear her nagging
when I'm dead. And, so she'll know I can hit back – I forbid
her to kiss me when I'm dead!'

75. When his fulminations ended, Habinnas tried to calm him
down. 'No one's perfect. We're mortals, not gods.' Scintilla
said the same thing through her tears and, calling him 'Gaius',
begged him by his guardian angel to relent.

Trimalchio couldn't hold back the tears any longer. 'Please,
Habinnas, as sure as you hope to enjoy your own nest-egg, spit
in my face if I've done anything wrong. I gave the boy a very
frugal kiss – not because he's beautiful – but because he's frugal!
He can do division or read a book at sight; he saved enough
from his daily allowance to buy a suit of Thracian armor! He's
also bought himself an easy chair and two punch ladles! Now
doesn't he deserve to be the apple of my eye?

'But Fortunata forbids it! Don't you, my high-heeled Caesar?
I warn you, magpie, enjoy what you've got! Don't make me
show my teeth, lovebird, or you'll get a piece of my mind. You
know me: when I make a decision, it's nailed to the ground.
But let's remember the living!

'Please, friends, enjoy yourselves for I, too, was once what
you are, but thanks to my native talents I ended up here. Brains

---

[74.5] Spitting in one's own bosom was like knocking on wood, meant to head
off ill fortune. Trimalchio is accusing Fortunata of taking her own good luck, i.e.,
Trimalchio, for granted.

make a man, the rest is garbage! I buy low and sell high. Everyone has his own pet wisdom, I guess. I'm just lucky as hell.

'Are you still crying, my snorer? I'll give you something to cry about.

'But – as I was about to say – frugality was the key to my success. When I left Asia I was no bigger than this candelabrum here. In fact, I used to measure myself by it every day and rub its oil on my lips to get a beard on my beak a little sooner! I was still my master's pet for fourteen years. To do your master's bidding is nothing to be ashamed of.[1] And I gave my mistress equal time! You know what I mean. I say no more because I'm no braggart!

76. 'Then I became the master of the house, as the gods willed; I simply had my patron in the palm of my hand. Why waste words? He made me his heir – along with the emperor – and I came into a senator's fortune. But no one is ever satisfied: I just loved doing deals. I won't bore you with the details: I built five ships and loaded them with wine – it was worth more than gold at the time – and shipped it to Rome. Every ship sank. You'd have thought I'd planned it that way. A fact, not a fable. On a single day Neptune gulped down thirty million!

'Do you think I fell apart? No, by god, I didn't even blink. I built more ships – bigger, better and luckier! No one could deny I was tough. And you know, a big ship is tough too! I loaded them up again with wine, bacon, beans, perfume from Capua and slaves. This time Fortunata did the right thing: she sold off all her gold and all her clothes, and put a hundred gold pieces in my hand. This was the seed-money for my fortune. What the gods will happens quickly: I scooped up ten million on a single voyage!

'I promptly bought back all the estates that had belonged to my patron. I built a house and bought up some mules and slaves. Whatever I touched grew like a honeycomb. Once I owned more than the whole country, I threw in the towel. I

[75.1] Cf. Seneca, *Epist.* 47.14 (tr. Gummere): 'Each man acquires his character for himself, but accident assigns his duties.'

gave up doing deals and started lending money through my freedmen.

'I already wanted out of handling my own business, and a Greek astrologer named Serapa happened into our town and convinced me. He was on intimate terms with the gods. He even told me things about myself that *I* had forgotten. He explained me right down to my buttons: he knew my insides. The only thing he didn't tell me was what I'd had for dinner the day before. You'd have thought he'd always lived with me.

77. 'Say, Habinnas, weren't you there when he said, "You acquired your wife with your wealth." "You are unlucky in your friends." "No one ever returns your favors." "You own enormous estates." "You are nursing a viper in your armpit!" And something I should never tell you – right now I have thirty years, four months, and two days to live! And I shall soon come into a legacy. My horoscope says so. If I could only extend my estates to Apulia, I will have gotten somewhere in this life!

'At least I built this house while Mercury watched over me. As you know, it was a hut; now it's a temple.[1] It has four dining rooms, twenty bedrooms, two marble colonnades, a series of servants' bedrooms, my private bedroom, this viper's lair, and a superb porter's lodge. And there's room enough for a hundred guests. In fact, when Scaurus visited here, he would stay nowhere else, and he has his father's place by the sea. There are lots of other things, which I'll show you in a minute.

'Believe me, if you have a nickel in your pocket, you're worth a nickel. You are what you own. Just like your friend – first a frog and now a king.

'Meanwhile, Stichus, bring out my funeral clothes – the ones I want to be buried in, and bring some perfume and a taste from that jar I want poured over my bones...'

78. Stichus didn't waste any time: he returned to the dining room carrying a white shroud and a purple-striped toga ...

---

[1] Cf. Suetonius, *Aug.* 28, on how Augustus found Rome a city of brick and left it one of marble.

Trimalchio urged us to feel if they were made of good wool. Then with a wily smile, he said: 'Stichus, make sure no mice or moths get at these – or I'll have you burned alive! I want to have a glorious funeral so that the whole town will shower me with blessings!

He promptly opened a flask of exotic oil and anointed us all: 'I hope I like this as well when I'm dead as I do now!' He then had wine poured in a bowl: 'Now pretend you were invited here for my funeral banquet!'[1]

The whole thing was getting positively nauseating when Trimalchio, now sloppily drunk, ordered some trumpeters into the dining room for more entertainment. Propped up on a pile of cushions he stretched out full length along the edge of the couch, saying, 'Pretend I'm dead: play something beautiful.' The trumpeters blared out a funeral march. One fellow – the slave of the undertaker who was the most respectable person there – played so loud that he woke up the entire neighborhood. This caused the local fire brigade to think Trimalchio's house was on fire. They promptly broke down the door and wielding axes and water proceeded as usual to turn everything upside down. We seized this golden opportunity, gave some excuse to Agamemnon, and raced out of there as fast as if it *were* on fire.[2]

*

78.1 Cf. Claudius' preternatural attendance at his own funeral in Seneca's *Apocolocyntosis* 12. Compare also Pacuvius, who, according to Seneca, *Epist.* 12.8–9, made a habit of rehearsing his own funeral; and Sextus Turannius, who, according to Seneca, *De brevitate vitae* 20.3, had his household mourn him as if dead.

78.2 Conflagration Survived, a persistent Imperial theme from Augustus (the Roman Civil War) to Vergil (Troy's fall) to Nero (Rome's burning; cf. Chapter 89, n. 1), served up here with a farcical twist, perhaps?

79. We had no torch handy to light our way, and little hope of meeting someone with a light in the dead of night. In addition, we were drunk, not to mention the fact that this neighborhood would have been bewildering to us in broad daylight.[1] So we marched our bleeding feet over sharp rocks and shards of broken pottery for almost an hour until we were finally delivered by Giton's cunning. Our wily boy was afraid of getting lost even in the daytime and so had marked every post and column with chalk; even in the thick of night his marks were visible and their bright color showed the way to us wanderers.

But even when we'd found our lodgings, our sweaty ordeal wasn't over. The old innkeeper had spent so long swilling wine with her lodgers, she wouldn't have noticed if you'd set her on fire! We might have spent the night on her doorstep if one of Trimalchio's couriers hadn't turned up ... After making quite a racket, he simply broke down the door and ushered us in ...

*

> Ah, what a night, you gods and goddesses;
> how soft the sheets! We coupled heat to heat
> and lip to lip this way and that we poured
> our flitting souls. With all your cares, farewell
> Mortality! So I rehearsed my dying.

My hymn of thanks was premature: as soon as I gave into the wine and loosened my grip, Ascyltos, that master of misdeeds, stole my boy and carried him off to his own bed in the

---

[1] In effect this inscrutably nondescript town just extends the 'new labyrinth' of Trimalchio's villa (cf. Chapters 6, 73). Only somewhat ironically cast as a new, female-lead Ariadne (who unravelled the labyrinth of Crete for her fickle love Theseus), Giton cunningly marks the way out.

middle of the night! Then after taking a free tumble with someone else's lover – who either didn't mind or pretended not to – he just fell asleep in his arms oblivious of right and wrong.

And so when I woke up and groped for the delight plundered from my bed ... if you can ever believe a lover, I had half a mind to run them both through with my sword and marry their sleep to death.[2] But I followed a saner plan and woke Giton up with a beating, and looking sternly at Ascyltos said, 'Since you've broken faith and raped our friendship, get your things now, and find someplace else to pollute!'

He didn't argue, but after we'd split up our loot very fairly he said, 'Okay, now let's divide the boy!'[3]

80. I thought that would be his parting jest, but then he put his ruthless hand on his sword and said, 'You're not gonna be the only one to enjoy this booty you've been hovering over. I'm gonna get my share even if I have to chop it off with my sword!'

I responded in kind – wrapped my cloak around my arm and got ready for a fight. Caught between two desperate lovers the poor boy begged us like a tearful suppliant not to make that shabby inn the setting for a Theban tragedy,[1] or stain the sanctity of a brilliant friendship with each other's blood. 'If you must commit a crime,' he shouted, 'look, my throat is bare, turn your hands to this, bury your blades here! I deserve to die if I've corrupted the sacred bond of friendship!'[2]

At his pleading we put down our swords, and Ascyltos spoke up: 'I'll put an end to this quarrel. Let the boy go with whomever he wants; at least he should be free to choose his lover.'

I had no fears – I thought our longstanding intimacy as good as a tie of blood – on the contrary, I jumped at the offer and

---

[79.2] Cf. 89.63.

[79.3] *Dividere* can apparently also mean 'open up', 'split' in a more graphic sexual sense (cf. Plautus, *Aul.* 286, and here, Chapter 11).

[80.1] A reference to the fratricidal strife of Oedipus' sons Polynices and Eteocles dramatized in Aeschylus' *Seven against Thebes*. Since the *fratres* ('brothers') of this text are sexual partners and rivals, the reference is archly germane here in more ways than one (cf. also Chapters 11 and 119.163).

[80.2] Cf. the Sabine women's intervention in Livy 1.13.

happily referred our case to the judge. But as soon as the words were out of my mouth, Giton had stood up and chosen Ascyltos as his lover, without even pretending to deliberate! I was so shattered by this sentence I simply collapsed on the bed. And I would have done myself in then and there if I hadn't begrudged my enemy such a triumph. Ascyltos walked out exulting in his prize and simply abandoned me in despair in a strange town, me who just moments before was his dearest comrade-in-arms, and his mate in misfortune!

> Friendship endures no longer than it pays,
> no longer than a shifting gamepiece stays;
> you stand fast, friends, while fortune keeps its place;
> when *that* gives out, you fall off in disgrace.[3]

. . . .

> A stage-troupe acts a mime, the father this,
> that one the son; a third 'the rich man' is;
> but when the farce that each performs is ended,
> back to plain truth and off with the pretended![4]

81. I didn't indulge myself in tears for long for fear that on top of my other troubles Agamemnon's assistant, Menelaus, would find me alone at the inn. I sadly gathered up my things and took a private room near the beach. There I holed up inside for three days haunted with feelings of loneliness and humiliation. I beat my aching breast and over the din of my own moaning would often shout aloud, 'Why couldn't the earth simply open up and swallow me whole? Or the sea, so cruel to the innocent? Did I escape the law, cheat the arena, and kill my host to end up, after so many proofs of daring, deserted in an inn – a beggar, an alien in some Greek town?[1] And who condemned me to solitude? A boy teeming with filthy desires, deserving exile in his own opinion, a free man – in depravity – well-bred – in depravity – who sold his youth for small change and was hired as a girl even by those who thought him male! And

[80.3] Cf. Ovid, *Epist. ex Ponto* 2.3.23.
[80.4] Cf. Lucretius 3.55–8 (in hard times masks are dropped, the truth remains).
[81.1] Cf. Vergil, *Aen.* 2.664–72.

what about his friend? Who came of age in a skirt, not a toga?
Whose mother convinced him not to become a man? Who did
woman's work in a sweat shop? Who, after he'd gone broke and
acquired novel appetites, abandoned his old friend and – most
shameless of all – sold out everything for one night in the sack,
like some camp follower! Now the lovers lie entwined all night –
every night! And perhaps, when they've exhausted each other
sexually they chuckle over my loneliness. They won't get away
with it: for either I'm not a man, let alone a free one, or I'll make
them pay for my suffering with their own damn blood!'

82. In this state of mind I belted on my sword and, to insure
my martial vigor, fortified myself with an unusually large lunch.
Soon I was out on the street prowling like a madman through
all the arcades. Wearing a frankly murderous expression I
looked daggers in all directions and frequently touched the
handle of my sword, which I had dedicated to the task, when
some soldier – who was probably a con man or a thug –
happened to notice me and said, 'Say, soldier, what legion are
you in? Whose unit?'
    I confidently fabricated a legion and a commanding officer.
'Well then, tell me, do soldiers in your army go around in
Greek slippers?' My guilty look and nervous manner instantly
gave me away: he ordered me to hand over my sword and stay
out of trouble! Disarmed and deprived of revenge, I went back
to my room, but, as soon as I calmed down, I began to feel
grateful to that pushy thug!

*

      Waters waist-deep, undrunk; unplucked the fruit;
      poor Tantalus, whom his wishes destitute!
      So mighty rich men fare, their stores immense,
      who feed on hunger, fearful of expense.[1]

Don't trust in plans: Fortune has a mind of her own ...

*

[1] Tantalus' punishment for some violation of guest-host relations (serving up
his own son to the gods to test their omniscience or revealing their secrets to men;
cf. Pindar's *Olymp.* 1.1–32, and more generally Apollodorus, *Epit.* 2.1) was most
often depicted as an endless torment of temptation by food and drink always

83. I happened into an art gallery with an amazing collection of paintings.¹ I actually saw some originals by Zeuxis, unscathed by all the years, and sketches by Protogenes that so rivalled the truth of nature herself that I trembled to touch them. But when I got to Apelles – the piece [the Greeks] call 'The Goddess on One Knee' – my admiration began to verge on worship.² So precisely did the look of his creations conform to nature, you would have thought they were animated! Here a soaring eagle bears Ganymede to heaven; there fair Hylas fights off a wicked Naiad; Apollo damns his own murderous hands and adorns his unstrung lyre with the first hyacinth. Surrounded by these painted lovers I exclaimed as if alone: 'Look, even the gods are touched by love! When Jupiter cannot find what he desires in heaven, he harms no one by erring on earth. The nymph who ravished Hylas would have mastered her desires, had she thought that Hercules would intervene. Apollo invokes his lover's shade in a flower. In all these stories the embraces of love are unimpeded by a rival! But I befriended someone crueler than Lycurgus!'³

Even as I contended with the winds, a grey-haired gentleman entered the gallery. His face bore the stamp of experience and

placed just out of reach (cf. Homer, *Od.* 11.582–92). Just as Tantalus' offense bears on many of the *Satyrica's* themes (food, deception, hospitality, moral trespass, forbidden knowledge), so his punishment was frequently moralized as the commonplace wages of avarice or some other intemperance, and is similarly applied to the fleeting delights of boy-love in Achilles Tatius 2.35. Yet Encolpius' whole series of farcically anti-climactic priapic travails, oddly like Humbert Humbert's bedeviled pursuit of Lolita, is itself one long Tantalean tease (see especially Chapters 11, 79–80, 128, and *Carm.* 48, along with the perhaps spurious *Carm.* 57).

⁸³·¹ Art collections are often the venues for crucial or central encounters and reveries in ancient romance (cf. Achilles Tatius 1.1–2, and Winkler's note in Reardon *ad loc*). In this gallery the themes that Encolpius reflects on are all violent or star-crossed boy-love (on star-crossed homosexual love as a subplot in ancient romance see Winkler's note on Achilles Tatius 1.12). Facile moral or immoral application of painted *exempla* seems to be fairly standard in antiquity (see Augustine, *Confessions* 1.16.26, citing Terence).

⁸³·² Famous painters of the Classical period (5th and 4th centuries BC). Ernout speculates that the 'Goddess on one Knee' was a running Diana the Huntress, but a crouching Venus is more probable.

⁸³·³ The main reference is probably to the importunate host by this name whom

seemed to hold out the promise of something great. Not that
he was well dressed; in fact, it was plain from his appearance
that he was one of those literati rich men love to hate. He
walked up and stood beside me . . .

'I am a poet,' he said, 'and, one, I hope, of no mean talent,
if the garlands of victory still mean anything when favoritism
so often crowns the undeserving! "*Then why are you so badly
dressed?*" you wonder. For just that reason: a passion for beauty
never has made a man rich!

> 'The trafficker at sea brings back a bundle;
> the soldier for his pains wears cloth-of-gold;
> the two-bit yes-man lounges drunk in purple;
> even the marriage-breaker sins for hire;
> eloquence alone, left shivering in its rags,
> invokes forgotten arts with pauper's pleading.'⁴

84. 'No doubt about it: if any man is averse to all the popular
vices and insists on following his own steep path through life,
that very fact – his being different – makes him hated. For who
really likes what's at odds with himself? So those whose goal
in life is to pile up interest-bearing accounts want it believed
that there is nothing in the world better than what they themselves possess. So they attack those who love literature however
they can in order to make them seem inferior to money, too!¹

*

'I don't know why but the sister of talent is poverty . . .

Encolpius apparently slew in some lost earlier episode (cf. Chapters 81, 117). But
his name may echo that of 1) the legendary Lycurgus of Sparta, a tough but fair
ruler, or more plausibly 2) the Lycurgus of Thrace who, maddened by Dionysus,
chopped up his son thinking he was destroying a vine (Apollodorus 3.5).

⁸³·⁴ A conventional plaint (cf. Juvenal 7, on the hardships of poets especially).

⁸⁴·¹ Here and elsewhere Eumolpus is prone to present his own artistic plight in
a philistine age as a culture-war extraordinaire or an ultimate contest of cultural
darkness and light; cf. his orchestrated Orphic exit in Chapter 141, and n.2, and
note how his occasionally self-serving perspectives ironize even as they in some
ways support his accounts of more general abuses. On Eumolpus as a poet of
blame and therefore a near-satirist, see below, Chapters 96, 113, 141 nn.1–2.

'I wish the enemy of my discipline were so harmless that he might somehow be mollified. But in reality, he is a seasoned thief and shrewder than any pimp.

*

85. 'When I went to Asia to serve on the quaestor's staff, I was put up as a guest in Pergamum. I was happy to stay there, not only because my lodgings were elegant, but also because my host's son was truly beautiful. So I hatched a plan to insure that I would never be viewed with suspicion by the paterfamilias: whenever the conversation at dinner even hinted at the sexual attractions of beautiful boys, I would blush like a virgin and object in the severest tones that my ears were offended by such obscene talk. The mother came to regard me as a veritable philosopher! So I started taking the boy to the gym, I organized his studies; I was his teacher and warned him not to let any sexual predator into the house.

*

'Once we were lying around the dining room on a holiday when the long hours of play had made us too lazy to retire; around midnight I noticed that the boy was still awake and so, in the softest whisper, I said a prayer: "Venus, who art in heaven, if I can kiss this boy without his noticing, tomorrow I will give him a pair of doves."

'When he heard the price of pleasure, the boy started to snore. So I went over to the little faker and stole some kisses. Happy with this beginning, I got up early the next morning and, as he expected, brought him a choice pair of doves, and so fulfilled my promise.

86. 'When the same opportunity arose the next night, I changed my prayer and said, "If I can caress this boy with my naughty hands without his feeling it, I will give him two ferocious fighting cocks for his patience."

'At this promise the boy came over to me on his own and, I think, he was even afraid that I had nodded off! I reassured him on this point and gorged myself on his entire body, stopping just short of the summit of pleasure. The next morning I gave him what I'd promised and he was elated.

'When my moment came the third night, I whispered ... in his ear as he pretended to sleep: "Immortal gods, if I could enjoy in full the complete satisfaction of my desires while the boy sleeps, in return for this bliss, tomorrow I will give him a choice Macedonian thoroughbred,[1] so long as he has felt nothing!"

'Never has a young man slept more soundly! So, first, I filled my hands with his milky breasts, then I inhaled kisses, and, finally, all my desires converged into one.

'In the morning he sat in his room waiting for my usual visit. Well, you know very well how much easier it is to buy doves and cocks than a thoroughbred. Besides, I was afraid that so extravagant a gift would make my kind attentions look suspicious. So after wandering around a few hours I returned home and gave the boy nothing but a kiss. He hugged me round the neck as he looked about and said, "Please, sir, where is my thoroughbred?"

*

87. 'Because of my broken promise the door I had opened was slammed shut, so I resorted again to wheedling. A few days later a similar occasion put us in the same lucky situation. Since I could hear his father snoring I started asking him to be friends again, to let me make it up to him, and all the other things a swollen libido inspires one to say. But he was obviously angry with me and only said, "Go to sleep or I'll tell my father."

'There's no obstacle a lack of scruples can't overcome. While he kept threatening "to wake up father", I wormed my way around him and took my pleasure by force in spite of his half-hearted resistance. He was not entirely displeased by my ambush, and after he'd complained for some time that he'd been deceived, and then was laughed at and reviled by his fellow students (to whom he had boasted of my wealth!), he said, "But look, I'm not going to be like you, if you want to, do it again."

[86.1] Possibly a standard boy-lover's gift (see Achilles Tatius 1.7 ff.).

'So with all my sins forgiven I was back in business on friendly terms; I enjoyed his favors and then slipped off into postcoital slumber. But the boy was ripe for pleasure – at that age, they're insatiable – and he wasn't satisfied with a mere repetition. So he woke me up saying, "Well, don't you want something?" And I admit, it was no unpleasant task. So somehow I panted, sweated, and banged away till he got what he wanted, then I fell asleep again, exhausted with pleasure. Less than an hour had passed when he started jostling me with his hand and said, "Why aren't we doing it?"

'I was furious at being woken up so many times, so I gave him a taste of his own medicine. "Go to sleep", I warned, "or I'll tell your father!" '

*

88. The poet's lively conversation prompted me to ask him ... about the age of the paintings and the subjects of those unfamiliar to me. At the same time I questioned the causes of our modern decadence, since the finest arts had all but disappeared, including painting, which had scarcely left a trace of itself behind.

'Money,' he said, 'the sheer lust for money has caused this revolution. In the old days when mere excellence was still a source of pleasure, the liberal arts flourished and heroic effort was expended just to see that nothing of value to posterity would remain undiscovered. My god, isn't that why Democritus distilled the essence of all known herbs and spent his entire life performing experiments to discover the powers of stones and plants?[1] Isn't that why Eudoxus grew old on a lofty mountain top trying to grasp the motions of the heavenly bodies?[2] Isn't that why Chrysippus dosed himself three times with hellebore – just in order to strengthen his powers of invention?[3]

[88.1] The 5th–c. BC father of Atomism, also a devoted early naturalist, and, by the time of the empire, a legendary sage.

[88.2] Eudoxus, 4th–c. BC astronomer, most of whose *Phaenomena* survives in a verse paraphrase by Aratus (see Chapter 40, above).

[88.3] Famous 3rd–c. BC expounder of Stoicism. Hellebore was esteemed as a powerful purge known especially for clearing the intellect.

'But to return to artists: poverty killed Lysippus brooding over the lines of a single statue; and Myron, who could find the very souls of men and animals in bronze, could not find an heir.[4] We, on the other hand, are so mired in wine and whores that we can barely manage to appreciate the established arts. We despise the past, while we study and teach only its vices. Where is dialectic? Where is astronomy? Where is the path to wisdom? Who goes into a temple and prays to become eloquent or to drink at the fountainhead of philosophy? And that's not because they're busy praying for a sound mind in a sound body![5] No, as soon as they set foot on the Capitoline, one promises an offering if he can bury a rich relative; another if he should dig up a treasure; a third if he should live to make thirty million. The senate itself, that model of rectitude, is in the habit of promising a thousand pounds of gold to the Capitol and, lest anyone hesitate to lust after money, Jove himself is decorated with it! It's really no surprise that painting has declined when gods and men alike deem a lump of gold more beautiful than anything made by Apelles, Phidias,[6] or some other crazy Greek!

89. 'But I see you are utterly engrossed in that painting of the Fall of Troy. Let me try to expound the theme in verse:[1]

Harvest-season, the tenth of the siege around Troy,
and a doubt-haunted fear troubled all Trojan joy,

[88.4] Famous classical sculptors of the 4th and 5th centuries BC, respectively.

[88.5] See Chapter 61, above, and more generally Juvenal 10, De votis, on right and wrong objects of prayer. Eumolpus' complaint once more transfigures the commonplace (cf. Seneca the Elder, Controv. 1 pref. 1; Pliny the Elder, N.H. 14.1; Horace, Ars poetica 330 ff.).

[88.6] Phidias (5th-c. BC), the legendary sculptor of the Parthenon; Apelles (4th-c. BC), famous for his remarkable paintings.

[89.1] A reworking of Vergil's Aen. 2 in old-fashioned iambic senarii meter, the main meter of Roman tragedy and comedy (cf. the fairly full census of parallels from Vergil supplied in Ernout). We have rendered the Latin in an equally obtrusive dramatic-narrative meter derived in this case from a high-doggerel mode of English balladry. Eumolpus' title 'The Fall of Troy' (Troiae halosis [cf. Suetonius, Nero 38.2]) closely matches the name of the poem Nero famously sang at the burning of Rome (which in Roman lore was a new Troy), but Eumolpus stops just short of Troy's burning.

while in darkling fear's doubt seer Calchas' words hung,
till at Ida's top Phoebus bade axes be swung—
    timber dragged down and sawn in a pile
    soon to furnish a horse full of guile!
In it opened a huge hidden hollow, a pit
for an army to sink in, and sinking in it
a host hardened by ten years of fighting now hides;
heavy Greeks line their own votive offering's insides!   10
    Homeland! Alas – '*What* thousand ships?
    Peace! Free at last!' on all our lips;
so the horse's inscription and Sinon assert—
Sinon expert in ruin, cunning keen to do hurt!
From the gates free and clear of war now a crowd seeks
the wished offering, tears now pouring down people's cheeks,
tears long fettered by fear-fretted minds, now released
by relief. Hair unbound, Laocöon Neptune's priest
agitates the plebeians till everyone here
begins shouting, then takes careful aim with his spear,   20
and just grazes the belly, but Fate makes effete,
and the blow bounces off to support the deceit!
He attacks, nerving his feeble hand yet again,
the steep flanks of the horse with an ax, and within
    the young troop caught there grumbles and groans
    and the oak mass with others' fears moans,
a young cargo of captives, Troy's capture their goal,
one new trick to dispose of the war as a whole!
Now still more portents. There where high Tenedos hulks
off the coast, the strait surges together and bulks,   30
and across a calm sea shattered billows recoil
and resound as when oars' beating makes the waves boil
with sound heard from afar in night's calm, and complain
when ships press through the sea and their keels cut the main.
    Looking back, we see twin serpents' crests
    wave-born onto the rocks, tumid breasts
    like tall ships throwing foam left and right,
    thrashing tails, and their manes like their sight,
waveswept, wild, bright as lightning; they make the sea burn,
and with their very hiss make the waves seethe in turn!   40

We were dumbstruck. In sacred array,
    Phrygian-style, where they stand in the way,
Laocöon's twin sons are ensnared in the bands
of the bright serpents' backs, throwing up little hands
    to twin faces, but neither his own,
    each his brother's, and so not alone
    either dies, but from shared love and fear.
    Next the sire falls in death, the sons' peer
impotent to defend; fleshed in his dear ones' dying
the snakes turn to him next, overwhelmed leave him lying   50
among altars where he late the priesthood rehearsed,
now the ground-flailing victim, an offering accursed;
thus it was that doomed Troy turned her gods away first!
    Now the risen moon was shining full,
    with lesser stars that sensed her pull,
    but dead-asleep or drunk Troy's sons,
    when the Greeks let out their manly ones.
The chiefs brandish their arms, as an unhaltered horse
out of Thessaly's highlands prepared for the course
    shakes its head and high mane to and fro;   60
    swords drawn, shields at the ready, they go
to make war. One cuts off Trojans' wine-heavy breath,
and makes their sleep dead-end in an unending death;
from the altars another a firebrand ignites,
and against Troy Troy's own hallowed usage incites!'

*

90. As Eumolpus recited his verse, some of those strolling through the arcade started throwing stones at him. But he took this as a tribute to his genius, covered his head, and dashed out of the building. I was afraid that someone would call *me* a poet! So I followed Eumolpus as he fled toward the beach. As soon as we could stop safely out of range, I said, 'Tell me, why are you acting like a madman? You've spent less than two hours with me and have spoken more verse than prose! I'm not so surprised that people chase you with stones. I'm going to fill my pockets with rocks and whenever you start to take off for poetic heights I'll return you to earth with a knock on the head!'

Eumolpus winced saying, 'Young man, today was hardly my debut. On the contrary, I have often been accorded similar receptions after marching into a theater to recite something. But I want no quarrel with you, so I will abstain from sustenance for the rest of the day.'

'No need for self-denial,' I said, 'if you can swear off these humors, we will dine together . . .'

*

I gave the housekeeper our order for supper . . .

*

91. I saw Giton leaning against a wall with rags and scrapers in hand looking sad and confused. You could tell he just didn't take to slavery.[1] Since I could scarcely believe my eyes . . . As he turned, his face relaxed into a smile, and he said, 'Pity me, dear friend! Here where there are no weapons, I can speak openly. Rescue me from this sadistic kidnapper and demand any kind of penance you like from your former judge[2] no matter how brutal! It will be consolation enough for my suffering – just to die in obedience to your will!'

I told him to stop carrying on for fear someone would overhear our plans. We left Eumolpus behind – reciting poetry in the baths – and I quickly led Giton down a dark and dingy little passageway, and then raced back to my room. As soon as the door slammed shut I took him in my arms and brushed my face against the tears on his cheeks. We were both speechless; his lovable breast was still shaking with sobs. 'What a disgrace!' I said. 'To think that I was abandoned by you whom I love, and there is a gaping wound in my heart, but no scar! But what do you mean taking up with this fly-by-night lover? Do I deserve this kind of treatment?'

After he saw he was still loved, he raised his eyebrows . . .

'I asked no one but you to judge our love, but I won't complain; I'm ready to forget it all if you repent in good faith.'

[91.1] Contrast Chapter 26 (concl.); here Encolpius seems mainly intent on just cheering himself up.

[91.2] Giton served as a 'judge' in Chapter 80.

As I poured out these words sighing and crying, Giton wiped my face with his cloak: 'Please, Encolpius, be honest. Did I leave you or did you hand me over? I admit, I'll confess it openly: when I saw two armed men, I sided with the stronger.' I fondly kissed that breast so full of wisdom, and hugged him round the neck. And to show him that he was forgiven and that our renewed friendship could be counted on, I held him snug in my arms.

92. It was already getting late and the woman had taken our order for dinner, when Eumolpus banged on the door. I asked, 'How many are you?' and tried very hard to peek through a crack in the door to see if Ascyltos had come with him. When I saw my guest was alone, I promptly let him in. After he'd sat down on the cot and observed Giton setting the table right in front of him, he nodded his head and said, 'Say, I like your Ganymede! It should be a nice day!'

This calculated opening did not please me and I was afraid I had hooked up with another Ascyltos. Eumolpus persisted, and when the boy gave him something to drink, he said, 'I like you better than the whole bathful,' and greedily drained the cup dry. Then he said he had had a singularly unpleasant experience.

'I almost got a beating at the baths just because I tried to share a poem with some people sitting around the edge of the tub. After I was thrown out, I walked up and down every street shouting "Encolpius!" at the top of my lungs. Out of the blue came a young man, stark naked – he'd evidently lost his clothes – bellowing "Giton!" with equal ardor. While some boys mocked and mimicked me mercilessly like some kind of madman, an enormous crowd surrounded the young man with applause and a kind of awe: you see, the youth's sexual organs were so oversized that *he* looked like an appendage to *them*.[1] Talk about a hard worker! I think he must be the kind to start

---

[1] Thus Ascyltos is virtually Priapus incarnate, especially long on just what makes Encolpius fall short, one more instance in which the two members of this double-act, like the paired leads in much later farce, seem to vie for one functional identity. For another apt manifestation of this sort of twin-strife, see Chapter 80, above.

yesterday and finish tomorrow! Anyway, he was soon saved by
the cavalry: some Roman knight – a notorious one, I hear –
wrapped the vagrant in his own cloak and took him home, in
order to enjoy his good fortune alone, no doubt. But I couldn't
even have gotten my own clothes back from an officious bath
attendant, if I hadn't produced a witness! It just goes to show
how much more advantageous it is to have your genius between
your legs than between your ears!'

As Eumolpus told his story the expression on my face kept
veering from delight – at the misfortunes of my enemy – to
sorrow – at his being rescued. But I kept quiet as if I knew
nothing about it, and then explained what we'd ordered for
dinner . . .

*

93. 'What is permitted, I hold cheap; my soul delights in going
off the beaten path and finding trouble:[1]

> 'The Black-Sea pheasant and
> the Guinea-hen delight
> because they're scarce; white geese
> and gaudy ducks taste trite.
> Hauled home from distant seas
> or scratched from shoals of sand
> by way of shipwreck, *these*,
> not *standard* seafood, please.
> Far-out and Foreign win;
> what's out-of-bounds is in.

'Is this how you keep your promise not to versify today?' I
said. 'Please, spare us, at least: we didn't stone you! If someone
drinking in this inn gets even a whiff of a poet, he'll rouse the
whole neighborhood and bury us all! Take pity, remember the
art gallery and the baths!'

My gentle Giton scolded me for talking this way. He said it
was wrong to reproach my elders, to forget the duties of a

---

[1] A rather Cole-Porteresque variation on a favorite Petronian theme (cf. here,
Chapter 55 and 119. 33–8, along with Ovid, *Amores* 3.4. 17, and for line 6, see
Pliny the Elder, *N. H.* 19.52).

host, and to spoil with insults the dinner I had so generously
provided. He gave much sensible and modest advice of this
kind that only served to enhance his beauty still further ...

*

94. [*Eumolpus to Giton*] 'How fortunate your mother was to
bear a child like you, what a blessing! The combination of
wisdom and beauty is a rarity.[1] And so you won't think all
your words were wasted, behold, you have a lover! I will fill
my poems with your praises! As your tutor and bodyguard I
will follow you beyond the call of duty. Encolpius won't be
hurt: he is in love with someone else!'

Eumolpus was lucky that that soldier had taken my sword.
Otherwise I would have worked off that rage I had mustered
against Ascyltos in Eumolpus' blood. Nor did this escape Giton.
He left the room on the pretext of fetching water and his timely
exit quelled my anger.

So, after I'd cooled down a bit, I said, 'Eumolpus, I would
even rather hear you speak in verse than entertain desires like
these. Just as I tend to be irate, you are priapic: look how ill-
suited our dispositions are! So just consider me a maniac and
get out of harm's way: that means, *leave now*!'

Eumolpus was shocked by my outburst, but, instead of
asking why I was angry, he promptly left the room and then
suddenly slammed the door shut on me. I was caught completely off-guard when he snatched the key and rushed off to
look for Giton.

There was no way out, so I decided to end it all and hang
myself![2] I had just tied a belt to the frame of the bed next to
the wall and had put the noose around my neck, when Eumolpus and Giton walked in the door and called me back to life
from the very verge of death. Giton's grief abruptly converted
to rage and he shouted as he pushed me down on the bed with
both hands: 'You're wrong, Encolpius, if you thought you'd be

---

[1] Formulaic praise, mainly (see Vergil, *Aen.* 1.605 [to Dido], 9.641–2, and
Juvenal 10.298).

[2] Cf. Apuleius, *Metam.* 1.16, for another farcical attempt at suicide by
hanging oneself from a bedpost.

the first to die. I was first to try: I looked for a sword in
Ascyltos' room. And if I hadn't found you the other day, I
would have thrown myself headfirst over a cliff! Just so you'll
know how near death is for those who really seek it: look at
the sight you would have had me behold!'

With that he snatched a razor from Eumolpus' servant, and
slashed repeatedly at his throat, before collapsing at our feet. I
cried out in horror, rushed to his side, and sought the road to
death with the very same blade. But there was not even a trace
of a wound on Giton and I felt no pain. The razor was a
dummy! It was blunted and safely sheathed for boys to learn
barbering. That's why the servant didn't panic when Giton
grabbed it, and why Eumolpus hadn't interrupted our comic
death scene.

95. While the lovers were playing out this comedy, the innkeeper came in with the rest of our supper. After observing our
filthy wallow, he said, 'What are you? Drunks or runaways?
Or both? And who tied up that bed? Just what on earth are
you up to? By god, you'd rather run off in the middle of the
night than pay your bill, wouldn't you? Well, you won't get
away with it: I'll have you know this boarding house doesn't
belong to some widow but to Marcus Mannicius!'

'Are you threatening us?' shouted Eumolpus and slapped the
man hard in the face with the palm of his hand. The innkeeper
responded by lobbing an empty wine jug at the poet's head,
cleaving his forehead in mid-scream, and dashing from the
room. Eumolpus was not one to suffer insults gladly: he chased
after his assailant with a wooden candelabrum and avenged
his pride with multiple blows. The whole household was roused
now, including a crowd of drunken guests. I seized the opportunity for revenge and locked Eumolpus out. With the tables
turned on that ruffian, I enjoyed both the room and the night
free of my rival.

Meanwhile the cooks and boarders lit into the poet: one
stabbed at his eyes with a spit of sizzling sausages; another
threatened him like a gladiator with a fork he'd snatched from
the kitchen. Then a bleary-eyed old woman wrapped in a filthy
apron and wobbling along on an uneven pair of clogs dragged

in an enormous dog on a chain and proceeded to sic him on Eumolpus. But he successfully parried every attack with his candelabrum.

96. We were watching all this through a hole in the door (where the handle had been before we'd broken it off a little while earlier). I was just delighted to see Eumolpus get this beating. Soft-hearted Giton felt sorry for him though and actually thought we should open the door and rescue him. I was still so angry, I couldn't keep myself from giving Giton's compassionate head a sharp rap with my knuckles! He sat down on the bed in tears, but I kept watching through the hole – first with one eye, then the other, and feasted myself on Eumolpus' suffering just like a fine meal!

I was telling him to get a lawyer, when Bargates, the manager of the house, was interrupted at dinner and had himself carried by two litter-bearers right into the middle of the fight. Evidently, he had gout. He had launched into a rabid denunciation of drunks and runaways in a barbarous voice when he spotted Eumolpus: 'Is that you, most eloquent of poets?' he said. 'Then these worthless slaves had better quit fighting and get out of here now!'

*

[*Bargates to Eumolpus*] 'My mistress has taken on airs. So please bad-mouth her in your verse, so she'll show a little respect...'

*

97. While Eumolpus was conferring in secret with Bargates, a town crier entered the inn along with a policeman and a fair sized crowd. Waving a torch that shed more smoke than light, he issued this proclamation:

'WANTED: A BOY RECENTLY LOST IN THE PUBLIC BATHS. AGE: ABOUT 16. CURLY-HAIRED; DELICATE; HANDSOME; CALLED "GITON". WHOEVER TURNS HIM IN OR REVEALS HIS WHEREABOUTS WILL RECEIVE ONE THOUSAND IN COIN.'

Near the crier stood Ascyltos wearing a motley-colored shirt and holding up the proclamation and the reward money on a silver tray. I told Giton to jump under the bed and hook his hands and feet in the straps that hold the mattress to the frame; that way, like old Ulysses clinging to the ram, he could hang beneath the frame and dodge the hands of the search party.[1] Giton didn't waste any time. In a split second, he had his hands bound in place – and Ulysses beaten at his own game! To leave no room for suspicion, I stuffed the bed with clothes and arranged them in the shape of a man about my size.

Meanwhile, after Ascyltos had gone through everyone's room with an assistant he reached mine and his hopes rose seeing how carefully the door was bolted shut. The policeman stuck an axe in the joints and dislodged the bolts. I knelt before Ascyltos' knees and in memory of our friendship and all the trouble we'd been through together I begged him to let me at least see my dear friend. In fact, to make my feigned prayers more credible, I said, 'Ascyltos, I know you've come to kill me. Isn't that why you brought the axe? So, quench your anger: look, here is my neck! Spill my blood! That's what you came for under the pretense of this search!'

Ascyltos brushed my charge aside saying that he really sought nothing but his 'runaway' and desired the death of no suppliant, let alone one whom he had continued to cherish even after a nasty quarrel.

98. But the cop wasn't so easily handled: he got a cane from the innkeeper, rammed it under the bed, and probed every nick and cranny along the wall. Giton squirmed out of reach and, while desperately trying to hold his breath, stuck his face right into the bedbugs . . .[1]

Next Eumolpus burst in – the broken door couldn't keep anyone out – talking very excitedly: 'I just picked up a thousand in cash! All I have to do is go after that official and tell him you have Giton – betraying you as you so richly deserve!'

He persisted in making this threat until I was hugging his

97.1 From Odysseus' escape from the Cyclops in *Odyssey* 9.420 ff. Lichas, too, is compared to a Cyclops in Chapter 101.

98.1 Ascyltos disappears from the story at this point.

knees and begging him to spare the dying: 'Your excitement
would be understandable, if you knew the boy's whereabouts.
But he ran off in the crowd. I haven't the faintest idea where
he went. Be my guest, Eumolpus, bring the boy back, hand him
over to Ascyltos even!'

I'd almost gotten Eumolpus to swallow this, when Giton,
who was still holding his breath, suddenly let loose a torrent
of sneezes that shook the bed to its frame. Eumolpus turned
toward the commotion and said drily, 'Bless you, Giton.' When
the mattress was pulled back, he saw a Ulysses even a hungry
Cyclops would have pitied.

Eumolpus turned on me next: 'What is this, you thief? You
didn't have the nerve to tell me the truth even when you were
caught red-handed. No, if god in his wisdom hadn't excited a
sneeze from our pendant hero, I'd be wandering around the
local dives on a fool's errand.'

*

Giton was far smoother than I. First, he treated a cut over
Eumolpus' eye with spider webs soaked in oil. Then he removed
Eumolpus' torn jacket and gave him his own little cloak; finally,
he hugged Eumolpus, who was already softening up, and
applied kisses like a soothing salve. 'Dearest father, we are in
your hands. If you love your Giton, now is the time to save
him. I wish hungry flames would devour me alone, or a stormy
sea engulf me. I am the motive of all these crimes. I am the
cause. If I were gone, you might be reconciled...'

*

99. [*Eumolpus*] 'So I have lived in all times and places as if
each day I spent would be my last and never return...'[1]

*

My eyes brimming with tears I begged and prayed for him
to be my friend again, too. Lovers can't control the madness
of jealousy, I insisted, and I would do my utmost to avoid

[99.1] A traditional Epicurean position often developed by Horace (see for
instance *Epist.* 1.4.13–14, and Epicurus, *Vatican Sayings* 14).

saying or doing anything else that would offend him. Only he must heal every sore in his own soul and leave no scar behind, as befits a man of culture: 'Snows linger longer in harsh uncultivated regions, but where the earth shines tamed by the plough, a light frost vanishes as you speak. So it is with anger in our hearts: it obsesses savage minds but rolls off the cultivated.'[2]

'Of course,' said Eumolpus, 'What you say is true. Look, I kiss my anger good-bye, so may our affairs prosper! Get your gear together and follow me, or if you prefer, lead the way.'

He was still talking when the door creaked open and a sailor with a shaggy beard stood in the doorsill: 'You're holding us up, Eumolpus, like you don't know we're in a hurry.'

Without a moment's delay, we all stood up and Eumolpus ordered his man, who had been asleep for sometime, to get his bags. Giton and I readied what we had for the journey and I boarded the ship with a prayer to the stars...

*

100. [*Encolpius to himself*] 'It's annoying that our guest fancies the boy. But what's new? Aren't nature's most beautiful creations free to all? The sun shines on everyone. The moon with countless stars in train leads even wild beasts to pasture. What can you name more beautiful than water? Yet it flows for everyone.[1] Will love alone be stolen, not bestowed? Exactly – I certainly don't want what the world won't envy. One man, and an old one at that, shouldn't be any problem. And if he tries anything, his heavy breathing will give him away!'

When I had made these dubious assertions and defrauded my dissenting intellect, I covered my head with my tunic and pretended to sleep.

But suddenly, as if Fortune were determined to shatter my resolve, a voice groaned on the ship's deck: 'So he's made a fool of me?' Yes, it was a man's voice and familiar enough to

---

99.2 Possibly parodic (cf. Ovid, *Epist. ex Ponto* 2.9.37–8).

100.1 A rather hapless erotic inflection of Pindar, *Pyth.* 1.1, and the commonplace 'water-rights' plea found for instance in Ovid, *Metam.* 6.349 ff. (cf. also Chapter 11, n. 1 and 91, n. 1).

make my heart pound. But then a woman, equally outraged, exclaimed more fervently, 'If some god should put Giton in my hands, what a welcome I'd give the exile!'

The shock of hearing these voices knocked the blood out of us both. I felt lost in a bad dream and could no longer find my own voice; finally, with trembling hands I tugged on Eumolpus' collar just as he had fallen asleep: 'Please, Father, can you honestly tell me whose ship this is, or who's on board?'

He was quite annoyed at being disturbed. 'Was this what you had in mind? Did we take the most remote spot beneath the deck, so you could keep us from sleeping? And what would it mean to you if I said the ship belongs to Lichas of Tarentum, who's bringing a certain Tryphaena back from exile?'

101. His words hit me like a thunderbolt. I shuddered, bared my throat and said, 'At last, Fortune, you have completely undone me!' In fact, Giton fainted right on top of me.

When we were revived by the sweat pouring over us, I embraced Eumolpus' knees in supplication: 'Take pity on the doomed! Lend your fellow scholars a helping hand. Death is on the way, and unless you avert it, it may be a blessing.'

Taken aback by my desperate charge, Eumolpus swore by all the gods and goddesses that he had no idea what had happened, and had planned no treachery. In all innocence and good faith he had led his companions onto the very ship he himself had been planning to take all along.

'Where is the treachery? Who is the Hannibal sailing with us?[1] Lichas of Tarentum is a very respectable man. Not only is he owner and captain of the ship, he also has several large estates and a business run by his slaves. He's under contract to deliver some cargo to market. This is the Cyclops, this the Bluebeard, to whom we owe our voyage. Then there is Tryphaena, loveliest of all women, who travels hither and yon for the sake of pleasure.'

'These are the people we're running away from,' Giton interjected. He promptly explained to a frightened Eumolpus the

---

101.1 Carthaginian perfidy was proverbial (cf. *punica fides*).

reasons for the enmity between us and the imminent danger we faced.

Confused and at a loss Eumolpus suggested that we each give our own opinion.

'Pretend we've entered the Cyclops' cave,' I said. 'We simply must find a way out, unless we stage a shipwreck, which would certainly free us of every kind of danger.'

'No,' said Giton, 'persuade the pilot to put in at some port – for a reward, of course – and claim that your brother can't take the sea and is at the end of his rope. You can cover up the lie by crying and looking upset. The pilot will feel sorry for you and do what you want.'

Eumolpus didn't think this was possible. 'Large ships need deep harbors and it's hardly credible that my brother would collapse so abruptly. And, besides, as captain Lichas might want to visit the sick man. You can see how much it would help our cause to lead the master back to his runaways voluntarily! But, suppose the ship could be diverted from its long voyage, and Lichas did not come around to the sickbeds after all: how can we get off the ship without being seen by everyone? With heads covered or bare? If we cover them, then who wouldn't want to lend a hand to the sick? And if we don't cover them, we might as well make a public confession!'

102. 'Why don't we be rash,' I said, 'and take a risk, slip down a rope into the lifeboat, cut her free, and leave the rest to fortune? I'm not asking Eumolpus to share this risk. What's the point of involving an innocent man in someone else's troubles? I'll be happy if luck is with us on the way down.'

'A clever plan,' said Eumolpus, 'if it were possible. But who wouldn't notice you leaving? Particularly the pilot, who's on watch all night tracking the stars. Now, it might be possible to escape his notice, if you went off another part of the ship. But in fact you must slide down over the stern by the rudder, where the rope is hanging. Besides that, I'm surprised it didn't occur to you, Encolpius, that a sailor is always posted in the lifeboat on watch, night and day. The only way to get by the guard is to kill him or throw him overboard. You have to ask yourselves whether you're up to this. As for my own role, I shirk no

danger that holds out hope of deliverance. I assume even you
don't want to risk your lives for nothing, like a trifle.

'See how you like this plan: I'll stick you into two leather
bags, tie them up with straps, and stow them among my clothes
like so much baggage; we'll leave the tops open, of course, just
enough for you to get air and food. Then in the middle of the
night, I'll raise a ruckus saying that two slaves of mine have
gone overboard fearing a more severe punishment. When we
arrive at port, I'll take you off like baggage without exciting
any suspicion.

'Oh, I see,' I said. 'You're going to pack us like cargo, as if
we had no stomach to trouble us, and neither sneezed, nor
snored; just because this kind of trick may have worked well
once?[1] But even if we could stand being tied up for one day,
what if a calm sea or bad weather holds us up longer? What
will we do? Even clothes get wrinkled if they're tied up too
long. Even bundles of paper lose their shape. Are two young
men who have never worked a day in their lives supposed to
put up with packing rags and ropes like a couple of statues?

*

'There must be another way out. Listen, I have an idea: like
any man of letters, Eumolpus has plenty of ink. So we'll use it
to change our color from our hair to our toenails! We will be
on hand as your Ethiopian slaves happy to have escaped
torture, and we will deceive our enemies by simply changing
colors.'

'Why don't you circumcise us while you're at it,' said Giton,
'so we'll look like Jews. And bore holes in our ears, so we'll
resemble Arabs? Or paint our faces so that Gaul would take
us for natives? As if color alone would change our shape. As if
many other things must not agree in order for our lie to be
credible. Suppose that the color on our faces could last long
enough. Suppose that no drop of water would spot our skin,

[101.1] Conceivably a reference to Menelaus' disguising himself as a seal in *Od.*
4.435 ff., if we read *Menelao* with certain texts. Others more plausibly compare
Cleopatra, who had herself delivered to Caesar wrapped in a rug (Plutarch,
Caesar 49), while the reference to sneezing suggests the escape from Ascyltos-as-
Cyclops in Chapter 98.

and that our clothes would not stick to the dye, although they stick to us often enough anyway. What then? Can we stretch our lips into shape? Can we change our hair with curling tongs? Part our foreheads with scars? Spread our legs into a bow? Or walk on our ankles? And cut our beards in a foreign fashion? An artificial dye stains our bodies, but can't transform them. Listen, I have a desperate idea: let's wrap our heads in our clothes, and jump in the ocean.'

103. 'Heaven forbid that you should take such a disgraceful way out of life,' Eumolpus exclaimed. 'You'd best do as I say; as you learned from his razor, my man here is a barber. Let him give you both a shave right now – not just your heads but even your eyebrows. Then I'll mark some clever inscription on your foreheads so that you'll look like slaves punished with tatooing.[1] These letters will both divert suspicion from you and hide your faces under the shadow of punishment.'

We wasted no time on the trick sneaking off into a corner of the ship, where the barber shaved our heads and eyebrows clean. Eumolpus then covered our heads with large block letters drawing the notorious signs tatooed on runaway slaves in broad strokes right across our faces. By chance, one of the passengers was leaning over the side of the ship to relieve a queasy stomach, and in the moonlight he noticed the barber busy with his ill-timed task. He cursed the omen, because it resembled the last offering of shipwrecked sailors, and then threw himself back in his cabin. We pretended not to hear the sick man's curse, and returned to our gloomy chores. Keeping very still we spent what was left of the night in a fitful slumber.

*

104. [*Lichas*] 'I dreamt Priapus said to me: "As for your search for Encolpius, know that I have led him onto your ship." '

Tryphaena shuddered and said: 'You'd have thought we slept

---

[1] Standard treatment for slaves (cf. Cicero, *Pro Roscio comoedo* 7.20). Winkler p. 225 cites Nonnius' statement, 'Slaves who gain their freedom shave their head because they seem to be escaping the storm of servitude, as do people who escape shipwreck.' Shaven eyebrows were regarded by Scipio (Aulus Gellius 6.12.5) as the marks of *cinaedi* or 'queens' (cf. here Chapters 21–3).

together: I too dreamt that a statue of Neptune that I'd noticed in a temple at Baiae said, 'You will find Giton on Lichas' ship!" '

'You can tell from this,' said Eumolpus, 'what a godlike man Epicurus was, since he condemns this kind of foolery with such witty logic...'[1]

But to avert any danger posed by Tryphaena's dream Lichas said: 'Who will stop us from searching the ship? We wouldn't want to appear to reject the workings of providence...'

A man called Hesus, the one who had seen our desperate subterfuges the night before, suddenly shouted: 'Those are the men who were getting shaved in the moonlight! God knows it's a bad omen! They say no mortal should cut his nails or hair aboard ship unless the wind is angry with the sea!'

105. Lichas was outraged by this news: 'What? Did someone cut their hair on my ship, and in the very dead of night? Bring the offenders here immediately! I want to know whose heads will have to roll to purify the ship!'

'It was I who gave those orders,' Eumolpus calmly declared. 'Since I was going to be travelling on this ship too, I wouldn't have done anything inauspicious. But because they had long, shaggy hair, and I didn't want to make your ship into a prison, I gave orders to clean up these convicted criminals. I also wanted to make sure that the marks branded on them were not covered by their hair, so they can be readily identified by anyone. What's more, they squandered my money on some girlfriend they shared. It was just last night when I had to drag them away from her still reeking of wine and perfume. In fact, they still smell of the remains of my inheritance...'

It was decided that we should both receive forty lashes in order to appease the tutelary deity of the ship. So no time was wasted: some furious sailors came at us with ropes and tried

---

[104.1] Eumolpus' scepticism is ironically placed since these dreams from Priapus and Neptune are clearly by way of the gate of Horn, strictly veridical. Cf. Chapters 9, 17, and *Carm.* 30, which some editors actually place here; dreams can be seen as analogies for the Tantalean tease plaguing Encolpius throughout the whole book (above, Chapter 82, n. 1). Tryphaena's dream (sent by Neptune-Poseidon) recalls the plot-premise of the *Odyssey*, where Poseidon, instead of Priapus, is the hero's divine adversary.

to placate the god with our cheap blood. I even stomached three of their blows with Spartan indifference. But the first blow made Giton cry so loudly that the familiar sound of his voice filled Tryphaena's ears. Not only did this shock her, but that familiar voice drew all her attendant slave girls toward the man being flogged. Giton had already disarmed the sailors with his remarkable beauty and was trying to appeal to his tormentors silently, when the chorus of slave girls shouted in unison:

'It's Giton! Giton! Get your brutal hands off him! Hurry, mistress, it's Giton!'

Tryphaena's ears had already convinced her and she quickly flew to the boy's side. Lichas, who knew me best, ran up as if he, too, had recognized a voice. He studied neither my hands, nor my face, but looked down and placed his officious hand right on my groin saying, 'Greetings, Encolpius!'[1] Now will anyone be surprised that after twenty years Ulysses' nurse recognized him by his scar, when this clever man so shrewdly hit on the one sure way of identifying a runaway slave, even if his looks have changed in every other way? Deceived by our appearance, Tryphaena wept hysterically – she thought we had been kidnapped and the marks were actually tatooed on our foreheads – and started to ask us rather gingerly what prison had intercepted our wanderings, and whose cruel hands had inflicted our punishment. Of course, she added, as runaway slaves we had deserved a scolding, especially for responding so hatefully to our own good fortune...

106. Lichas leapt up in anger: 'You simple woman – as if they got these letters from a tatooing needle! I wish they had – that would be some consolation, at least. As it is, we are the butts of a farcical plot, mocked by a mock-inscription!'

Tryphaena wanted to take pity on us since she hadn't forgotten all her pleasure; but Lichas still remembered the

---

[1] A variation on standard recognition-by-tokens, with the most famous precedent here actually cited from Homer (*Od.* 19.467 ff.); since Encolpius' name could be rendered 'McGroin', he is also recognized for his namesake.

seduction of his wife and the wrongs that he suffered in the portico of Hercules.[1] He scowled and cried out feelingly: 'I think you now understand that the immortal gods oversee the affairs of men, my dear Tryphaena. For they led these reckless malefactors right onto our ship and warned us of what they had done by the coincidence of our dreams. So how can we forgive those whom god himself has brought to punishment? As for me, I am not a cruel man, but I am afraid I will suffer whatever penalty I spare them.'

This superstitious bit of oratory changed Tryphaena's mind. She denied that she was interfering with our punishment; on the contrary, she favored the most exacting retribution. Had she not suffered as great a wrong as Lichas when her virtue had been publicly besmirched?

*

107. [*Eumolpus*] 'They chose me for this task, I assume, as a man of no little standing and begged me to reconcile them with their dearest friends of old.[1] Don't imagine that they just stumbled into this trap by accident, when the first question every traveller asks is into whose care he is entrusting himself. Don't be unbending when satisfaction has been given; allow these free men to go their way unmolested. After all, even savage, unforgiving masters refrain from cruelty when a change of heart brings their runaways home; we even spare enemies who surrender. What more could you ask for? What do you want? Before your eyes kneel two young suppliants, free-born gentlemen, and, what is far more important, once joined to you by the intimate bonds of friendship! For god's sake, even if they had robbed you of money or betrayed your confidence, you would still have been satisfied with the punishment you see. Look at the slavery inscribed on their foreheads! Look

---

[106.1] It seems Lichas was wronged (in a missing part of the novel) by an open-air tryst of his wife and Encolpius, perhaps in the style of the Cynics' 'dog-marriages' (cf. here, Chapter 11, and Apuleius, *Flor.* 14). On the other hand, lusty Tryphaena blames Encolpius for staining her honor, though here she promptly takes up with Giton (below, Chapter 113).

[107.1] Here the argument shifts to the style of a quasi-*controversia* (cf. Chapter 48, Introduction xxiv–xxv) and Chapter 2, n. 3.

at those free-born faces banished from society by their own hands!'

Lichas interrupted his plea: 'Don't confuse the issue and, please, keep the facts in order. First of all, if they came here deliberately, why did they shave their heads? Whoever disguises himself is engaged in an act of fraud, not of penance. Furthermore, if they were planning to make a formal apology through you, why did you do everything possible to keep your clients safely hidden? It is perfectly obvious that the malefactors stumbled into a trap and that you have devised this stratagem to elude the force of our displeasure. As for your attempt to intimidate us by pronouncing them "free-born gentlemen", be careful that your audacity doesn't damage your case. What should the injured parties do, when the very flight of the guilty brings them to justice? Of course, they were our friends, which makes them all the more deserving of punishment! For if someone harms strangers, we call him a thug; but if he harms his friends, he's little better than a parricide!'

Eumolpus tried to counter this vicious tirade. 'I can see that nothing incriminates these poor young men so much as the fact that they shaved their heads at night. This suggests that they came aboard the ship accidentally rather than deliberately. But I want an account to reach your ears as guileless as the deed was simple. Before they came on board, they wanted to rid themselves of a troublesome and superfluous mass of hair, but the wind came up too soon and they put it off. They didn't think it made any difference where they did what they had already decided to do; what did they know of sailors' omens or the law of the sea?'

Lichas interrupted: 'But why on earth should suppliants shave their heads? I suppose bald men are more pitiable! But what's the point of interrogating some middleman? What do you have to say for yourself, you thug? What salamander singed off your eyebrows? What god received your hair as an offering? Answer, you snake in the grass!'

108. I was paralyzed with fear at the thought of being punished: we were so obviously guilty, I could think of nothing to say. Panic-stricken and disfigured – for besides the disgrace of

my pillaged head my eyebrows were as bald as my forehead –
there was nothing I could do or say without appearing absurd.
But as my tearful face was wiped with a wet sponge and the
ink streamed down my cheeks reducing all my features to a
veil of soot, anger gave way to disgust...

Then Eumolpus intervened declaring that he would permit
no one to lay a finger on free-born men in violation of both
custom and law. He cut short their angry threats, at first with
words, then with blows. His valet sided with him as well as a
couple of feeble looking passengers, but they provided moral
support rather than physical strength. I said nothing on my
own behalf, but poked my fist at Tryphaena's eyes and said
loud and clear that I would use violence against her if the bitch
didn't lay off Giton; *she* was the only one on the ship who
deserved a good flogging.

My outburst made Lichas even madder: he was furious that
I would simply drop my own case only to raise my voice for
someone else. Tryphaena was no less outraged by my assault
and drove everyone aboard to take sides. On our side the valet,
armed with the tools of his trade, handed out razor blades to
the rest of us; on their side, Tryphaena's slaves bared their fists
for a fight. And not even her shrieking slave girls deserted the
front line. The pilot alone objected, threatening to abandon his
post if the madness stirred up by the lust of these scoundrels
didn't stop. But the rage for a fight prevailed: they were out for
revenge, we to save our lives.

Many went down alive on both sides, and still more retreated
with bloody wounds, as they would in war, but no one's anger
slackened. Then, Giton the brave, brandished a deadly razor
over his own genitals and threatened to chop them off as the
cause of so much misery! Tryphaena averted so heinous a crime
with offer of an unconditional pardon. I too held the barber's
blade to my throat repeatedly – with no more intention of
harming myself than Giton had. But he could play the tragic
role with more daring: he knew he had the same razor he'd
used last time he cut his throat!

Both sides stood their ground and it was obvious that it
would be no ordinary battle, when the pilot prevailed on
Tryphaena to signal a truce like the herald of an army. When

the traditional pledges had been exchanged, Tryphaena held
out an olive branch plucked from the ship's patron deity and
boldly entered the parley:

> 'What madness,' cries she, 'turns the peace to blows?
> Is this our due? No Trojan hero goes
> in this ship with an Atreid's stolen wife;
> no mad Medea takes her brother's life.[1]
> Your scorned love makes you fierce? Still, why should you
> tempt fate with arms? Won't simple drowning do?
> Must you die *twice*? Must you outdo the flood
> in hate, and overwhelm its gulfs with blood?'

109. When the woman poured out these excited, clamorous
words, there was a momentary lull in the fighting and we
turned our hands from war to peace. Our leader Eumolpus
took advantage of their change of heart and, after chastising
Lichas roundly, sealed a formal peace treaty worded as follows:

> 'Article I: It is hereby agreed that you, Tryphaena,
> will drop all complaints lodged against Giton, and if any
> wrong was committed before this date, you will pursue
> the matter no further by word or deed. Furthermore, you
> agree to refrain from imposing anything on the boy against
> his will, including hugs, kisses, and venereal embraces,
> unless you have paid one hundred pieces of gold in cash.
>   Article II: It is hereby agreed that you, Lichas, will
> refrain from harassing Encolpius with either abusive words or looks.
> Nor will you inquire where he is sleeping at night. For each and
> every violation of this agreement, you agree to pay a fine of two
> hundred pieces of gold in cash.'

When the wording of the treaty was agreed upon, we laid down
our arms officially. To ensure that no animosity remained after
the oath was taken, we further agreed to put the past to rest
with a round of kisses. Our anger subsided as the crowd cheered
us on; and the food brought as provisions for battle served
instead to unite us all in a jovial mood.

[108.1] Famous violent sea-faring precedents starting with the abduction of Helen.

The whole ship rang with song and, as a sudden calm had interrupted our voyage, one man used a trident to spear fish leaping in the waves, while another hauled in a fighting catch with baited hooks. Up above, seabirds even perched on the rigging and a clever craftsman caught them in a trap of reeds; snared in the twigs sticky with lime, they were lowered right into our hands. A breeze buoyed up their plumes and the sea spray spun their feathers across the waves.

Lichas was already beginning to get friendly with me again, while Tryphaena was sprinkling Giton with the last of her wine, when Eumolpus, now thoroughly soused, started cracking jokes about bald heads and tatooed men. When he ran out of lame jokes, he resorted to verse and started reciting a little elegy on hair:[1]

> 'The body's crowning ornament, its hairs
> are gone; dull winter, spring's bright tresses tears.
> The temples mourn, denuded of their shade;
> your pate a sunburnt threshing-floor is made.
> Born cheaters! Gods! First gifts you take away
> are those you gave us on our natal day.'

*

> 'Poor head, you gleamed with hair,
> than sun and moon more fair;
> bronze-bald, as tuber round,
> rain-born in garden ground,
> now mocking girls you dread;
> to teach how soon you're dead,
> there goes part of your head.'

110. Eumolpus was about to offer us even more ludicrous verses, I believe, when Tryphaena's maid took Giton below deck and dressed him up in one of her mistress's curled wigs. In fact, she even furnished him with eyebrows from a little chest, and then she traced the outlines of his other losses until she had restored all his former beauty. Tryphaena recognized

[109.1] An unpromising but not an unparalleled theme; cf. Ovid, *Amores* 1.14.

the real Giton and gave him her first bona fide kiss, as tears came to her eyes.

I too was delighted to see the boy's pristine beauty restored, but I kept trying to hide my own face. I realized how hideously disfigured I must be when not even Lichas thought me worth talking to! But the same maid rescued me from my shame; she called me aside and dressed me in an equally becoming wig. Indeed, my face was especially flattered by the blonde wig she gave me.

*

But Eumolpus, our defender in danger and the author of the present peace, didn't like a party with no stories. So he started telling jokes about the fickleness of women – how easily they fall in love, how quickly they forget even their own sons, and how none has ever been so virtuous that she couldn't be driven mad with desire for some perfect stranger.[1] Nor was he talking about ancient tragedy or names known from legend, but an incident lodged in his own memory, which he would tell us about if we were curious. So when he had everyone's eyes and ears, he began his story:[2]

111. 'There once was a lady of Ephesus who was so famous for her virtue that women came from foreign countries just to get a look at her. So when this woman buried her husband, it wasn't enough for her to grieve in the usual way by walking behind the corpse with her hair down or by beating her bare breast before a crowd of mourners; instead she followed the dead man right into his tomb. She had the corpse placed in a

---

[110.1] This is also the favorite theme of the boy-lover Orpheus in Ovid's *Metam.* 10 (see esp. ll 152–4).

[110.2] 'The Widow of Ephesus' (Chapters 111–12), like 'The Pergamene Boy' (85–7), is traditionally considered a 'Milesian Tale', a variety of bawdy short tales first attested in the 1st century BC. All we know of them apart from their name is that they were compiled or invented by one Aristides and that they were considered quite scandalous (Plutarch, *Life of Crassus* 32.5; 'Lucian', *Amores* 1). They were translated into Latin by Cornelius Sisenna. 'The Widow of Ephesus' predates Petronius (it first appears in Phaedrus) and has been reproduced and imitated more often than any other part of the *Satyrica*. In this century it was dramatized by Christopher Fry in *A Phoenix Too Frequent*.

vault underground, in the Greek fashion, where she tended it and continued to mourn night and day. She was so grief-stricken that neither her friends nor her parents could dissuade her from seeking death by starvation. Finally, even the local magistrates went away, their pleas rebuffed; everyone had given her up for dead, this exemplary woman, who had already gone five days without a bite to eat. The poor widow's only company was a faithful maid, who shared her tears and refilled the lamp in the tomb as often as it went out. Soon all Ephesus talked of only one thing; men of every rank agreed: this woman was the sole true embodiment of wifely love and devotion.

'Meanwhile the provincial governor gave orders that some thieves be crucified not far from the little tomb where the widow was mourning the body of her husband. On the next night a soldier, whose job it was to make sure no one took one of the criminals down and buried him, noticed a light flickering among the tombstones and heard the sobs of someone crying. He was naturally curious to find out who was there and what she was doing. So he walked down into the vault, and the rare beauty of the widow struck him with all the force of an apparition from the underworld. At first he was bewildered, then he noticed the corpse lying there, and the tears and marks of grief on the widow's face, and he understood exactly what he saw: a woman overcome with longing for her dead husband. So he brought his own little supper into the tomb and began to console her; he urged her not to compound her grief with pointless mourning. What good would it do to weep until she broke her heart? Doesn't the same end await us all, the same resting place? And so he reasoned with her using all the arguments that restore sick minds to health.

'But the stranger's attempt to console her only upset her; she tore at her breast more violently, ripped out fistfuls of hair and laid them on the body. Yet the soldier didn't go away. He kept trying to comfort her and give her food; finally, the servant gave in to the scent of the wine and stretched out her hand to his kind offer. Invigorated by food and drink, she began the assault on her mistress' will:

'"What good does it do you to starve to death, to bury

yourself alive, to breathe your last breath before the fates demand it?

'"Could ashes or dead souls care less for mourning?[1] Don't you want to live again? Don't you want to shake off this womanish weakness and enjoy the good things of life while you can? Let this corpse lying here be a warning to you – to live!"

'Who can resist it when they're urged to eat or enjoy life? So too the widow, thirsty after days of fasting, lost her resolve and began to fill herself with food no less greedily than the maid who gave in first.

112. 'But you know what appetite remains when our stomachs are full. So the same beguiling arguments that the soldier had used to make the widow want to live, he used again to lay siege to her virtue. Nor did the chaste lady find the young man unpersuasive or uncomely. The maid, too, was trying to win her favor for him and kept saying:

"Will you fight welcome love, as well?
[Have you forgotten in whose lands you dwell?"][1]

'Well, why beat around the bush? The woman didn't starve that part of her body either. The persuasive soldier was victorious on both fronts. And they celebrated their marriage not only that night, but the next one as well, and the one after that! (Of course the doors to the tomb were closed!) Indeed, any friend or stranger who came to the tomb would have thought that most virtuous wife had finally expired over the body of her dead husband.[2]

'Well, the soldier took great delight in the widow's beauty and their secret tryst. He kept buying whatever food he could and bringing it to the tomb as soon as night fell. And so it happened that the parents of one of the crucified thieves, seeing

---

[111.1] Vergil, *Aen.* 4.34, spoken by her sister Anna to a more famous widow, i.e., Dido.

[112.1] Vergil, *Aen.* 4.38–9.

[112.2] Possibly an ironic inversion of the scene in Homer, *Od.* 23.133–51, where Odysseus consolidates his victory over the loyal Penelope's suitors as the passers-by think they are hearing the sound of her wedding-banquet.

there was no one on guard, took their son down one night and gave him the last rites. Tricked while off duty, the next day the soldier discovered that one of the crosses was missing a corpse. Scared to death of being punished, he explained to the widow what had happened. He said he would not wait for a judge to impose a sentence on him, but would punish his negligence with his own sword, if she would kindly make room for a man about to die and use the same fateful tomb for both her lover and her husband!

'But this widow was no less compassionate than she was virtuous! "Heaven forbid that I should have to look upon the bodies of both the men I love at the same time! I would rather sacrifice a dead man than execute a live one!" And she followed her speech with orders that the body of her husband be taken out of his coffin and hung on the empty cross! The soldier adopted this sensible woman's plan, and the next day everyone wondered how a dead man had climbed up on that cross!'

113. The sailors greeted the story with laughter; Tryphaena turned bright red and leaned her head fondly on Giton's shoulder. But Lichas didn't even crack a smile, he just shook his head in anger saying, 'If the governor had cared about justice, he would have put the paterfamilias back in his tomb and nailed that woman to the cross!'

No doubt the story had reminded him of his Hedyle and how his ship had been plundered when she eloped.[1] The terms of the treaty forbade such memories, as the good mood we shared left no room for rancor.

Meanwhile, Tryphaena was perched in Giton's lap covering his chest with kisses and occasionally sprucing up his hairless look. I was feeling depressed and uneasy with this new arrangement; I took no food or drink, and out of the corner of my eye I was giving them both hateful looks. Every kiss wounded me, every flirtatious move that insatiable woman made. I still didn't know whether to be madder at my boyfriend for stealing my

---

[1] Hedyle is presumably Lichas' wife (106), and the 'plunder' presumably that of the tokens of Isis remembered in Chapter 114.

mistress or at my mistress for seducing my boyfriend![2] Both acts were hateful in my eyes and more painful than my own imprisonment. On top of this, Tryphaena didn't speak to me like a friend – who used to please her as a lover – nor did Giton bother to toast my health in the usual way, or at the very least, to include me in the conversation. I imagine he was afraid of reopening a fresh wound when our reconciliation had barely taken hold. Tears of resentment streamed down my breast and I almost choked trying to hide my groans under sighs...

*

[Lichas] asked to share in our pleasure, not like a proud master, but more like a needy friend...

*

[*Tryphaena's maid to Encolpius*][3] 'If you had any free blood in your veins, you'd think him no better than a whore! If you were a man, you wouldn't chase after a male harlot...'

*

Nothing made me more ashamed than the thought that Eumolpus might get a whiff of our antics and use his razor-sharp tongue to punish me in verse...

*

Eumolpus swore in the most solemn terms.

*

114. While we were chatting about this and that, white caps appeared on the sea and storm clouds enveloped us from all sides, blotting out the light of day. Frightened sailors scrambled to their posts and took down the sails before the storm hit. But the winds blew the waves every which way and the

113.2 Cf. 'Shakespeare's' (perhaps no less parodic?) predicament in the last several sonnets involving the Dark Lady and the poet's male friend.

113.3 Though the MSS. refer this to Tryphaena's servant speaking of Giton, it could equally well be Encolpius speaking of Tryphaena. If the servant is speaking, the point is no doubt to turn jealousy into aversion-therapy till Encolpius is ready to forget about Giton altogether.

pilot couldn't find his course. One moment we were blown straight toward Sicily, at the next, the wind whipped around from the north and spun our helpless ship back toward the Italian coast.[1] But even more dangerous than all the gale winds, were the dark, heavy clouds that suddenly occluded the sky so completely that the pilot could scarcely see over the prow!

Just as the storm was reaching its height, Lichas came to me in abject fear and held out his hands in supplication: 'You, Encolpius,' he cried, 'save us from these perils – restore to our ship the goddess' robe and holy rattle![2] For god's sake, take pity on us, as you have before!'

Just as he uttered this prayer a gust of wind knocked him overboard, the storm churned him round and round in an enormous whirlpool and then swallowed him up! Loyal servants grabbed Tryphaena, on the verge of collapse, put her in a lifeboat with most of her baggage, and so saved her from certain death...

Clinging to Giton, I wept aloud and said 'Did we deserve this fate? To be united only in death? But the cruel game of Fortune isn't over, look! The storm is swamping the ship! This angry sea will sever our embraces! If you ever really loved your Encolpius, kiss me now while you can, steal this last pleasure before the fates harry us to our deaths!'

As I spoke, Giton took off his clothes, huddled under my tunic, and held up his face to be kissed. For fear the spiteful sea should tear us apart, he looped his belt around us both and said, 'Whatever happens now we'll be borne together longer united in death! And if a more merciful sea washes us up on the same shore, either some traveller will heap a pile of stones over us out of common decency, or, if the angry sea does its worst, the indifferent sand will inter us.'

I accepted this final bond and, like a man laid out on his funeral bier, I faced death without regrets. Meanwhile the storm carried out the fates' decrees shattering all that was left of our

---

[114.1] This detail recalls *Od.* 12, where Odysseus shipwrecks, a scene often placed between Italy and Sicily (= ? Homer's *Thrinakiē*) in the Straits of Messina; correspondingly, here Lichas drowns in a Charybdis-like whirlpool.

[114.2] See Chapter 113, n. 1.

little ship. No mast, no rudder, no rope or oar remained. Her timbers scattered across the waves like so much driftwood...

*

Fishermen had already set out in little boats to net some booty; when they saw survivors who might defend their property, their raid became a rescue...

*

115. We heard a strange murmur – from the pilot's cabin came a kind of groaning like a wild animal trying to escape.[1] When we followed the sound we came upon Eumolpus sitting there, inscribing verses on a huge sheet of parchment. Astonished that he would take the time to compose a poem in the face of death we dragged him out, shouting all the way, and begged him to come to his senses. But he was furious at being interrupted: 'Let me finish this line! The poem's having trouble ending.' I grabbed the madman and told Giton to help drag the howling poet ashore.

*

When we finally finished the job we sadly entered a fisherman's hut. We somehow made do on food ruined in the shipwreck and spent an utterly miserable night. The next day when we were trying to decide where in the world to take our chances, I suddenly noticed a man's body floating toward the beach on a gentle swell. I stood there for a moment downcast and with tears in my eyes I reflected on the faithless sea, 'Somewhere in the world, perhaps, this man has a wife waiting for him safe at home, or a son, maybe, or a father, who knows nothing of the storm. At least there was someone he kissed good-bye. But here lie the plans and prayers of mortals! See how he bobs in the water!'

So I mourned him as a stranger until a wave heaved his unmarked face toward the shore and I recognized the once stern and unforgiving Lichas cast almost at my feet! I couldn't

---

[115.1] An especially humorous comparison in view of Eumolpus' connection with Orpheus; see Chapter 84, here, and cf. Ovid, *Metam.* 10.

hold back the tears any longer. I struck my breast again and again and cried, 'Where is your anger now! Where is your rage – now that you've become food for fish and wild animals! Just a little while ago you flaunted your powers of command, but now, a castaway, you have not one plank from that great ship of yours.

'Go ahead, mortal friends, fill your hearts with great desires! Come, you shrewd investors, bank your pilfered profits on the next millennium! But just yesterday this man audited his estates' accounts! Yes, he calculated the very day that would bring him home. Gods and goddesses! How far he lies from that destination!

'But it isn't just the sea that deceives mortals. Arms betray the man at war, the collapse of his family shrine entombs another – as he thanks the gods! The busy man slips from his coach and gasps out a hurried life! Food chokes the glutton, fasting the frugal! If you add it all up, shipwreck is everywhere!

'*But only those who drown at sea receive no burial?* As if it matters to a corpse whether water, fire, or time devours it! Whatever you may do, it's all one in the end! But wild beasts may claw the corpse, you say? As if fire were any gentler! When we're angry at our slaves, don't we threaten them with fire? What folly it is to move heaven and earth only to be sure our burial leaves nothing behind!'

*

So Lichas burned on a funeral pyre built by his enemies' hands. Meanwhile, Eumolpus composed an epitaph for the dead and cast his eyes about in search of a metaphor ...

*

116. We willingly dispatched this duty and set off on the path we had chosen. Very soon we were sweating our way up a mountain; on the next horizon we could make out a town lodged on a lofty hilltop. Lost as usual, we had no idea what town it was until we learned from a hired hand that it was Croton, a very ancient city, once the foremost in

Italy.¹ So we proceeded to make further inquiries as to what people inhabited this worthy place and what business they practiced now that frequent wars had exhausted the city's ancient wealth.

'Strangers', he said, 'if you really are businessmen, change your plans, find another way to make a living. But if you're the clever city type, and can lie till you're hoarse, you're headed straight for a gold mine! Now in this city, culture counts for nothing. Eloquence has no place. Frugality and goodness are not rewarded or honored – no, any men you meet there you can be sure are one of two kinds: either fortune hunters or their prey. No one raises children in this city! If you have your own heirs, you'll never be invited to dinner or asked to the games. You'll be deprived of every advantage and relegated to slavish obscurity. But those who never take a wife and have no near relations climb right to the top; they are the conquering heroes there! Yes, indeed,' he said, 'you're coming to a city that's like a land racked with plague. There's nothing else there but corpses being ravaged and ravens ravaging them.'

*

117. As the wiser head, Eumolpus took note of the novel situation and admitted that this kind of business was much to his taste. At first, I thought the old man was taking poetic license to tease us, until he said, 'I wish I could set the scene more fully – with more civilized clothes and the lavish accoutrements needed to make such a fiction plausible. By Jove, I wouldn't postpone the plundering. I'd lead you straight to a fortune! Anyway, I promise...'

[So we agreed] to do whatever he asked, as long as the cloak, my old partner in crime, actually fit and while the spoils from

¹¹⁶·¹ Croton's slow but relentless decline perhaps makes it another unflattering mirror for Neronian Rome. Having once been a colony of Pythagoreans (who were vegetarians) and the fictional scene of Pythagoras' sermon on universal flux and reparative metempsychosis in Ovid, *Met.* 15, Croton is also an ironically appropriate setting for the ultimate act of transgressive predation and meateating. Legacy-hunting is a stock theme in Roman verse satire, e.g., Horace, *Sat.* 2.5, with occasional parallels in Juvenal.

Lycurgus' villa lasted. I was sure the mother of the gods would be happy to make good by supplying some cash to meet our present needs...

'Well then,' said Eumolpus, 'why don't we get on with the farce? Make me the director, if you like the plot.'

No one dared object to a scheme where we had nothing to lose. So to keep our lie completely secret, we swore an oath that Eumolpus composed: to be burned, bound, beaten, beheaded, or anything else that Eumolpus ordered. Just like real gladiators, we solemnly pledged our bodies and souls to our master. After taking this oath, we pretended to be slaves saluting their master! We also agreed on the following story: Eumolpus had lost a son, an enormously eloquent and promising young man; in his inconsolable grief the old man had left his home town to avoid seeing his son's clients and friends, or his tomb, which brought tears to his eyes every day. To add to his sorrows, he had recently suffered a shipwreck and lost over two million in cash. While the monetary loss was nothing to him, he felt that his lack of attendants detracted from his dignity. On top of that, he had thirty million invested in Africa in farms and loans. In fact, he had so many slaves scattered over his estates in Numidia that they could take Carthage itself!

In accordance with this plan we told Eumolpus to cough a lot, to get first constipation, then diarrhea, and to complain constantly and loudly about all the food. His talk would be of gold and silver, of disappointing investments, and invariably unproductive land. And he must go over his holdings daily and revise his will once a month. To complete the setting, he would use the wrong names whenever he tried to call one of us, so that it would be obvious that he was thinking of those he'd left behind.

With all this agreed on we prayed to the gods for 'luck and success' and started down the road. But Giton wasn't up to carrying his load, and Eumolpus' man, Corax, who frankly disliked work, kept dropping his bags and got surly when we tried to hurry him up. He even threatened to throw our stuff away or run off with the whole load. 'Do I look like a mule or a cargo ship to you?' he said. 'I was hired as a man not a

workhorse!¹ And I'm every bit as free as you are even if my
father did leave me a pauper.' Not content with his grumbling,
every so often he lifted his leg and cut a fart that filled the
road with his obscene noise and stench. Giton laughed at his
impudence and matched him fart for fart...

*

118. 'Yes, my young friends,' said Eumolpus, 'poetry has led
many of us astray. For as soon as someone has managed to write a
line of verse that scans, and woven some sense into a moderately
subtle turn of phrase, he thinks he's set foot on the top of Helicon!
So when they're tired of slaving away in court, they often turn to
the tranquility of poetry as if it were some kind of safe haven;
they believe that composing a poem is less demanding than dressing up a speech with those witty one-liners!¹ But the truly talented have no love of empty showmanship, and that mind can

---

¹¹⁷·¹ Cf Seneca's protest (*Epist.* 47.5) against treating slaves like beasts of
burden and not men.

¹¹⁸·¹ Cf. Agamemnon's poem (Chapter 5). Eumolpus' personal tragedy, such as
it is, seems to be that he knows more about diagnosing other poets' conventional
lapses than about rectifying his own; his phrasings too often fall back on the
stagey tricks that his own theories condemn; yet Eumolpus' near-misses may turn
out to be more telling by getting as close to the target as they often do. We
accordingly translate his main effort – his poem on the Roman civil wars – not
as a simple parody of Lucan's *Bellum civile*, despite numerous parallels of the
sort well surveyed by Ernout, but as a revealing attempt to treat Lucan's distinctly
unusual (though not unprecedented) subject, the civil war, in a quasi Vergilian
manner (even pointedly bringing back the gods' speaking parts after Lucan omits
them in a decisive break with tradition) but without Vergil's teleological reading
of Roman history. Thus Eumolpus embraces Lucan's novel project – an epic on
the Roman civil wars – while essentially inverting his revolutionary poetics. The
effect is both comic and anachronistic, as well as politically ambiguous (since
neither Eumolpus' nor Lucan's poem is actually completed; see Connors, 'Famous
last words: authorship and death in the *Satyricon* and Neronian Rome' in Elsner
et. al.). Eumolpus' neo-classicizing stance is made explicit by the precepts that
precede the poem (Chapter 118) including a verbal citation from Horace (*Od.*
3.1.1), a rejection of extraneous ornamentation (cf. *Ars poetica* 15–16), a double
appeal to *Romanus Vergilius* and *Horatii curiosa felicitas*, and, not least, his
hoary conception of the poet as an 'inspired seer' (cf. Coleridge *ad. loc.* in
Petronius and his Critics, p. 175, below). Fittingly, too, as the poems' formal
program is often at odds with the poet's own practice, so the poems' ethical
stance is at odds with the poet's life (see esp. Chapter 119.19–38 and Chapter
93).

neither conceive, nor give birth that is not steeped in the great
river of literature! One must flee every syllable that smacks, so
to speak, of vulgarity and use only those expressions remote
from plebeian speech to realize the Horatian dictum: 'I despise
and shun the common crowd.' Besides this, one must be very
careful that the aphorisms do not stand out from the body of the
work, but glow with colors actually woven into its fabric. Homer
and the lyric poets illustrate this, as do our Roman Vergil and
the fastidious felicity of Horace. The others either didn't see the
path that leads to poesie, or lost heart when they did.

'For example, anyone who undertakes a theme as vast as the
Civil War will sink beneath its burden, if he isn't brim-full of
literature. One can't simply report what actually happened –
the historians do that far better – no, the spirit must soar fancy-
free through the labyrinths of divine intervention and mythical
thought. The result will be more like the prophetic words of
an inspired seer than some sober statement of fact before
witnesses. Take this daring attempt as an example, if you like,
even though it still lacks the final touches:

119. 'The Roman victor held the world in thrall,
      land, sea, the sun and moon's whole circuit, all,
      but wanted *more*. The straits were overworked
      with laden ships; if any inlet lurked,
      if any land with tawny gold in store,
      it was the foe; by Fates disposed to war,
      riches were won. The common pleasures palled,
      delights by vulgar currency worn bald.
      Corinthian bronze was prized by men at sea;
      earth rivalled shellfish-purple's finery.   10
      Here Afric's stones, there China's silken yields;
      the Arabs too had plundered their own fields.

          Lo new destruction, peacetime's bloody clashes;
      gold traps wild beasts; man distant Ammon thrashes
      for elephantine prey, its tusk a treat
      to die for; alien hungers fill the fleet;
      the stalking tiger comes in gilded gear
      to drink men's blood, while all the people cheer.

It shames me to speak out, detail our fate
of ruin – the way they seize, emasculate   20
young men half-grown (if that), break them to lust
à la Persane, and by forestalling, trust
to halt the hastening years and manhood's flight
while nature lacks itself. So all delight
in catamites, their jaded mincing air,
the *tousled* look, new words for things to wear,
all that's unmanly!
                              Culled from Nubian plots,
dearer than gold, and splashed with golden spots
reflecting table-slaves and lavish dresses,
a table made of citrus-wood impresses;   30
a sodden rout surrounds such useless woods,
and soldiers thirst, then fight, for just such goods.
Ingenious gluttony! Sicilian fish,
served living, in an oceanic dish;
Lake Lucrine's clams, a plate of them so dear
that once we pay to eat, starvation's near.
The Black Sea's shore lies mute, its pheasants gone;
only the wind in lonely leaves breathes on.

   Madness in public life is just as great:
for touted profits Romans sell their state,   40
Senate and populace both keen to sell;
their vote's for cash. Yes – SENATORS AS WELL
sold out 'free' virtue! Lucre swayed their might;
even *their* honor fell to money's blight!
Then Cato's banished, beaten by the crowd—[1]
the victor crushed at seeing Cato bowed—
the people's shame, their character's ruination—
just Cato banished, and in him the nation
reft of its might and light! Abandoned Rome,
defenseless prey to Avarice at Home!   50

[119.1] Marcus Porcius Cato Uticensis, renowned martyr to the Roman republican
cause; these lines probably bear on an election he lost to Vatinius, a henchman
of Caesar's.

The plebs besides, caught in the double jaws
of usury and high interest, fed those maws;
no house was safe, no one not deep in debt,
anxieties like barking dogs beset
them all, like some bone-wasting chronic sore.[2]
Despair drives them to fight, their wounds restore
what squandering lost; bankrupts can lose no more.
Sleep-drowned in turpitude and somnolence,
what arts could waken Rome but violence,
war-fever, and the lust bred by offense?   60

120.   Fortune three generals bore; War sank them all,
each heaped with arms, in different ports of call:
Crassus haunts Parthia, Pompey Egypt's shore,
while Caesar stained ungrateful Rome with gore,
as if the earth, her heavy load to ease,
scattered their ash – of Fame the wages these![1]

There is a place deep in a plunging cleft
'Twixt Naples and Dicarchus' precincts left[2]
drenched with Cocytus' water; for a draught
suffused with its dire spray emerges there.   70
This ground is never gold with crops; quite bare
of grass this hapless field; no thickets ring
with springtime songbirds' clamorous chattering;
chaos is here, black pumice, jagged stone
joying in cypress-trees that form its crown.

[119.2] For the image, c.f. Sallust, *Cat.* 36, and Livy 2.23.6.

[120.1] The three members of Rome's first triumvirate all met violent ends: Crassus
in an attempt to win glory by fighting the Parthians, Pompey after his final loss
in a long bloody contest with Caesar, and Caesar himself in the Senate at the
hands of republican assassins. Petronius' conceit here is especially close to Lucan
6.817–18. Also Lucanic is this poem's obvious taste for invoking personified
concepts like Fortune, often in lieu of more mythic divinities.

[120.2] Dicarchus' precincts: Pozzuoli. Its more precious alias, *Dicarchis* – serving
here the same way that *Parthenope* is used to mean 'Naples' – harks back to the
name of the town's plainly Greek founding hero. The region around the two cities
is known for its volcanic features, suggesting close links with the infernal regions;
it is also (cf. Chapter 6, n. 1) the scene of most of the extant adventures comprised
in Petronius' novel.

Here Hades rose, his face tinged with a dash
of funeral flames, and there some hoary ash,
and stirred winged Fortune up with this address:
"Of men's and gods' affairs the arbitress,
Chance, no firm friend of power without duress,   80
lover of change, quick leaver of your own,
do you not feel how Rome's weight bears you down,
how you can hoist no higher its tottering bulk?
Young Rome hates its own strength, inclines to sulk,
bears ill the wealth that its own hands compiled;
see plunder squandered everywhere, wealth wild
to spend itself. In gold, sky-high, they build,
shut water out with stone, or flood a field,
make war on nature, making things trade place.
See how they even raid my realm: earth's face   90
is gouged for monstrous projects; caverns groan
in mountains hollowed out for ill-used stone;
hell's ghosts expect a glimpse of heaven soon.
Then, Chance, arise; turn placid looks to strife;
harry the Romans; glut us with their life.
Too long it is since blood last crossed my lips
and my chief Fury waded to her hips,
not since the sword of Sulla drank, and fed
a record crop the life-blood of the dead!"[3]

121. He ended thus,[1] and as he strove to take   100
her hand, gave earth an even broader break.
    Then slippery Fortune gushed out this reply:
"O father whom Cocytus' depths obey,
if I may truly speak without offense,
your wish will speed as mine for all intents:
my anger is as great, my fire as killing;
all I gave Rome I hate, hereby unwilling
the very gifts I gave. The very god
that raised those walls will smash them back to sod.

[120.3] The dictator Sulla slaughtered adherents of his rival Marius in 82 BC.
[121.1] A formulaic hexameter half-line (see Chapter 61, n. 2 here).

I, too, like toasting men and tippling blood;   110
now I see Philippi twice-corpse-strewn² – *good*! –
Thessalian pyres, and funerals in Spain.
The clash of arms assails my ears again,
and Libyan Nile, I see your channels groan,
dismayed by Actium and Apollo's own.³
Now, Hades, clear your kingdom's thirsty reach
for new recruits! Charon to ferry each
unbodied wraith will scarcely have the strength –
you'll need a fleet. Enjoy the crush, at length!
Dig in, pale Fury – right behind the blades!   120
A mangled world will join the Stygian shades."

122.   She finished, and at once a mighty jolt
kindled a cloud struck by a thunderbolt!
With fear of brother's blow quite bloodless left,
the Lord of Darkness sank and closed the cleft.
Omens at once made plain the deaths of men
and ruins to come. The sun with bloody wen
disfigured and in darkness hid his face,
as if a civil war were taking place;
the moon for her part staged a full eclipse,   130
denying the crime her light. The upmost tips
of mountain ranges thunderingly give way;
beyond their usual banks doomed rivers stray.
War's noise makes heaven rage; amid the stars
the throbbing trumpet's roar arouses Mars;
with new fires eaten, Etna blasts on high;
where tombs stand, and where bones unburied lie,
see specters gibbering threats that more will die.
A firebrand mounts with novas in its train
and a new Jove descends in bloody rain,   140

[121.2] A confusion found also in Vergil, *Georg.* 1.489, between Pharsalia and
Philippi, two towns in different parts of northern Greece and the scenes of decisive
defeat for Pompey and Brutus, respectively.

[121.3] Apollo supposedly aided Octavian, the future Augustus, in his victory at
Actium over ships of Cleopatra and Antony (cf. Vergil, *Aen.* 8.704–6).

portents borne out apace! Revenge in mind,
Caesar abruptly leaves Gaul's broils behind
for civic blood as penalty-in-kind.[1]

In the high Alps, traversed by that Greek god
on rugged ways that mortals too have trod,
there stands a hallowed shrine to Hercules
hemmed in with vaulting wintry snowcaps; these
hint at a height past heaven's remedies.
Full sunlight never warms it, nor spring's breeze,
tight in the grip of ice and winter curled;   150
its hulking shoulders could support the world.
When Caesar marched here with his vaunting crew,
he chose the spot, surveyed the fields below
of widespread Italy, raised voice and hands
up to the stars, and listed his demands:
"Almighty Jove, and Saturn's land, once thrilled
and freighted with my trophies from the field,
hear ye: this time, not willingly at all
I take up arms and Mars to battle call;
outrage compels me – banished, though I stain   160
the Rhine blood-red, and make the Gauls abstain
from sacking Rome anew.[2] That seals my fate;
dead Germans and my sixty wins to date

[1] 'Leaves Gaul's broils behind': i.e., crosses the Rubicon, the boundary
between Italy and Cisalpine Gaul. As Ernout notes, a large part of the following
passage on Caesar traversing the Alps is apparently patterned on Livy's account
(31.36 ff.) of a much earlier crossing by Hannibal, while the opening three lines
here allude to a mythical crossing by Hercules en route from killing the man-
monster Geryon in Spain. Caesar did cross the Alps fairly peacefully. Caesar's
crossing of the Alps and the Rubicon is more briefly versified by Lucan in *Bellum
civile*, Book 1.

[2] Saturn's land: Italy, here so-called because mythically it is Saturn's place
of exile. Caesar claims he himself has been banished; in fact he was simply denied
an exemption from Rome's standard rule that a general could not run for the
office of consul without first giving up his *imperium* or direct military authority.
The Gauls' first sack of Rome took place *c.* 390 BC. 'Dead Germans' or *sanguine
germano* can here also mean 'brother's blood', unsurprisingly hinting (at Caesar's
expense) that this civil war verges on fratricide (cf. Chapter 80, above). 'Pawns
without a name': perhaps gangs of political thugs like the ones whose fights gave
rise to Cicero's *Pro Milone*.

were my first crimes. But just who fears my fame?
Who wants to stop me? Pawns without a name –
bought and sold, cheap – stepsons of mother Rome!
No weakling holds without it hitting home
this hand of mine. To victory, men! Rage on,
blades busy till the righteous cause has won!
One charge arraigns us all; the same doom you   170
as me awaits; they want to thank you, too –
you won, as well. So since they punish winning,
and victory is counted sordid sinning,
let Fortune cast the dice, the war begin
and try your hand. I rest my case here, men,
and armed with such firm friends, feel sure to win."
    This said, direct from Delphi's deity
a raven fluttered past auspiciously,
and from the left part of the gloomy wood
strange voices issued and a flame ensued.   180
The sun himself glowed with a special grace
and wrapped a golden halo round his face.

123. By this encouraged, Caesar pressed ahead
and in this strange dare took an active lead.
    At first the ice and hoarfrost-fettered ground
stayed hospitably cool without a sound,
but once the troops the packed clouds loosened up
and shivering horses cracked the ice's grip
a thaw began. Soon from the summits new
rivers streamed down, then *stopped*, as if on cue,   190
frozen in place, a flood bound to the spot,
a stream before, now hard enough to cut.
But then, more treacherous still, it tricked them all
and gave troops, men, and arms alike a fall
on its slick face, pathetic, piled pell-mell.
Clouds knocked around by icy blasts expel
their stuffing; violent twisting winds, as well,
barrage them with whole Heaven-loads of hail.
Clouds burst and fall upon the men *en masse*,
and ice comes crashing like a wave of glass.   200
Deep snow had overwhelmed the earth, the stars

in heaven, the rivers frozen to their shores;
Caesar, not yet. Propped on his mighty spear,
he broke the ice with steps devoid of fear,
as Hercules sped down the towering face
of Caucasus, or Jove with angry grace
made his descent from great Olympus' height
to make a rout of the doomed Giants' fight.[1]

   While wrathful Caesar treads the swollen peaks,
Rumor flies (winged with fear), the summit seeks   210
of Palatine, and jolts the images
of all the gods there with her messages,
how ships now flood the sea, and how the Alps
seethe with troops dripping blood from German scalps.
Arms, bloodshed, slaughter, fire, and war *tout court*
fuddle their vision; men feel insecure,
and take two different courses in their fright:
by land some, some by water take their flight
(sea safer now than home), some choose to try
the chance of war, embracing fate's decree.   220
All flee as far as fear prompts, sad to say,
the populace unites to run away
where panic leads, abandoning the town.
Rome takes up running; Romans beaten down
by rumor's rumble leave their walls to groan.
With shaking hand some hold a child; some cleave
to household gods, forlorn their thresholds leave,
and call down curses on the absent foe;
some clasp their wives in sorrow; others, though
unused to loads, bear aged parents, this   230
all they can bear, all they most fear to miss,[2]
while, walking spoils, fools leaving nothing flee;
as when a great south wind blows up at sea

[123.1] The two earlier descents mentioned here are from Hercules' rescue of
Prometheus, hung on Mt Caucasus, and Jove-Jupiter's journey to defeat the
Giants. In line 261, nonetheless, we are told Hercules sides not with Caesar but
rather with Pompey.
[123.2] A fairly precious reminder of Aeneas' carrying his father out of Troy on
his shoulders in Vergil, *Aen.* 2.

churning the waves, the seamen uselessly
man either tackling or the helm, but here
one lashes planks, one makes as if to steer;
one runs before the wind, to Chance leaves all.
Why grieve at trifles? Pompey, whom they call
the Great, the Pontic scourge, Hydaspes' light,
the pirates' nightmare, who gave Jove a fright   240
with his three triumphs, whom the Pontus rough
and Bosporus reverenced fawningly enough,[3]
broke ranks – for shame! – two consuls with him, – *ran*,
that Fortune's whim might rout so Great a man.

124.   Such vast ills touch the gods, as well; their fear
augments the flight. Benign gods far and near
in their disgust leave the mad world behind
and turn from the doomed corps of humankind.
Peace first, white arms bruised, hides her vanquished head
beneath a helmet, *cuts the planet dead*,   250
and goes to ground in ruthless Hades' land;
with her, crushed Faith, bedraggled Justice, and
Concord in mourning with her garments torn.
Where Erebus, though, bursts its shattered bourn,
Hell's chorus looms: a Fury dreadful stands;
threatening Bellona; brandishing her brands,
Megaera; Doom; Deceit; and Death's sick grey!
Among them, Madness like a runaway
tosses her bloody head, her face inside
a helmet that a thousand scars must hide;   260
her left hand grips a well-worn Martial shield
with countless spear-points sticking in its field;
her threatening right, a torch to fire the world.
Earth felt gods move; stars shift, thrown off their poise,
for everywhere the palace of the skies
runs to take sides. Venus, the first to sign,

[123.3] Lines recalling Pompey's victories in the eastern Mediterranean, notably against Mithridates VI of Pontus, and against pirates throughout the region. The Hydaspes is a river in India to which Alexander the Great once advanced, but to which Pompey actually did not.

joins Caesar, Pallas her, and next in line
stands Romulus with his enormous spear,
while Hermes, Phoebus, and his twin adhere
with Hercules, to Pompey, his *Great* peer.[1]   270

   The trumpets shook; Discord with her torn hair
raised Stygian head aloft. Caked blood was there,
and tears ran down her face from her bruised eyes;
a rusty scurf her teeth rigidifies;
her tongue drips gore; her face is ringed with snakes;
heart twisted, dress all shot-to-Hell, she shakes
a torch of blood-red in her palsied hand.
When she had left Cocytus' dismal strand,
she strode to mount the noble Apennines,
peered down on all the lands earth's coast confines,   280
one solid surge of armies on the move,
and from her rabid breast these words she hove:
"Nations, to arms! To arms! In passion's heat
take up the torch and cities' hearts ignite.
Whoever lurks, must lose; leave none exempt,
women or children, old folks, time's contempt;
let earth itself quake; falling walls, rebel!
Lay down the law, Marcellus; Curio, tell
the plebs to panic; Lentulus, help Mars;
and you, Lord Caesar, why delay the wars?   290
Break gates down, flatten city walls, steal gold!
Since, Pompey, you seem ill-equipped to hold
the hills of Rome, seek Epidamnus then[2]
and dye Thessalian bays with blood of men."
So Discord spoke, and bade the games begin.'

While Eumolpus poured out these verses in a voluble stream

[124.1] Basically a schematic alignment: Venus here sides with Caesar as his supposed forbear, Minerva as his tactical sponsor, and Romulus or Mavortius as his strictly Roman *force majeure*, whereas Hermes joins Pompey as (presumably) Republican eloquence, Diana and Phoebus as sheer personal glory, and Hercules as heroic persistence (at least of a sort), almost evening the odds, but not quite.

[124.2] Epidamnus, a Pompeian bastion in Epirus; Plautus famously treats 'Epidamnus' in *Men.* 262–3 as a name meaning roughly, 'At a Loss'.

of words, we finally entered the town of Croton,[3] where we
recuperated in a little inn. The next day, while searching for
more prosperous-looking lodging, we happened onto a crowd
of fortune hunters who wanted to know who we were and
where we came from. So, according to plan, a full account of
where we were from and who we were streamed forth ready-
made. They believed every word of it evidently since they
immediately made a contest of pushing their own resources on
Eumolpus ... All the fortune-hunters competed at wooing
Eumolpus with their gifts ...

*

125. It went on like this in Croton for quite some time ... and
Eumolpus got so carried away with his newfound success that
he completely forgot his unfortunate past and took to boasting
that no one could oppose what he favored and that if 'his
people' got into trouble here, 'his friends' would get them off
scot-free!

For my part, although I enjoyed stuffing myself on more and
more luxuries every day and even began to think that Fortune
had at last averted her evil eye, I worried as often about my
usual bad luck as its cause and asked myself: What if one of
these cagey fortune-hunters sent a spy to Africa, for example,
and exposed our lie? Or what if Eumolpus' valet should tire of
his present good fortune and inform on us to his friends, thus
betraying the whole scam from sheer envy? We'd be on the run
again; we would have rid ourselves of poverty only to be
reduced to beggary. Goddamn, it's hard to live outside the law!
You're always waiting to get what you really deserve ...[1]

*

[124.3] In a sense, the three arch-rogues' advance on the city of Croton (a town
taken much earlier by Hannibal) here converges with Caesar's advance on pre-
Civil-War Rome. On the city of Croton see further Chapter 116 and n. 1.

[125.1] Cf. Seneca, *Epist.* 105.7.

126. [*Circe's maid, Chrysis, to Encolpius/Polyaenus*] 'Because you know you're sexy, you flaunt it: you don't *give* hugs, so much as market them! Why else is your hair so carefully combed, your face so made-up, the look in your eyes so provocative? Why else would your walk be so artful that never a step is out of place, unless you were advertising your beauty – for sale? Look at me; I'm no prophet of divination and I don't care about astrology, but I can read a man's character in his face, and when I see him walk, I know what he's thinking. If you're selling what we want, you've found a buyer; if, however, you are nicer than that, and are giving it away, go ahead and put us in your debt. For when you say you're a lowly slave, you merely inflame my mistress's passion. You see, some women like to slum it. They can't get excited unless they see some slave or messenger-boy half-naked! Some of them lust for gladiators in the arena, or mule-drivers covered in dust, or actors parading themselves on stage! My mistress is like that: she doesn't have time for the elites in the orchestra seats, she's busy finding what she loves with the lowliest pleb in the house!'[1]

Flattered by her seductive proposal, I said: 'Tell me, the woman in love with me, isn't she *you?*'

She laughed out loud at the awkwardness of my question and said, 'Please don't flatter yourself! I haven't yet fallen on my back for a slave – God forbid that I should take a common criminal in my arms! Let the merry matrons see to that; they can kiss away the scars from your floggings.[2] Even if I am only

---

[1] See Suetonius, *Jul.* 39, on the *Lex Roscia* of 67 BC barring all but members of the equestrian order from the first fourteen rows behind Senatorial seating in the theater.

[2] An upper-class feminine quirk also satirized in Juvenal 6.

a maid, I don't sit on anyone's lap – unless he's at least a knight!'

I was astonished by the symmetry of their desires. What a couple of oddballs! The maid was as aloof as any mistress, the mistress as accessible as any maid!

The joke didn't stop there. I asked Chrysis to bring her mistress into the grove of plane trees. She liked my plan. So she gathered up her skirt and took off through the laurel grove that grew beside the path. She didn't waste a moment leading her mistress out of her hiding place and bringing her to my side. And the woman was more perfect than any work of art. No tongue could do justice to such beauty, and whatever I say will fall short of reality. Her hair had a natural curl and literally cascaded over her shoulders; her forehead was small and her hair curled away from it; her long eyebrows reaching almost to her cheekbones all but met between her eyes, which were brighter than stars on a moonless night. Her nostrils were slightly flared, and her lips were like those Praxiteles gave Diana.[3] Chin, neck, hands, and ivory feet were adorned by a thin gold band – each in turn outshone the finest Parian marble. That was when I realized how little I really cared for Doris, my old flame!

*

How comes it, Jove, your hardware laid aside,
you loll in heaven as if the stories lied?
Now is the time in borrowed horns to scowl,
or hide your grey hair in a feather cowl;
Meet a real Danaë; just touch her skin,
and feel your members meltingly give in[1]...

*

[126.3] A sculptor of the 4th century BC famous for his Aphrodites. Lucian (*Essays in Portraiture* 4) tells the story of a man who fell so completely in love with Praxiteles' Aphrodite of Cnidos that he tried to ravish her (cf. also 'Lucian', *Amores* 16).

[127.1] He alludes to Jove's guise as a bull for Europa, a swan to woo Leda, and a shower of gold to win over Danaë (cf. below, Chapter 137, n. 2). None of these analogues in Encolpius' phrasing bodes particularly well for his potency.

127. She was delighted and laughed so charmingly that her face reminded me of a full moon peeking out from behind a cloud. Punctuating her words with her gestures, she said 'If you don't disdain an elegant woman without any experience of men (until this year), I present you with a mistress,² young man. I know you have a boyfriend – I'm not ashamed of making inquiries – but why not adopt a mistress too? I'll keep right in step. All I ask is that you deign to enjoy these lips, when you're so inclined.'

'On the contrary,' I said, 'I pray by your beauty that you will deign to admit a stranger among your worshippers. You will find me devout, if you allow me to adore you. And don't expect me to enter your temple without an offering; for you I will give up my boyfriend.'³

'What?' she exclaimed, 'the one you can't live without, on whose lips you hang? The one you love as I would have you love me?'

As she spoke, her voice was so gracious, the sound of her words so caressed and charmed the very air, you would have thought you heard the Sirens' harmonies floating on the breeze. As I stood there lost in admiration, the sky seemed somehow to shine more brightly, and it occurred to me to ask the goddess her name. 'Didn't my maid tell you? I am called Circe. Not because I am the daughter of the Sun, nor because my mother could stop the moving world at will. But I will owe something to heaven if the fates bring us together. Even now the gods are at work, as silent as thought. Not without reason does *Circe* love *Polyaenus*. Between these names a great torch burns forever!⁴ Please, hold me tight. You needn't worry about anyone seeing us: your boyfriend is far from here.'

So spoke Circe as she entwined me in her two arms softer than eiderdown and pulled me down on the lush grass.

---

¹²⁷·² The word translated here as 'mistress' is *soror*, 'sister' (cf. the use of *frater* as 'lover' in Chapter 9 and elsewhere).

¹²⁷·³ The religious language of this passage casts Giton as a sacrificial offering.

¹²⁷·⁴ Circe's name connects her with the temptress-enchantress of *Od.* 10, just as Encolpius' pseudonym Polyaenus ('much fabled'), applied to Odysseus by the Sirens in *Od.* 12.184, connects him to that poem's famous wandering lover (cf. below, Chapter 128). See Glossary of Important Names.

When Jove on Ida's heights his mistress knew
in lawful love that fired him through and through,
our mother Earth in molten splendor flowed
of rose and violet; bloomy rushes showed,
and from the meadow's green, white lilies glowed;
such was the place, soft grass inviting love,
while bright day blessed our trysting from above.[5]

Lying side by side in the grass we traded countless little kisses on our way to more robust pleasures ...

*

128. [*Circe to Polyaenus*] 'What's wrong?' she said, 'Has my kiss offended you? Is my breath stale from fasting? Or my armpits sweaty, perhaps? If not, then are you afraid of Giton?'

I blushed with obvious embarrassment and instantly lost whatever potency I had mustered, as if my whole body went limp. 'Please, princess, don't mock my misery. I've been bewitched!'[1]

*

[*Circe*] 'Tell the truth, Chrysis: Am I unattractive? Badly made-up? Does some natural defect mar my beauty? Don't deceive your mistress: I must have done something wrong!' She then snatched a mirror from her silent maid and after trying every look that makes a lover smile, she shook the wrinkles out of her dress and rushed into the temple of Venus ...

[127.5] An allusion to the lusty 'sacred marriage'/regenerative coupling of Zeus and his wife-sister Hera on Ida in Homer, *Il.* 14.346–51. With Aphrodite's help Hera seduces Zeus to distract him from the war; thus in narrative terms the seduction is an act of deception not love.

[128.1] This debacle begins another comically magic misadventure in which our new Ulysses, 'bewitched' (*veneficio contactus*) in more ways than one, withstands his Circe's charms while intending to do quite the opposite. Encolpius/Polyaenus' magically induced failure to rise to the occasion comically inverts Odysseus' overcoming of the witch Circe with the help of a magical drug provided by Hermes (*Od.* 10.230–347). Encolpius' claim that witchcraft *per se* is to blame is supported by Chrysis' comments in Chapter 129, by the measures the witch takes against evil-eye fascination in Chapter 131 (cf. Chapter 74) and of course by the potent herbal medicine and *fascinum*-magic of Chapter 138 (cf. Chapter 22); see our notes on both these later therapies.

Personally I felt like a convicted criminal or like a man frightened by a nightmare. I began to wonder whether I had been swindled out of the real thing – or not?

> As when in night's deep sleep, dreams hypnotize
> our errant sight, and earth turned to the skies
> bares gold; our greedy hands the theft embrace,
> and grab the goods; sweat too runs down our face,
> and deep fear grips the mind lest someone know
> gold stashed, and through our loaded pockets go.
> Such joys but tease and run, but even so,
> truth once restored, we long for what we lost,
> engrossed completely in the phantom past.[2]

*

[*Giton to Encolpius*] '... I certainly am grateful to you for loving me so Socratically. Not even Alcibiades lay as chastely in his teacher's bed...'[3]

*

129. [*Encolpius to Giton*] 'Believe me, little brother, I don't think I'm male any longer. I don't feel it. That part of my body where I was once a veritable Achilles is dead and buried...'

The boy was afraid that it might make people gossip if he were found alone with me; he jumped up and hurried to another part of the house...

*

Chrysis came into my room and gave me a letter from her mistress which read as follows:

Dear Polyaenus:

If I were a lustful woman, I would complain of being misled by you. But, as it is, I'm grateful to you, feeble as you are. At least we played in the shadow of pleasure for a while. But how are you? Did you make it home on your own two feet? Doctors say men in your condition even lose the ability to walk! I tell you, young man,

---

[128.2] Cf. *Carm.* 30.
[128.3] Cf. Plato, *Symposium* 217–19.

beware of complete paralysis. I have never seen a sick man in graver danger. You are half dead already! If this frigidity spreads to your knees and hands, you may as well send for the funeral trumpeters!

What is to be done? Well, even if I have been deeply hurt, I won't begrudge a wretched man his cure; if you want to get well, banish Giton from your bed. You will recover your strength, I say, if you sleep without your lover for three days.

As for me, I have no fear of meeting someone who finds me less pleasing. My mirror doesn't lie, nor does my reputation.

Get well – if you can!

When Chrysis saw I had finished reading the whole insulting thing, she said 'This isn't unusual, especially in this city where witches pull the moon out of the sky . . .'[1] So the matter will be taken care of. Please answer my mistress in gentle terms. Be magnanimous, cheer her up. To tell the truth, she hasn't been herself from the moment you wronged her.'

130. I happily obeyed and inscribed the following letter on a tablet:[1]

Dear Circe:

I admit that I have often made mistakes. I'm only a man, and a young one at that. But until today I have never committed a capital offense. I admit it – I'm guilty. Whatever punishment you wish to impose, I deserve. I have committed treason, killed a man, and robbed a temple – punish me for these crimes! If you sentence me to death, I will come with my sword; if a mere flogging will satisfy you, I will run naked to my mistress. Only remember one thing: the fault lies not in me, but in my tools. I was a willing soldier but disarmed! Who did this to me? I don't know. Perhaps my mind outstripped my body; perhaps I desired so many things, I squandered our pleasure in delay. I don't know what I did wrong. You tell me to beware of paralysis – as if anything could be worse than what has already robbed me

---

[129.1] Cf. Vergil, *Ecl.* 8.70.
[130.1] Cf. Ovid, *Amores* 3.7, esp. 63–8.

of the power to possess you! My apology comes down to this: I promise to satisfy you, if you allow me to atone for my crime.

Your faithful servant,
Polyaenus

*

After dispatching Chrysis this promissory note, I took very good care of my ailing body. I skipped my bath and anointed myself with a modicum of oil; then I fed myself healthier food – I mean onions and snails' heads (without sauce). And I cut down on my wine. Finally, I took a stroll for my digestion before going to bed – without Giton. I was so determined to please Circe that I was afraid the boy might sap my strength.

131. The next day I got up feeling well in body and mind and went down into the same grove of plane trees. Although I feared the location was inauspicious, I waited among the trees for Chrysis to come and lead the way. After pacing about for a minute I sat down where I had been the day before, and Chrysis appeared with an old woman in tow. After greeting me she said, 'Well, my fastidious lover, have you started to come to your senses? ...'

The old woman pulled out a bundle of colored threads and tied them around my neck. Then she put some spittle on her middle finger, mixed it with dust, and made a sign on my forehead, despite my disgust ...[1]

<hr>

[131.1] Here there follows in Burman's and other earlier editions this elegiac couplet, first attributed to Petronius by Scaliger in his *Catalecta*:

Where there is life there's hope; O garden watch,
upstanding Priap, come, stand by this crotch!

On both spitting and multicolored thread (*periammata*) as correctives or counters for evil-eye magic (*fascinatio*, affective contagion), see Pliny the Elder *N. H.* 28.38–9 and Bonner, *Studies in Magical Amulets* (Ann Arbor, 1950) 4. For stones as love charms, see Philostratus, *Life of Apollonius* 7.39. The middle finger is also a favored evil-eye apotropaic; see esp. Persius, *Sat.* 2.31–4 and our note on Chapter 138. Pre-Enlightenment scholars were well aware of the concern of these chapters with evil-eye magic; see G. Voss, *Etymologicon Linguae Latinae*, 2nd ed. (Amsterdam, 1695) *s. v.* fascinum and the comments in Burmann's edition *ad*

When she finished the incantation, she instructed me to spit three times and to drop some pebbles in my lap three times after she had wrapped them up in purple and cast a charm on them. Finally, she started to test my sexual prowess with her hands. Before you could say a word, my nerves obeyed her command and a surging motion filled the old woman's hands. She was jumping for joy: 'Look, Chrysis dear,' she said, 'see how I've started a hare for others to hunt?'

*

> The lofty plane tree cast a summer shadow,
> the laurel wreathed with berries, trembling cypress
> and the sheared pine trees with their waving tops.
> Among them played a stream's meandering waters
> that foamed and murmuring churned among the pebbles,
> real love-nests all; ask sylvan Philomel
> and city Procne singing in the grass
> and tender violets of their stolen kisses...[2]

She lay there with her marble limbs stretched out on a golden couch fanning the quiet air with a sprig of myrtle in flower. As soon as she saw me, she blushed slightly, embarrassed at the thought of yesterday's debacle. When all the servants had left, she asked me to sit down by her and then laid the branch of myrtle over my eyes. This made her bolder as if there were a wall between us: 'Well my poor paralytic, are you all man today?'

'You may ask,' I said, 'but wouldn't you rather try me?' I let

---

locc. Outside Plutarch's *Sympotic Questions* 5.7 probably the best treatment in brief of the seminal and intricate matter of fascination or evil-eye magic is A.-M. Tupet, *La magie dans la poésie latine* (Paris, 1976) 178–81, noting how it afflicts through both vision (*invidia*) and speech, producing unnerving or wasting effects (cf. Vergil, *Ecl.* 3.102–3); impotence was of course often the most dreaded effect of all. On these and related topics, cf. C. A. Barton, *The Sorrows of the Ancient Romans: The Gladiator and the Monster* (Princeton, 1993) esp. Chapters 3–5.

[131.2] More ill-omened allusions to events in the mythical past of the nightingale and swallow respectively. Philomel was the sister-in-law Tereus furtively raped, Procne was the abused wife who served up her own son to Tereus to avenge herself.

my whole body sink into her arms and enjoyed her kisses to my heart's content – free of magic![3]

*

132. The sheer beauty of her body summoned me and she pulled me down to make love to her. Our lips met again and again in a shower of kisses; our hands met and explored every kind of love; our bodies were so intertwined they seemed to mix our souls together...[1]

*

Exasperated by such palpable insults the lady finally hurried to take her revenge: she summoned her servants and ordered them to hoist me up on their shoulders for flogging. But this outrageous punishment didn't satisfy the woman: she called all the old women who spun her wool and the dregs of her slaves and ordered them to spit on me. I put my hands in front of my eyes, but didn't beg for mercy because I knew what I had coming. I was beaten, spat upon, and thrown out the door. They even tossed out Proselenus; Chrysis was beaten. The whole household was upset now; the slaves walked around muttering, 'Who ruined the mistress's good mood?'

*

After thinking it all over I cheered up a bit and craftily covered the marks from my beatings. For I knew if I didn't, Eumolpus would be as delighted by my disgrace as Giton would be distressed. But there was only one way to hide my shame effectively, so I pretended to be ill. As soon as I got into bed, I turned the full fire of my rage against that which was the root of all my troubles:

> Three times I whip the dreadful weapon out,[2]
> and three times softer than a Brussels sprout

131.3 Cf. Catullus, 5.12, 7.12.

132.1 The manuscript tradition flags this excerpt with the rubric *Encolpius de Endymione puero* ('Encolpius on the boy Endymion'), making it at least possible that it was moved here from a now-lost adventure to offset Encolpius' present poor showing.

132.2 Cf. Vergil, *Aen.* 2.479.

I quail, in those dire straits my manhood blunted,
no longer up to what just now I wanted;
fear-frosted worse than all mid-winter's colds—
holed up in me, lapped in a thousand folds—
it lurks so I can't bare its head to beat it;
fear-stymied by that craven, next I meet it
with verbiage far more potent to defeat it.

Propping myself up on my elbow, I berated that pig-headed hold-out in no uncertain terms: 'What do you have to say for yourself? All gods and men are ashamed of you! Why, it's uncivil even to mention your name in serious conversation! Do I deserve this kind of treatment from you – to be dragged kicking and screaming from heaven to hell? To have my youthful vigor slandered while the debility of senility is thrust upon me? Speak up; you'd better have something to say for yourself!'

> Its *eye fixed on the ground it turned away,*
> *as little roused by what I had to say*
> *as willows limp or poppies drooping sway.*[3]

As soon as this foolish outburst was over, I began to regret it, and even felt ashamed that I could forget my better self so completely as to 'have words' with that part of myself that men of sterner stuff scarcely deign to notice.

Then after rubbing my forehead for quite a while I said: 'What harm does it do to relieve my sorrow with some perfectly natural abuse? After all, we often curse other bodily parts – our stomachs, throats, and even our aching heads. So what? Didn't Ulysses quarrel with his own heart?[4] Don't some tragic heroes chastise their eyes, as if they could hear? Don't gouty

---

[3] A Vergilian pastiche, parody in the strictest (ancient) sense (cf. *Aen.* 6.469–70 – Dido shunning Aeneas in Hades; *Ecl.* 5.16, *Aen* 9.436).

[4] Odysseus briefly debates with his own heart, e.g., in *Od.* 20.17–22. Ehlers notes that the reference to tragedy suggests Oedipus, who of course treats his eyes as Encolpius (almost) treats his penis. For a similarly antic debate with a penis, see Montaigne's *Essais* 1.17 (cf. also *Auct. priap.* 83 as included in Buecheler's edition of the *Corpus priapeorum* and elsewhere).

people curse their feet, people with arthritis their hands, people
with sties their eyes? Don't people who stub their toes blame
their feet?

> Censors, why look askance
> on my fresh, frank romance?
> Gay gracefulness, pure speech,
> tells straight the deeds of each;
> don't all know sex, Love's charms,
> and how a warm bed *warms*?
> sage Epicure's own voice
> called love *Life's wisest choice*.[5]

*

There is nothing falser than the silly prejudices of mankind,
nothing sillier than affected virtue...

*

133. When I had finished my speech, I called Giton and said,
'Now tell me, dear, on your honor: that night when Ascyltos
stole you from me, did he stay awake to molest you or was he
content with a chaste and spinsterish night?'

The boy touched his eyes and swore up and down that
Ascyltos had used no violence against him.[1]

*

I knelt on the threshold and prayed to the hostile deity:

[132.5] Following hard on Encolpius' argument with his penis, Petronius, by way
of Encolpius, aims this wide-eyed, good-natured aside at the hypocritical Catos
of his age and ours. What Petronius/Encolpius has to say here about Epicurus
and love comically conflates Epicurus' sceptical evaluation of sexual love (*eros*)
with his lofty assessment of friendship (*philia*; cf. *K. D.* 27; *Vatican Sayings*, 18,
51, 80), but may reflect a strained reading of Lucretius 1.21–53, linking love with
fertility, peace (cf. 1.31–7), and the saving acceptance of things as they are. This
indeed is one goal of the master's own teachings. Lucretius calls Epicurus a
'father' and 'finder of truth' (*pater, rerum inventor*) at 3.9. See Courtney 11–14.

[133.1] Of course it may well be that no violence was needed, an unpleasant
alternative reading of Giton's behavior, and one that Encolpius works hard to
avoid (cf. Chapters 26, 91, 100).

The nymphs and Bacchus' friend, broad forests' lord,
fair Venus' choice – *Priapus!*[2] Famous Lesbos
and leafy Thasos serve you; ever-praising,
the Lydian builds you shrines in his Hypaepa.
Bacchus' defender and the Dryads' darling,
come hear my fearful prayer. Not stained with blood
come I; not as a sacrilegious foe
have I laid siege to shrines; my want and hunger
drove me to sin (but not with my whole body);
whoever sins from want is less to blame.
I beg you by this prayer, forgive my guilt;
allow the lesser fault; when fortune smiles
 I will not leave your glory unregarded.
To your altars, holy one, a reverend goat
with horns shall go; a suckling sacrifice
from squealing sow; with new wine bowls shall froth,
and drunken youth dance three times round your temple ...

*

While I was busy with this and worrying over my moribund
member, the old woman walked into the shrine – a mess of
dishevelled hair dressed in black. She put out her hand and led
me from the vestibule ...

*

134. [*Proselenus to Encolpius*] 'What witches have turned your
nerves to jelly?[1] Did you step in something rotten or dead in a
crossroad last night? You haven't even protected yourself from
the boy! You're as delicate, frail, and tired as an old nag going
uphill, puffing, and sweating for nothing. And not content to
ruin yourself, you roused the gods' wrath against me.'

*

I made no objection as she led me again into the priestess'

[133.2] Some myths actually make Priapus the offspring of Bacchus and Venus, or
wine and desire, a fairly transparent symbolic ancestry. The form of Encolpius'
hymn is traditional; nothing else here comports quite as comically with this ritual
solemnity as Priapus' own trademark indecency. See Introduction, xxvi.
   [134.1] Cf. Chapter 63.

cell, pushed me down on the bed, took a cane from behind the door, and gave me a thrashing I took in silence. And if the cane hadn't broken on the first blow, blunting the force of her attack, she might well have broken both my arms and cracked my skull. I screamed out loud when she used her fists, and weeping uncontrollably I covered my head with my right arm and leaned it against a pillow. She was also upset and crying. She sat on the other side of the little bed and in a trembling voice complained bitterly of living too long until the priestess entered.

'Why have you come into my room as if you were visiting a fresh grave? And on a holiday when even mourners laugh...'

[*Proselenus to Oenothea*][2] 'Oh, Oenothea,' she said, 'this young man you see here was born under an unlucky star. He can't sell his family jewels to either sex! You've never seen a man so unfortunate. He's a soggy strap of leather – no balls at all. To make a long story short, what kind of man do you think could get up from Circe's bed without a taste of pleasure?'

When she heard this, Oenothea sat down between us and just shook her head for a long time. Then she spoke:

'I'm the only woman in the world who knows how to cure this disease of yours. And so you won't think I'm bluffing, I want the young man to spend the night with me! [My name isn't Oenothea] if I don't make that thing as stiff as a stag's horn!

> 'By all you see in life I am obeyed,
> and when I will the flowery earth lies withering,
> and when I will pours forth its plenty; crags
> and rugged rocks spout Niles; the sea before me
> lays down its waves inert, and at my feet
> the winds lower their stilled gusts! Rivers obey me,
> Hyrcanian tigers, snakes told, "Stand erect!"[3]
> Why stick at trifles? The moon's face descends
> drawn down by spells of mine; a daunted Phoebus

---

[2] Possibly 'she who makes wine a god'; certainly not unlike the 'old crone stewed in wine' of *Frag.* 21.

[3] Possibly an important selling-point for Encolpius at least (cf. Chapters 131–2).

is forced to backtrack, turn his raging steeds;[4]
[so great the power of words. By virgins' rites
bulls' fire abates put out; with magic spells
Phoebean Circe changed Ulysses' crew
and Proteus turns to what he will. These arts –
and I – can transplant Ida's every copse
to sea, with rivers whelm high mountain-tops!]'

135. I cringed with fear at her fantastic promise, and started
to study the old woman more closely...

'Now,' cried Oenothea, 'do as you're told ...' After wiping
her hands carefully, she leaned over the bed, and kissed me
again and again.

Oenothea put an old table in the middle of the altar, which
she filled with live coals, and proceeded to use some melted
pitch to mend a cup cracked from age. Then she stuck back in
the smoke-stained wall a wooden nail that had fallen out when
she took the cup down. Next she put on a square apron, placed
a huge kettle on the fire and used a wooden fork to lift a bag
down from a meat-hook; inside were some beans and the
remnants of an old pig's jowl all carved up. After she untied
the bag's mouth she poured out some beans on the table, and
told me to clean them carefully. I followed her instructions and
methodically picked the beans out of their filthy shells. But she
rebuked my slowness, grabbed the beans, tore the shells off
with her teeth spitting them on the ground like so many dead
flies.

*

I marvelled at the ingenuity of poverty and the craftsmanship
that went into every detail.

No ivory gleamed here in a golden setting,
nor did the earth here flash with trodden marble,
beguiled with her own gifts; a willow pallet
on which is spread a sheaf of empty corn-husks,
new earthen cups quick-turned on humble treadles,

[134-4] Cf. Seneca, *Medea* 754–9, and here, Chapter 129.

a basin of soft linden, trenchers woven
of limber withes, and a jar steeped in Bacchus.
Circling it all, a wall at random daubed
with chaff and clay, and hung with rustic pegs
on which from rope of reeds a twig-broom dangled;
a low lean-to, as well, with smoky rafters
to guard its bounty; serviceberries ripe
hung up high entwined with fragrant garlands,
dried savory herb, and raisins by the cluster;
the hostess here like reverend Hecale,
that ever-celebrated Attic wonder
eternized by the muse of *Libya's laureate*...[1]

*

136. While she was nibbling on a bit of meat ... and putting
that pig's jowl – which looked as ancient as she was – back on
the rack, the rotten stool she stood on collapsed and threw the
old woman down on the hearth with all her weight. The spout
broke off the kettle putting out the fire that had only just
revived. The old woman burned her elbow on a hot coal, while
her face was covered with the ashes stirred up by her fall.
Alarmed, I jumped up and helped her to her feet, though not
without a smile ...

She promptly took off for some neighbors to relight the fire,
so our sacrifice would not be delayed ...

So I went up to the door of the cottage ...

Then all of a sudden three geese – who I imagine, usually
demanded their daily bread from the old woman around
midday – actually charged me, and to my horror, pressed
around me with their hideous, rabid cackling. One of them
tore at my tunic; another tugged the straps off my sandals and
dragged them away. And a third – evidently the ringleader and
a real savage – didn't hesitate to peck me on the calf with his
toothy beak. I lost my temper at this point, grabbed the leg off
a little table, and lit into the aggressor with weapon in hand.

[135.1] Hecale's homely hospitality as extended to Theseus was extolled in a now
largely lost but still quite clearly mock-naive poem by Callimachus, native of
Libya.

But I wasn't satisfied with a mere swat: I avenged myself by killing that goose!

Doubtless this was the way the Stymphalian birds flew
into heaven before Hercules' skill, *Harpies*, too,
dripping filth, when *chez* Phineus the moveable feast
flowed with foulness; the sky above trembled distressed
with strange cries, and *the palace of heaven shook through*...[1]

*

The rest of the geese had gotten at the beans that were spilt and scattered across the floor and, then, deprived of their leader, as I saw it, they retreated into the temple.

Proud of my booty and my revenge, I threw the dead goose behind the bed and washed the little bite on my leg with vinegar. Then, fearing a scolding from Oenothea, I decided to run away; so I got my gear together and started out the door. I hadn't yet crossed the threshold when I spotted Oenothea coming back with a jar full of live coals. I abruptly reversed course, threw off my jacket, and stood in the doorway as if I'd been waiting for her impatiently.

She built a fire with some dry reeds, and, after piling some wood on top, started to explain her delay: her friend wouldn't let her go until she had drained three glasses, as was the custom. Then she said, 'What did you do while I was gone? And where are the beans?'

Since I thought what I had done was almost admirable, I narrated the whole battle for her from beginning to end, and, to cheer her up, I held up the goose as compensation for her losses. As soon as the old woman saw the dead bird she let out such an ear-piercing scream, you would have thought the geese had invaded the house again. I was flustered, and bewildered by the novelty of my crime, I asked her why she was so mad

---

[1] 136.1 In this mock-epic inset Encolpius likens the geese he defeats to the Harpies defeated in one of the labors of Hercules. Phineus was the seer whom the Harpies were sent to annoy. Could these geese be descendants of those – consecrated to Juno, not Priapus – who once saved Rome (in Livy 5.47.4)?

and why she seemed to care more about the goose than she did about me.

137. But she slapped her hands together and cried 'You criminal! You dare to speak? Don't you understand the enormity of the crime you've admitted to? You've murdered Priapus' pet, the goose cherished by all married women![1] Don't kid yourself: if the authorities hear of this, you'll be crucified! And you've polluted with blood my once sacrosanct house! You've made it possible for my enemies to get me thrown out of the priesthood...'[2]

*

'Please, stop screaming,' I said. 'Let me give you an ostrich to replace the goose.'

*

I was dumbfounded by all this. Oenothea sat on her little bed and bewailed the goose's fate. Meanwhile, Proselenus arrived with the makings of a sacrifice. When she saw the goose was dead, she asked why. Then she, too, started weeping bitterly and even commiserated with me – as if I had killed my own father, not a common goose.[3]

Finally, I was getting fed up and said, 'Please, let me expiate my crime with a fine, a blood price ... [as I might] if I had provoked you somehow, or even slain a man. Look, here are two gold pieces: this will buy you both gods and geese!'

When Oenothea saw the money, she said, 'Forgive me, young man. But it's you I'm worried about. That shows love, not ill

[137.1] Geese were good garden sentries, like Priapus, and clearly phallic birds, though less glamorous than swans like the one that sired Helen on Leda. Cf. modern English 'goose' as a verb and Pliny the Elder, *N. H.* 30.143, specifying goose tongue as stimulant for feminine libido. These associations along with the connection between geese and Juno, goddess of marriage, may explain the reference here to 'all *married* women' in particular. See D'Arcy Thompson, *A Glossary of Greek Birds* (Hildesheim, 1966) *s. v.*

[137.2] Here there follows *Carm.* 41 in Burman's and earlier editions.

[137.3] Now the goose as a potency symbol becomes linked with Encolpius' father, with Encolpius himself now allusively (and parodically) cast as a new tragic Oedipus? Cf. Chapter 136, n. 1.

will. We'll just have to make sure that no one hears of this.
Only you'd better pray that the gods forgive what you've done.'

> It's all clear sailing if you have the dough,
> so you can tell your fortune where to go.
> Go marry Danaë, and make her dad
> believe what *she* believed when she was had;
> write verse or speechify; win one and all
> those lawsuits, and give Cato too a fall;
> play judge, and cry 'sustain' and 'overrule',
> an all-star one-man jurisprudence-school;
> in short, make any wish; with cash on hand
> it's done! Jove's in the bag, *Yours to command*...[4]

*

   She put a bowl of wine under my hands and purified my
outstretched fingers by rubbing them with leeks and celery.
Then she recited a prayer and dropped some hazelnuts into the
wine. She made her predictions according to whether the nuts
floated on top or sank to the bottom. But I couldn't help
noticing that the empty husks, missing their kernels, floated on
top, while those that were heavy and full of fruit sank straight
to the bottom...

*

   She cut open the goose's breast, pulled out its bulging fat
liver and foretold my future from it. Then, to wipe out any
trace of my crime, she butchered the whole goose, spitted the
slices, and prepared a sumptuous feast for a man, who, only
moments before, she had said was doomed...[5]

   Meanwhile, draughts of unmixed wine made the rounds
quickly...

*

[137.4] On Danaë, see Chapter 126 and n., above; on the shower of gold as a
payoff, see Ovid, *Amores* 3.8.29–34. The Cato named here is most likely the
highly renowned legal expert, Marcus Porcius Cato *Licinianus*, son of Cato the
Censor, and not the republican martyr.

[137.5] Here there follows *Carm.* 41 in Burman and earlier editions.

138. Oenothea brought out a leather dildo,[1] which she smeared with oil, a little pepper, and crushed nettle seeds. She then proceeded to push it little by little into my anus...

The sadistic old woman repeatedly sprinkled the juice over my thighs...

*

She mixed the juice of watercress with absinthe, and after soaking my genitals in it took a bunch of stinging nettles and started gently lashing my whole body from the navel down...

*

Although the old girls were giddy with wine and lust, they took the right road and chased me for blocks shouting 'Stop the thief!' I lost them, but all my toes were bleeding from my rash escape...

*

Chrysis, who once looked down on your humble condition, is now bent on following you even at the risk of her own life.

*

What did Ariadne or Leda have to compare with her beauty? How could Helen or Leda surpass her? If Paris himself, the judge of rival goddesses, had laid his roving eyes on her for comparison, he would have given up Helen *and* the goddesses

---

[138.1] The *fascinum*, which can refer variously to a human penis (e.g., Chapter 92), a phallic shaped amulet, an artificial phallus (e.g., on a statue), or a dildo, is typically linked with the figure and cult of Priapus (F. W. Adams, *Latin Sexual Vocabulary* [London, 1982] 63–4) and quite clearly it functions magically here. Most of the herbs employed here were well known for their curative and Aphroditic powers: see Ovid, *AA* 2.514–19; Pliny the Elder, *N. H.* 21.92. Penetration with the *fascinum* may be meant to serve as Priapic expiation as well as therapy for impotence. In view of the two crones' mounting excitement, the magical cure seems to work (see our notes on Chapters 128, 131). For more detailed discussions, see F. T. Elworthy, *The Evil Eye* (London, 1895) esp. 148–55; C. Johns, *Sex or Symbol: Erotic Images of Greece and Rome* (London, 1982), esp. Chapter 3; the editor's comments on 19.50 and 28.39 in Pliny, *Histoire naturelle*, ed. J. Beaujeu et. al. 34 vols. (Paris, 1950); and K. W. Slane, M. W. Dickie, 'A Knidian Phallic Vase from Corinth', *Hesperia* 62 (1993) 482–505.

to have her.² If I were allowed to give her a kiss, if I could put
my arms around her divine torso, perhaps my body would
regain its strength and those parts that I'm sure were paralyzed
by witchcraft might return to their senses. No insulting treatment can deter me. I was thrashed? Forget it. I was thrown out
the door? It's part of the game – if she would only be friends
again.³

*

139. I tossed and turned on my bed as if I were chasing an
imaginary lover...

*

> God and relentless Fate plague on and on
> not me alone; from Argos, Tiryns' son
> felt the world's weight bear down; Laomedon
> profane bore *two* gods' rages; Pelias, one
> (Juno's), and fighting blindly, Telephus,
> and dashed by Neptune's realm, Odysseus.
> So drives me, prone by land or sea to *trap* us,
> the *lowering wrath* of Hellespont's *Priapus.*¹

*

I started by asking Giton whether anyone had asked for me.
'No one today,' he said, 'but yesterday a rather elegant woman
came to the door. She talked with me for some time and wore

---

¹³⁸·² Here Encolpius' gallery of great mythical beauties is female, not male,
further marking the new sexual focus remarked on more briefly in Chapter 126;
contrast the array of boy-beauties engaging Encolpius in Chapter 83.
¹³⁸·³ Introduced as a narrative bridge here there follows in some early editions
the spurious *Carm.* 63.
¹³⁹·¹ In this mock-epic précis Encolpius likens his sorrows from the wrath of
Priapus to those of past heroes run foul of some god: Hercules, persecuted by
Juno for being her husband's bastard; Laomedon, who angered Apollo and
Neptune by refusing to pay them for building the walls of Troy; Pelias, persecuted
by Juno for killing Sidero, her protégé; Telephus, in some tales foiled by Bacchus
for trying to reinforce Troy; and Ulysses/Odysseus, of course, persecuted by
Neptune for blinding his son, the Cyclops Polyphemus. A final comic touch comes
with the picture of phallic Priapus actually 'driving' or harrying Encolpius (cf.
Introduction, xxvi), something other gods generally do with more epic solemnity.
For the last line, cf. Vergil's phrasing in *Georg.* 4.11.

me out with her idle chatter. Finally, she did say that you deserved to be punished and would be tortured like a slave if the offended party persists in his complaint...

*

I wasn't through complaining when Chrysis came in, gave me a bear hug, and said 'I've got you now – exactly what I'd wanted! You are my sole desire, my only pleasure, and you will never put out this fire unless you quench it in my blood.'

*

One of the new slaves suddenly ran up and said the master was very mad at me because I hadn't been at work for two days. I'd better have some good excuse ready; he was foaming at the mouth and somebody was sure to get a beating.

*

140. There was a very respectable married woman called Philomela,[1] who in her youth had made it her business to win many a legacy. She was old now and past her prime and was forcing her son and daughter on childless old men as a way of passing on her trade. So she came to Eumolpus and entrusted her children ... herself and her hopes to his 'wisdom' and 'goodness'. He was the only man in the world who could teach children a wholesome philosophy on a daily basis. In short, she was leaving her children in Eumolpus' house to listen to his eloquence – the only legacy that could be bestowed on youth. She did exactly that: she left in the old man's bedroom an unusually pretty girl along with her brother, just on the verge of manhood, and pretended that she was going to the temple to offer prayers of thanks.

Eumolpus, who was so sexually frugal[2] that he would regard even me as a boy, didn't hesitate to initiate the girl in the rites of anal Venus. But since he had told everyone that he suffered

---

[1] 140.1 In this case the name hints at a whole repertoire of self-serving domestic abuse (see Chapter 131 n).

[2] 140.2 Arch-poseur that he is, Eumolpus at times actually boasts of his *frugalitas* ('discipline'; see above, Chapter 84).

from gout and weak loins, he risked ruining our whole plot if
he wasn't careful to maintain the pretense. So, to keep up
our lie, he persuaded the girl to sit down on top of his duly
commended 'goodness', and ordered Corax to get under the
bed he was lying on and keep his master in motion by putting
his hands on the ground and thrusting his own loins against
the bottom of the bed. He obeyed the command reluctantly
and the girl was skillful enough to match him, thrust for thrust.
When the business was nearing a climax, Eumolpus ordered
Corax in a loud voice to 'redouble his efforts'. So old Eumolpus,
sandwiched between his valet and his mistress, was riding a
kind of seesaw. Eumolpus played the game again and again
amid much uproarious laughter including his own. Well, use it
or lose it, I thought, as I made an attempt to breach her brother's
virtue, while he was watching his sister's antics through the
keyhole. The well-schooled boy did not shun my advances but
even there the gods were against me.

*

'There are greater gods who have made me whole again. For
Mercury, the courier of souls, by his good will has restored to
me what an angry hand had chopped off: consider me more
favored than Protesilaus or any of the ancient heroes.'[3] With
that I lifted my tunic and commended all of me to Eumolpus.
At first, he was appalled, but then, to be fully convinced, he
took the gifts of the gods in both hands...

*

'Socrates, considered the wisest of us all by both gods and
men, used to boast that he never looked inside a tavern or
thought great crowds of people worth glancing at. Nothing is
preferable to a continual conversation with wisdom...'

[140.3] According to legend the first Greek to be killed at Troy, Protesilaus, was
brought back to life for a brief tryst with his grieving wife, who had slept with
his effigy in the interim (see Apollodorus, *Epit*. 3.30). This version of Protesilaus'
story is thus an inversion of that of Orpheus or Alcestis (G. W. Bowersock, *Fiction
as History* [Berkeley, 1994] 112). But in the empire the legend of Protesilaus
continued to grow until he became 'the polytheists' new representative of bodily
resurrection' (Bowersock, 113). See esp. Philostratus' *Heroikos*.

'All this is true,' I said, 'and no one deserves to get into trouble faster than those who crave what isn't theirs. How would con men and pickpockets survive if they didn't cast little boxes and purses jingling with coins before the crowd like baited hooks? Just as game is caught with bait, so men can't be taken in if they don't get a taste of hope...'

*

141. 'The ship with your money and slaves has not arrived from Africa, as you had promised. The fortune-hunters are already drained dry and their generosity is shrinking. Either I am deceived or our usual luck is about to return with a vengeance...'

*

'All those who are named in my will (except my own freedmen) will get what I have left them on this condition: if they cut my body into pieces and eat it in front of the whole town.[1]

'We know that among some peoples the custom is still observed that the dead be eaten by their own family. Consequently, sick people are often blamed for spoiling the meat! So I warn my friends not to object to my demands: consume my flesh with the same fervor with which you prayed for my last breath...'

His legendary wealth blinded the eyes and souls of the poor fools. Gorgias was ready to comply...

*

'I have no fear of turning your stomach: it will obey you if

[141.1] Eumolpus' parodic last grab for an Orphic preeminence, in this case through a sort of *sparagmos/mactatio* akin to that suffered by Orpheus himself (see Chapter 84, n. 1 and Ovid, *Metam.* 11.1–55; at 11.93 Ovid actually mentions the Orphic disciple Eumolpus). The Dickensian requirement (cf. *Great Expectations*) that his heirs eat his corpse plays on their appetite for his goods, a satiric exposé of the dog-eat-dog ethos prevailing in Croton and thus *a fortiori* in Rome (see here Chapters 79, 116 and note, and the early Roman law [Aulus Gellius 20.1.39–49, on *Twelve Tables* 3.6] that the body of a non-paying debtor could be cut up and shared by his creditors).

you promise to compensate it with many fine things in return
for a single disgusting hour. Just close your eyes and pretend
you are munching on millions instead of on human flesh.
Besides, we'll find some appetizing condiments to change the
flavor. After all, no meat really tastes good by itself: it must be
artfully disguised to be acceptable to our fastidious palates!
And if you wish me to justify my plan with precedents, consider
the people of Saguntum:² when they were besieged by Hannibal
they ate human flesh – and they had no hope of an inheritance!
The people of Petelia did the same thing when they were on
the verge of starvation, and they sought nothing from their
feasting – except, of course, to end their hunger! And when
Numantia fell to Scipio, mothers were found cradling in their
arms the half-eaten bodies of their own children . . .³

141.2 For cannibalism as a satiric topos, see Juvenal's fifteenth satire, not to
mention Swift's *A Modest Proposal*. Bowersock (134–8) argues persuasively that
Petronius deliberately parodies both Herodotus 3.99 and the Christian New
Testament (*Kainē Diathēkē*) in his representation of the 'Will of Eumolpus'. The
siege-stories recalled here by Eumolpus are famous from Livy and elsewhere,
although cannibalism is rarely alleged in the sources except for Numantia. Saguntum and Petelia both fell to Hannibal in the course of the second Punic War (Livy
21.14–15, 23.30; cf. Silius Italicus 12.431–2, for Petelia as a 'second Saguntum'),
and Numantia fell to Scipio Africanus in 133 BC (Appian, *Rom.* 6.96–7). Though
Saguntum and Numantia were both cities in Spain, the small town of Petelia lay
conveniently not far from Croton.

141.3 The text breaks off here. The 'Wilde' version supplies a conclusion based
on *Frag.* 1, in which Eumolpus becomes the scapegoat first feasted then thrown
from a rock: see our note *ad. loc.*

Testimonia and Fragments (Müller's numbering where not stated)[1]

1. Servius on Vergil, *Aen.* 3.57: *auri sacra fames* ['accursed gold-hunger']; *sacra*, that is, 'accursed' [actually, 'blasted' and 'blest']. The phrase derives from the Gauls' custom. For whenever the Massilians were afflicted by plague, one of their paupers would offer himself to be sumptuously maintained for a year at the public expense. Afterwards, decked with sacred boughs and vestments, he was led with curses all through the town, so that all the town's ills would be transferred to him, and in this fashion he was thrown off a cliff. So we read in Petronius.[2]

4. Sidonius Apollonaris, *Carm.* 23:

> No need to list them, though I do,
> Latin's great names, including you,
> Tully, Livy, and Vergil ... and Arbiter, too,

[F1.1] The poetic fragments that here follow the *Satyrica* may well generally belong to the same manuscript tradition but cannot reliably be placed in the narrative. We have translated only those fragments with an evident bearing on the lost sections' plot or Petronius' performance in meter.

[F1.2] A standard reference to scapegoating-ritual quite clearly derived from some lost episode of Petronius, presumably the same one Sidonius has in mind in *Frag.* 4 (see Dennis H. Hughes, *Human Sacrifice in Ancient Greece* (London and New York, 1991) 157–60. In Sidonius the scapegoat's blest-blasted or blessed-cursed ambivalence appears to be borrowed or shared by some sort of phallic fetish (cf. Lat. *fascinum* and Gk. *baskanon*); also note the equation in *Frag.* 4 of Petronius and his fictional protagonist, as well as the apparent connection between the Massilian scapegoat's short-lived regal privilege and the *carte blanche* enjoyed by Eumolpus and his fellow swindlers while living in Croton on borrowed largesse (Chapters 116–41). (The 'Wilde' version makes Eumolpus the scapegoat, concluding the plot with Eumolpus' ritual death by being thrown from a rock.)

of Marseilles' gardens' blest (blasted) fetish[1] a fan,
and a match for Priapus the Hellespont's *Man*.

13. Fulgentius, *Expositio sermonum antiquorum* 61: *Aumatium* means a public privy as in theaters or the arena. Hence Petronius says, 'I hurled myself into the privy.'

16. From a Glossary of Saint-Denys: 'Petronius: "It was clearly their habit not to pass through the grotto of Naples without bending over." '

19. Cited by Terentianus Maurus, *De metris* (GL 6.399), and Marius Victorinus (GL 6.138) examples of catalectic iambic dimeter:

> the maidens of the Nile,
> prepared for holy rites.
> ...
> his skin dyed black as night,
> a boy whose gestures *spoke*
> ...
> Egyptian dancing-troupes

20. Cited by Terentianus Maurus, *De metris* (GL 6.409), as an example of anacreontics:

> you see how the three-faced moon
> whirls along her fiery course,
> and how in his flying coach
> Phoebus makes his own swift round

21. Cited by Diomedes (GL 1.518) as a species of short line or *comma*:

> an old crone, stewed in wine,
> with ever-trembling lips

[F4.1] Literally, 'sacred stump' (*sacri stipitis*); see *Frag.* 1 for the double-edged term *sacer* ('blessed'-'blasted').

24. Jerome in a letter to Demetrius 130.995: 'Let a virgin avoid like a plague and a poison for modesty boys with hair curled and crisped and skins smelling of foreign rodents, as in that comment out of Petronius, "He smells good all the time? We smell a *rat*." '[1]

25. Fulgentius, *Mythologiae* 2.6: 'But Nicagoras says that he [*sc.*, Prometheus] made the first idol, and treats the eating of his liver by the vulture as an image of envy; whence Petronius too says of it,

> That vulture charged with tearing up the liver,
> ripping away at breast and vital organs,
> is not the bird of witty poets' fictions
> but greed and envy, hearts' home-grown afflictions.[1]

Poems

26. [*AL* 690, Bu 26]:

> Nature's known 'laws' rule some affairs, not all;
> so ravens lay best when the corn is tall;
> so bears trot out their fresh whelps with the tongue,
> while fish as single parents bear their young;
> so Phoebus' tortoise, from Lucina's throes
> kindly released, broods eggs with her warm nose;
> so throbbing throngs of bees from webs of wax
> deploy in force, unmobilized by sex;
> not in one rut, but in a wealth of choices
> nature enlarged in curious ways rejoices.[1]

[F24.1] This line also appears in Martial 2.12.4 but may be a citation from Petronius.

[F25.1] A fairly standard moralization of a mythical punishment (cf. Lucretius 3.978–1010); but since a vulture rends Tityos in Tartarus while an eagle rends Prometheus on Caucasus this text seems to confuse the two punishments. Cf. Dio Chrysostom, *Or.* 8.33, who interprets the swelling of Prometheus' liver as a sophist's response to public opinion – an expression of his vanity and lack of Cynic autonomy. Hercules saves him from this plight.

[F26.1] The poem seems to be a pert hedonist retort to the Stoics' attempts to invoke observed natural 'laws' as a basis for standardized conduct, especially sexual conduct; in this sense, if not others, the poem may be yet another oblique program-statement. On ravens ('divining-birds' [oscines], though in Pliny apparently used to mean songbirds in general), see Pliny the Elder, *N.H.* 10.88; on

27. [AL 466, Bu 27]:

Fear it was first made gods, when sheer from heaven
lightning flashed down, dashed Maenalus with flame,
and stricken Athos blazed; when Phoebus sank
to rise, rounding the globe; the Moon grown old
renewed her state; hence signs spread through the skies,
the year divided with the months' succession.
The vice gained ground. Now empty error ordered
that farmers offer up first fruits to Ceres,
with laden vines wreathe Bacchus, and that Pales
rejoice in herdsmen's work; in Ocean's depths
Neptune installed rules *waves*; Minerva *shops*;
each thriving would-be, every world-class fraud,
takes turns inventing his own private god.[1]

28. [AL 476, Bu 28]:

People, you see, will sooner swallow fire
than keep a secret. Let it in one ear,
it leaks – the streets buzz! – at the speed of sound.
And telling's not enough; what gets around
outgrows its private source, adds to its weight;
so that slave, eager but afraid to prate
the secret of the ears King Midas hid,
buried his news, yet earth through many a reed
hummed with his exposé of Midas' head.[1]

bears 8.126; on fish 9.56, 166 (cf. Aristotle, *De gen. an.* 3.5, 755b7 ff.); on the
tortoise cf. 9.37 ('nose' [*sc.*, breath] may not be the right reading, in *Carm.* 26.6);
on bees cf. 11.46 ff. and Aristotle, *De gen. an.* 3.10, 759b33 ff.
    [F27.1] An essentially Epicurean account of the birth of religion (cf. Lucretius
5.1183–1240).
    [F28.1] On these rumorous reeds see Ovid, *Metam.* 11.183–93.

29. [*AL* 650, Bu 29]:

> Our eyes deceive us; wayward sense,
> oppressing reason, serves pretense.
> A tower that close-range rises square
> seems round, uncornered, from afar;
> full mouths spurn Hybla's honeycombs,
> and noses often loathe perfumes;
> nor could we choose now that, now this,
> but that to stray sense fated is,
> importing its own nemesis.[1]

30. [*AL* 651, Bu 30]:

Dreams which delude the mind with fleeting shadows
are neither shrine- nor heaven-sent dispatches;
each forms his own. Limbs wrapped in peace and slumber
and minds left unencumbered, free to sport,
each nightly re-enacts what was by day.
Who shakes down walls, puts poor towns to the torch,
dreams spears and routed ranks and dying kings
and fields awash with slaughter in profusion;
pleaders in court see law, the hall of justice,
and (fearfully) the bench ringed round with bailiffs.
The miser hides his wealth and digs up gold;
the hunter shakes the forest with his hounds;
the sailor saves his ship or goes down with it.
Whores write their lovers; cheating wives send favors;
even a dog in dreams barks after game;
and poor souls' toils last on into the night.[1]

[F29.1] Standard Sceptic examples of false or misleading sense-impressions (cf. Lucretius 4.353 ff.).

[F30.1] A fairly standard Epicurean account of dreams' content as dim reminiscence, not prophecy (cf. Lucretius 4.962–1036).

Poems not accepted by Müller

31. [AL 464, Bu 35]:

> Something for one and all, for not all lines
> converge; one plucks a flower, another spines.

32. [AL 465, Bu 38]:

> Autumn had broken summer's sweltering shadows
> and Phoebus steered a cooler course toward winter;
> the plane-tree had begun to shed, the vine
> to cast its leaves and reckon up its bunches;
> before our eyes there hung the whole year's promise.

33. [AL 467, Bu 33]:

> I'd rather not forever use
> one fragrance, or the same wine choose;
> bulls love to graze from here to there,
> and beasts delight in varied fare;
> The very sweetness of the day
> by darkness cut gets its bouquet.

34. [AL 468, Bu 34]:

> A wife is meant for love, like cash;
> but must I only love my stash?

35. [AL 469, Bu 37]:

> Youth, leave your seat and seek another shore;
> for you a grander prospect is in store.
> Take heart; the distant Danube will hear tell
> of you, and the cold North catch wind, as well,
> with Egypt's calms, from East to West, all lands!
> *A greater Ithacan, tread foreign sands.*[1]

[F35.1] Depite Müller's minor lexical cavils this poem seems distinctly Petronian, a mock-epic charter connecting its subject's adventures with not only Odysseus' broad wanderings but Aeneas' journey to found Rome (cf. Vergil, *Aen.* 3.159–62).

36. [*AL* 470, Bu 36]:

> Whatever is, may serve men's needs;
> in hard times, trash Recovery breeds;
> ship sunk, we drown with tawny gold,
> but lightweight oars for safety hold;
> when trumps sound, blades seek moneybags;
> war's blows are no big deal to rags.[1]

37. [*AL* 471, Bu 50]:

> Snug under its safe eaves, my little house,
> where on rich elm the grape hangs, big with wine;
> The boughs yield cherries, woods yield ruddy apples,
> and Pallas' grove groans under its crown's plenty.
> Now where a small space drinks the channelled spring,
> I grow Corycian kale and drooping mallow,
> and poppies which bestow untroubled sleep.
> Beyond this if I wish to lay a snare
> for birds, or rather trap unwarlike deer,
> or draw a trembling fish on silver line,
> no deeper wiles my humble homestead knows.
> Go on and sell your hours of fleeting life
> for living high; when my own death ensues,
> with life content here let me pay my dues.

38. [*AL* 472, Bu 32]:

> Why stop at letting mad youth bear along
> the lot, or shame-sunk scoundrels steer us wrong?
> See, even lackeys steeped in scum, their kin,
> find our crass wealth mire fit to wallow in;
> cheap slaves could ransom kings; a prisoner's cell
> beats Vesta's and Quirinus' place to hell.[1]

[F36.1] One of several only slightly overdone celebrations of the 'simple life', e.g.
Carm. 37, 48 (cf. notably Vergil, *Georg.* 4.116–38, and Horace, e.g. *Od.* 1.31,
37, *Epod.* 2).
[F38.1] Famous monuments to old Roman simplicity. Vesta's place is the temple
of Vesta the hearth-goddess, guardian of family integrity, while Quirinus' or
Romulus' place is a small ancient house thought in classical times to be that of
Rome's founder.

So virtue founders, overwhelmed with shite,
while evil's fleet flaunts sails of whitest white.

39. [AL 473, Bu 39]:

Thus, too, the limbs confine the belly's breezes;
these from the depths belaboring their releases
blast their way out, the shivers never-ending
that rule the hard-pressed limbs until, unbending,
the body's warm sweat proves relief is pending.[1]

40. [AL 474, Bu 51.1–6, 17–18]:

Shore sweeter than my life! O happy sea,
free visitor of my beloved country!
O glorious day! Here I once lingered often
to loll in lazy Iliads of claspings;
here flows a spring; there cove-kelp makes its landfall;
this was a place won to unspoken yearnings.
My life's complete; the blessings of past hours
ill fortune heightens even as it lowers.

41. [AL 475, Bu 40]:

He tore his trembling head's white hairs and scored
his cheeks once this was said; his eyes' rains poured;
and as swift floods when frozen snows give way
rush down, and mild airs ending ice's stay
make thawed ground sodden stream without delay,
so his face ran with copious tears, his breast
perturbed with moans a deep lament expressed.[1]

F39.1 More philosophy of flatulence (cf. Chapter 47). This poem may be revers-
ing a traditional explanatory analogy between visceral rumblings and earthquakes
(see Aristotle, *Meteorologia* 2.8, and Lucretius 6.577–84, 942–4). Courtney (57)
argues that this poem is a parody of the Senecan *Aetna* (true author unknown).
He compares Seneca's *NQ* 5.4.2 and Petronius' relation to Lucan's unpublished
work. Critics cited by Burman take this poem as referring to ejaculation; another
combines it with *Carm.* 41 (cf. here Chapter 137 n.).
F41.1 At least some early texts made this poem's subject feminine and assigned
it to one of the old crones entangled with Encolpius in Chapters 134–8.

42. [*AL* 477, Bu 51.7–16]:

> There sea and sky by turns collide;
> here rills trace smiling countryside.
> There sailors grieve while their ships sink;
> here shepherds guide their sheep to drink.
> There present death Greed's gaping chokes;
> here Ceres courts the sickle's strokes.
> There burning thirst prevails, afloat;
> here even on bad men, kissers dote.
> Let poor Ulysses fret the sea;
> on land seek fair Penelope.

43. [*AL* 478, Bu 52]:

> Who isn't in a rush to die
> and wants to let fate spin things out
> should just so far seas' anger try
> as he can wade without a doubt.
> Amid green kelp see mussels tossed,
> and conch-shells dragged with sucking roar;
> see sands in wave-turned spirals lost,
> bright stones laid bare on waveswept floor;
> play safe; tread here, and at the most
> sea-fare in walking-range of shore.[1]

44. [*AL* 479, Bu 52]:

> Looks aren't enough. You want to be a beauty?
> Don't flaunt what's merely in the line of duty.
> Words, witticisms, play, finesse, and laughter
> win the renown simplicity is after.
> Where looks entice, thank art's assists for that;
> artless, neglected, naked charm falls flat.[1]

[F43.1] Perhaps two parts of one even longer harangue against seafaring.
[F44.1] More defense of aesthetics-with-a-twist, and another obliquely apt program-statement.

45. [*AL* 691, Bu 31]:

> My place of birth was India's ruddy strand,
> where day with orb rekindled greets the land.
> Born here, with my divinity arranged,
> my barbarous tongue for Latin I exchanged.
> Now, Delphic Phoebus, tell your swans goodbye;
> to sound your temples' praise, far worthier I.[1]

46. [*AL* 692, Bu 42]:

> The naked shipwrecked sailor seeks a mate
> from the same boat to share his wretched state;
> a farmer, his whole year's work lost to hail,
> finds a like breast his sad lot to bewail,
> while deaths match mourners; parents through their tears
> pool their laments, whose protests make them peers.
> We too with plaints combined will strike the stars;
> it helps, they say, to synchronize your prayers.

47. [*AL* 693, Bu 44]:

> If you are Phoebus' sister, Delia, help me;
> tell him what I am asking, word for word:
> 'I built you, Delphic god, a shrine of marble –
> Sicilian – sang you fair with slender reed;
> now if you hear, Apollo, if divine,
> teach me to raise some cash; I've lost all mine.'[1]

48. [*AL* 694, Bu 45]:

> A friendly god all sad complaints to end
> a remedy for each placed near at hand.
> Cheap greens and berries off a bramble-bush
> suffice the stomach's hunger-pangs to hush.

[F45.1] As if spoken by a parrot, a bird sacred in India; swans, though sacred to Apollo, were thought to be mute until dying.

[F47.1] A prayer to Diana, the sister of Phoebus Apollo, both born on the island of Delos according to myth, while Apollo's great oracle was at Delphi. The poem's wit seems to lie in a too-glib agreement between ardent veneration and outright venality.

Fools thirst beside a stream, or freeze forsaking
when a hot pyre lends warmth there for the taking.
On others' wives' dire thresholds, law waits armed;
on licit couch, a girl lets go unharmed.
Rich nature serves enough all needs to ease;
rash pride serves up a never-ending tease.[1]

49. [AL 695, Bu 46]:

Doves in a soldier's helm to nest intend;
see just how plainly Mars is Venus' friend.[1]

50. [AL 696, Bu 47]:

A Jew may praise his god of pork
and heaven's highest ears invoke;
unless he also crops his groin
and frees the head there knotted in,
banished he'll leave his native state
and Sabbath's fasting violate.[1]

51.[AL 697, Bu ad 47]:

A noble mind's best reckoning:
hands bold enough for anything!

F48.1 In one sense a traditional riposte to Petronius' teasing and daring aesthetic (cf. Horace, Sat. 2.7, and here, Chapter 82 and Carm. 54 n.).

F49.1 A found emblem or trumped-up conceit: doves and helmets are obvious tokens of Love and War, Venus and Mars, whose celestial affair has been famous since Homer at least (Od. 8.265–366).

F50.1 Clearly references to Scriptural directives against eating pork and for practising ritual circumcision; it is hard to guess just how this poem may have borne on the (vaguely opposing?) taboos violated by Encolpius that helped earn him the wrath of Priapus (Chapters 17, 133).

Probably spurious poems (our numbering; texts in Courtney [C], Ernout [E], and De Guerle [G])[1]

52. [AL 698, Bu 48 (C)]:

> No sooner snug, eyes giving in to sleep,
> making the most of the first still of night,
> than fierce Love grips me, hales me by the hair,
> and tells me with hair torn to stay awake.
> 'Can you serve me, and love a thousand girls,
> yet still, you hard sort, lie alone – *alone*?'
> I leap up barefoot, just throw on a robe,
> dash every which way, get nowhere at all,
> stalled in mid-rush, as much point going home
> as standing in the middle of the street.
> Men's voices silent now, street noises, birdsongs,
> and the unflagging company of dogs,
> of all these only I shun bed and rest
> to roam, great Cupid, in your wandering quest.

53. [AL 699, Bu 49 (C)]:

> Forever cherish we that night, Nealce,
> the first that settled you in my embraces,
> the bedroom and the genius of the pillow,
> long stolen hours that made your freshness mine.
> Let us be true no matter how age alters,
> and use the little span our lot permits us.
> Custom and laws approve old love's remaining;
> prove our own sudden love no less sustaining.

54. [AL 700 (C)]:

> A quick, cheap thrill the Carnal Act;
> sex palls once an accomplished fact.
> Why gallop blindly to complete
> the course like quadrupeds in heat?

[F51.1] We translate only poems with especially clear bearing on Petronius and his textual or cultural legacy.

Love dwindles, and its flames decay.
So, so, unsated let us play,
and lie exchanging kiss for kiss;
no chore, no cause for blushing, this;
this is, was, always will be fun,
forever foreplay, never done.[1]

55. [*AL* 218, Bu 43 (C)]:

Marcia my sweet, you send me golden quinces;
you send rough chestnuts' offerings in the bargain,
and welcome all. But if you came in person —
pretty girl that you are — you'd grace your presents;
though you bring apples tart against the palate,
who eats them tastes of honey with the sour.
You don't deliver, dear? Then with the fruits
send kisses too; *those* I'll devour, and gladly.

56. [*AL* 701 (E)]:

Suspicious love, the one affair
too great for *Hercules* to bear.[1]

57. [*AL* 702 (E)]:

Awake, I seek you with my eyes, in mind
when night subdues my lonely limbs in slumber.
I had a dream that you could not refuse me;
come to me now, if but to disabuse me.

[F54.1] A much-translated poem; see the sampling of versions including Ben Jonson's in *Arion*, 2 (1963): 83–4. This might well be construed as another obliquely apt program statement, this time making a poetic virtue of teasing deferral (cf. Chapter 82, n.). Focusing on just one line, standard lexical cavils may not wholly rule out Petronius' authorship.

[F56.1] An allusion to Hercules' death thanks to Deianeira's jealousy.

58. [AL 703 (E)]:[1]

> Hesperie wrought these floral bands,
> industrious with her gentle hands,
> and, pretty wrap on pretty breast,
> now preens with twice the interest.

59. [AL 704 (E)]:

> Hesperie weaves with her own hands,
> worthy her ivory breasts, these bands.
> Pallas and Venus now embrace;
> Love's breasts Minerva's fashions grace.

60. [AL 705 (E)]:

> Rose-patterned, Tyrian-purple-dyed,
> the sash that binds her supple side
> from both her breasts sweet fragrance draws,
> rose-scent that renders it true rose.

61. [AL 706 (E)]:

> Julia just tossed a gleaming snowball at me;
> I thought snow didn't burn; this burned like fire.
> What is as cold as snow? And yet the snow
> *you* launched at me burns, Julia, to the quick.
> Where am I safe from sneak-attacks by Cupid
> if he can kindle even frozen water?
> No one but Julia, you can quench my flame,
> with – neither snow nor ice – more of the same!

62. [AL 707 (E)]:

> Delos, now moored to solid ground,
> once swam the wine-dark seas around
> here, there, breeze-driven endlessly,
> high on the waves, an easy prey;

F58.1 Quite unlikely to be by Petronius; worth including with some other poems in this section if only to show how Petronius' name came to be linked with all manner of (trifling) poetic eroticism.

soon God it bound with double chain,
first to high Gyaros and then
stout Myconos to rein it in.[1]

63. [AL 217 (E)]:[1]

Your bright eyes glow with starlike flair;
your throat sheds roses, gold your hair;
your soft cheeks with deep blushes dressed,
mixed red and white adorn your breast;
all honor's queen, with looks divine
Venus in figure you outshine.
Your hand is silver; silken line
your subtle fingers tease, rich twine;
fair foot unused to smallest stone,
whose steps the hard earth scorn to own,
on lilies (when you deign to walk)
lightly borne up, unharmed the stalk.
Load others' necks with necklaces,
bejewel them; you alone can please
undressed! None shines in all respects?
All dazzles who your All inspects.
The Sirens' song and Thalia's pluck
to my ear cannot match – worse luck! –
your love-dart accents honey-sweet.
I faint, flag, languish, feel the heat,
burn, sigh, sag, suffer, gasp for breath,
heartsick, inoperable, near death;
still may your lips attend to me,
purge heartache, and this remedy
retrieve me, lest nerves all but shred
give way, and leave me wrongly dead.

[F62.1] Much ado about floating; only after Apollo and Diana were born here,
according to myth (see *Carm.* 47 n.), did the island of Delos stop drifting. (Cf.
also Vergil, *Aen.* 3.73–7.)

[F63.1] Undoubtedly not by Petronius, though included in numerous early editions; retained here because in at least a few early editions it was made to do
narrative work, introduced as a missive from Encolpius/Polyaenus to Circe which
functioned to bridge the lacuna between Chapters 138 and 139.

If that seems much, permit me then
just this: once perished, take me in
those white arms, where I'll live again.

64. [*AL* 786 (G)]:

My mother while expecting me
it seems inquired what I would be.
Phoebus said 'boy', Mars 'girl'; their fight
Juno topped off, 'hermaphrodite'.
How would I die? She said, 'run through',
Mars 'hanged', 'drowned' Phoebus; all came true.
I climbed a streamside tree; my sword
and I let slip, myself I gored,
limb-caught, stream-foundered, met my loss,
girl-boy, by Water, Sword, and Cross.[1]

[F64.1] Possibly by Matthew of Vendôme (late 12th c. AD), an excessive, perversely suggestive, mysterious poem taking up more than one topic of seminal importance to Petronius; certainly most germane to the hermaphroditic epiphany in Fellini's strange homage to Petronius, *Fellini Satyricon*. For additional medieval developments of this 'threefold death' premise including a Latin poem often attributed to the late 12th c. Hildebert of Le Mans (*Patrologia Latina*, ed. J. P. Migne, 221 vols. [Paris, 1844–64] 171:1445–46) see the anonymous *Vita Merlini/Life of Merlin*, ed. B. Clarke (Cardiff, 1973), ll 323 ff., and notes.

GLOSSARY OF IMPORTANT NAMES

(in order of appearance)[*]

ENCOLPIUS, the narrator and protagonist (20); from the Greek verb *egkolpizo*: 'to form a bay, go into a bay, to inject into the vagina; to take in one's bosom, to embrace; to catch fish in the belly of a net; to conceive.'

AGAMEMNON, a professor of rhetoric who debates Encolpius in the first scene of the *Satyrica* and takes him to Trimalchio's banquet (3). His name recalls the Greek king who led the expedition to Troy to recover Helen, the wife of his brother, Menelaus. (The professor's assistant here is accordingly named Menelaus.)

ASCYLTOS, companion of Encolpius and rival for Giton's affections (6). His name is from the Greek *askultos*: 'not pulled about; undisturbed'.

GITON, Encolpius' boyfriend (9), who is also the object of Ascyltos' and Eumolpus' desires. From the Greek *geiton*: 'neighbor or borderer'.

QUARTILLA, priestess of Priapus (16). Hers is one of the few Italic names in the *Satyrica*, a diminutive from the Latin *quarta*: 'fourth in a series'. Except for Quartilla almost all the names in the *Satyrica* are Greek (or Semitic) in origin – including the dogs' (cf. Sedgwick 142). The exceptions (other than Quartilla) are Proculus, Scintilla and Fortunata.

PRIAPUS, a fertility god who originated in Lampascus on the Hellespont (16). He is the embodiment of lust. His symbol was the phallus. His statue was of a misshapen little man with huge genitals. He is often associated with Dionysus and satyrs. He is the subject of a poem by Encolpius (139).

C. POMPEIUS TRIMALCHIO MAECENATIANUS, the rich ex-slave whose party forms the longest surviving episode of the novel (26).

---

[*] Unless otherwise indicated the numbers in parentheses refer to the Chapter section in which the name first appears.

As a manumitted slave he took the praenomen and nomen of his master, C. (or Gaius) Pompeius (Pompeius is a common name in Campania). Maecenatianus shows that he had originally been a slave to someone named Maecenas (probably not the famous patron of Horace, but the comic suggestion must be deliberate). Trimalchio is his slave name and 'is probably derived from *tri-*, an intensive prefix, and a semitic word meaning "prince" found in Malchus, Melchios, Melek, Moloch, Melchizedek, Malachi, etc.' (Sedgwick 87).

HERMEROS, a guest at Trimalchio's party, who describes Fortunata to Encolpius (37). His name (first mentioned in 59) means 'a herm with a bust of Eros'. (A herm is a pillar that typically supported busts of Hermes and later of other gods.) But its most immediate reference would probably be to the famous gladiator mentioned along with Petraites (52).

FORTUNATA, Trimalchio's wife (37). This is probably a slave name given by her owner; it is from the Latin verb *fortuno*: 'to make fortunate or successful; to prosper'.

DIONYSUS, a young slave of Trimalchio's named after the Greek god of wine and ecstasy. The Latin for Dionysus, *Liber* ('Free') or *Liber Pater* ('Free Father'), permits Trimalchio's punning (in 41).

DAMA, a guest of Trimalchio's (41). His is a typical slave name found in satire and comedy and derived from the Greek verb *damazo*: 'to tame or subdue'.

SELEUCUS, a guest of Trimalchio (42). His name recalls the Seleucids, the dynasty that inherited the Asian conquests of Alexander the Great.

PHILEROS, a guest of Trimalchio (43); from the Greek *phileros*: 'prone to love, amorous'.

GANYMEDE, a guest of Trimalchio (44). In Greek myth Ganymede is a beautiful Trojan prince whom Zeus abducted to Olympus to be his cupbearer and lover. The English noun *catamite* is derived from his name.

ECHION, a guest of Trimalchio identified as a 'ragman' (45). His name recalls that of Pentheus' father, one of the heroes who sprang from the dragon's teeth sown by Cadmus, legendary founder of Thebes.

NICEROS, the guest of Trimalchio who tells the story of the werewolf (61–2). His name combines the Greek words for victory (*nike*) and desire (*eros*). In Martial (12.65.4) Niceros is the name of a fashionable perfumer.

PLOCAMUS, a guest of Trimalchio (64). His name is from the Greek *plokamos*: 'a lock or braid of hair'.

HABINNAS, the last guest to arrive at Trimalchio's (65); a close friend of the host, he is identified as a maker of tombstones. His name is probably Semitic. See Chapter 65 n.

EUMOLPUS, a poet and con man who befriends Encolpius (94); his name is from the Greek *eumolpos*: 'sweetly singing', and recalls the legendary Greek poet of the same name, often associated with Orpheus. See Chapter 141, note 1.

LICHAS, a ship captain from Tarentum who is looking for Encolpius (101). In Greek myth Lichas is the attendant of Heracles who brings him the fatal robe.

TRYPHAENA, a woman who travels 'in the service of pleasure' and is searching for Giton and Encolpius with Lichas (101). She and Lichas know them from a missing part of the novel. Her name is from the Greek *truphao*: 'to live luxuriously'.

CHRYSIS, Circe's maid (128). Her name is from the Greek *chrysis*: 'a vessel of gold'. It also recalls the name of the daughter of Chryses, whose capture by Agamemnon causes Apollo to send a plague on the Greek camp (in the first book of the *Iliad*).

CIRCE, the mythically beautiful woman who wants to be Encolpius' mistress (127). She is named after the witch in the *Odyssey* – the daughter of the Sun – who turns Odysseus' men into swine before Odysseus overcomes her power with the help of a magical plant given him by Hermes. They then become lovers.

POLYAENUS, the pseudonym used by Encolpius at Croton (127). It is an epithet for Odysseus in Homer and means both 'the man about whom many tales are told' and 'the man who has many tales to tell'.

PROSELENOS, an associate of Oenothea's who is the first to try to cure Encolpius' impotence. Like Oenothea, she may be a priestess of Priapus. Her name is from the Greek *proselenos*: 'older than the moon'.

OENOTHEA, a priestess of Priapus at Croton who tries to cure Encolpius' impotence (134). Her name may mean 'wine-goddess'; Ernout takes it to mean 'making a god of wine'.

PETRONIUS AND HIS CRITICS

In the opinion of our Arbiter almost the whole world is engaged in a mime [*fere totus mundus ... mimum videtur agere*; cf. the Globe Theater's motto, *mundus agit histrionem*].

John of Salisbury, *Policraticus* 3.8.25–6 (12th c.

Petronius, Plinius Secundus, and Tacitus speke best Latine.

Ben Jonson, *Conversations with Drummond* (1619)

Tanta gratia vocis famam conciliabat, saith *Petronius* [Chapter 127] in his fragment of pure impurities, I meane his *Satiricon, tam dulcis sonus permulcebat aera, ut putares inter auras cantare Syrenum concordiam*, Shee sang so sweetly that she charmed the Aire, and thou wouldst have thought thou hadst heard a consort of Syrens.

Robert Burton, *The Anatomy of Melancholy* 3.2.2.4 (1624)
(Here Burton echoes the judgement of Justus Lipsius, [1547–1606], in his commentary on Tacitus' *Annales* 16.18)

... like Petronius Arbiter in his *Satyricon*, a text which should have shared the same pyre as its author, the only light that book deserved.

P. Masen, S. J., *Palaestra styli romani* (1659). The Roman Catholic Council of Trent in the previous century had allowed (guarded) reading of authors like Petronius *propter sermonis elegantiam*,
i.e., as a resource for stylistic elegance. Cf. G. B. Marino, *L'Adone* (1622), 10.157–8.

I am no admirer of quotations; but you shall hear, if you please, one of the Ancients delivering his judgement on this question; 'tis Petronius Arbiter, the most elegant, and one of the most judicious authors of the Latin tongue; who after he had given many admirable rules for the structure and beauties of an epic poem, concludes all in these following words [118]:

*Non enim res gestae versibus comprehendendae sunt, quod longe
melius historici faciunt: sed, per ambages, deorumque ministeria...
praecipitandus est liber spiritus, ut potius furentis animi vaticinatio
appareat, quam religiosae orationis, sub testibus, fides.*

John Dryden, *Of Heroic Plays: An Essay* (1672)

Fancy and Art in gay Petronius please;
The scholar's learning, with the Courtier's ease;

Alexander Pope, *Essay on Criticism* 667–8 (1711)

To judg (sic) of the merit of *Petronius*, I would have perused what
Tacitus says, and without lying, he must be one of the most honest
men of the world, since he could oblige so severe an Historian,
to renounce his Nature, and enlarge himself in the praises of a
voluptuous person; not but that so exquisite a voluptuousness
contributed as much to the delicacy of the spirit, as to that of the
taste. That *Erudito Luxu*, that arbiter *Elegantiarum*, is the character of an ingenious politeness, much different from the grosser
conceptions of the vicious: Nor was he so given over to his pleasure,
as to become incapable of affairs; neither had the sweetness of
his life made him an enemy to business. He retained the merit
of a Governor in his Government of *Bythinia*, and the virtue of
a Consul in his Consulate; but instead of subjecting himself to his
dignity, as do most part of men, fetching thence all their per-
plexity, or all their joys; *Petronius*, with a spirit superior to his
charges, reduced them to himself: and to explain my self better,
according to *Montaigne*, he renounced not the Man in favour
of the Magistrate.

For his death, after having well examined it, either I am deceived,
or it was the most exemplary of all antiquity [...] He not only
continued his ordinary functions [...] but suffered himself to be
transported to any thing that might delight him; and his Soul, at
the point of so troublesome a separation, was more affected with
the sweetness and facility of Verse, than all the sayings of the
Philosophers. *Petronius* at his death only left an image of life; no
action, no word, no circumstance betray'd any trouble of a dying
man; of him may properly be said, that *dying is to cease to live*,
and to him the *Vixit* of the *Romans* justly appertains.

Saint-Évremond, *Judgement on Alexander, and Caesar; and also on Seneca, Plutarch, and Petronius,* tr. after J. Dancer (London, 1672)

The authentic Petronius displays a most elegant candor, a supple rapidity, and a fortunate daring in his phrasing; *this* displays only languid frigidity.

G. Leibniz to D. Tenzel (1693) on Nodot's spurious additions to Petronius

Petronius, the author of his era who knew human beings best and portrayed their behavior most vividly ... [followed by a citation of Chapter 88 of *Satyrica*]

Jacques Diderot, note on his 1745 French translation of the Earl of Shaftesbury's *Inquiry concerning Virtue or Merit.* There were not a few other Enlightenment prizers of Petronius. John Locke owned four editions of *Satyrica*; Thomas Jefferson owned two, not to mention the works of Petronius' disciple Saint-Évremond; Benjamin Franklin chose an epigraph from *Satyrica*, Chapter 37, for his 1722 essay 'On Titles of Honour.'

'Here's a book,' said he, taking one from his bosom, 'written with great elegance and spirit, and though the subjects may give offense to some narrow-minded people, the author will always be held in esteem by any person of wit and learning.' So saying he put into my hands Petronius Arbiter [...]

Tobias Smollet, *Adventures of Roderick Random* (1748)

It is from a very common but a very false Opinion, that we constantly mix the idea of Levity with those of Wit and Humour. The gravest of Men have often possessed these Qualities in a very eminent Degree, and have exerted them on the most solemn subjects with very eminent success. These are to be found in many Places in the most serious works of Plato and Aristotle, of Cicero and Seneca [...] Not to mention the Instance of St Paul, whose writings do in my Opinion contain more true wit, than is to be found in the works of the unjustly celebrated Petronius.

Henry Fielding, *Covent Garden Journal*
(Tuesday, 3 March 1752) Number 18

Petronius! All the muses weep for thee;
But ev'ry tear shall scald thy memory;
Thou polish'd and high finish'd foe to truth,
Grey-beard corruptor of our list'ning youth,
To purge and skim away the filth of vice
That, so refin'd, it might the more entice,
Then pour it on the morals of thy son,
To taint his heart, was worthy of thine own!

William Cowper, *The Progress of Error* (1782)

Behold the new Petronius of the day
Our arbiter of pleasure and of play!
[*var.*: Behold the new Petronius of the times
The skillful arbiter of modern crimes.]

Byron, *English Bards and Scotch Reviewers* (1809)

Praecipitandus est liber spiritus, says Petronius Arbiter most happily [118]. The epithet *liber* here balances the preceding verb; and it is not easy to conceive more meaning condensed in fewer words.

Samuel T. Coleridge, *Biographia Literaria* (1817)

Petronius – a charming and terrible book, for the thoughts and the doubts it provokes in sound souls! This *Satyricon* is surely the work of a demon. Say that it lacks cohesion, that its general intent does remain enigmatic; so what? Every fragment is exquisite; every detail is enough to engage. I do not flatter myself that I have totally broken its husk; and indeed, I have scarcely attempted to do so; I have read, I have skimmed, and this more or less facile assay was enough to bring me to appreciate at least, in the middle of all that escaped me, the swift, well-turned phrasings, the light touch, the elegant familiarity, the novelty that is not too far-fetched and does not labor for its effect (*curiosa felicitas,* as Petronius himself once described it in Horace [*Sat.*, ch. 118]), in a word, the *distinction* [*cachet*] that has always marked out those writers who are masters of the art of pleasing. Certain narrative segments, among which the tale of this most famous 'Matron' [*Sat.*, ch. 111–12] stands out, are accomplished productions, and the poems that the author had the whim to insert here and there in his prose, unlike similar

mélanges in French, have a substance and brilliance about them
that make them authentic inset pearls. Even so, this indulgence of
taste leaves an uneasy feeling behind it and raises a problem that
weighs down the spirit. Taste is not the same thing as morality;
that much we know full well; but can these have so little to do
with each other that the former's perfection coincides with the
latter's perversion and ruin? What, then? Can it be so? Such cor-
ruption to gain this perfection! For this flower, so much dung!
From what elements does it crystalize, then, this supreme, dying
grace that haunts only a *point* and a *moment*? For that delicacy is
the delicacy of the *end*; one has said it resembles those dishes that
cannot be kept one instant more. Let us promptly add: there is a
certain sound, primitive taste, a taste born of the heart and of
nature, less subtle at times, but yet noble throughout, and braced
with a clean savor that does not go stale. In sum, there is Lucretius,
Petronius' total opposite; there are others in between, and one's
choice is not only between the historian of Encolpius [*sc.*, Petronius]
and the virtuous scholar, [Antoine-Léonard] Thomas....

C. A. Sainte-Beuve, 'Le Chevalier de Méré' (1848), *Portraits littéraires* III (1862), the same year in which Baudelaire announced
                    his projected translation of Petronius

I also read Petronius Arbiter, which is a rum work, not so immoral
as most modern works, but singularly silly.

                    Robert Louis Stevenson in a letter to Sidney Colvin
                                             (9 March 1884)

The author he really loved, and who made him abandon Lucan's
resounding tirades for good, was Petronius.

   Petronius was a shrewd observer, a delicate analyst, a marvellous
painter; dispassionately, with an entire lack of prejudice or animosity, he described the everyday life of Rome, recording the
manners and morals of his time in the lively little chapters of the
Satyricon.

   Noting what he saw as he saw it, he set forth the day-to-day
existence of the common people, with all its minor events, its
bestial incidents, its obscene antics.

   Here we have the Inspector of Lodgings coming to ask for the
names of any travellers who have recently arrived; there, a brothel

where men circle round naked women standing beside placards
giving their price, while through half-open doors couples can be
seen disporting themselves in the bedrooms. Elsewhere, in villas
full of insolent luxury where wealth and ostentation run riot, as
also in the mean inns described throughout the book, with their
unmade trestle beds swarming with fleas, the society of the day has
its fling – depraved ruffians like Ascyltos and Eumolpus, out for
what they can get; unnatural old men with their gowns tucked
up and their cheeks plastered with white lead and acacia rouge;
catamites of sixteen, plump and curly-headed; women having
hysterics; legacy-hunters offering their boys and girls to gratify
the lusts of rich testators, all these and more scurry across the
pages of the *Satyricon*, squabbling in the streets, fingering one
another in the baths, beating one another up like characters in a
pantomime.

All this is told with extraordinary vigour and precise colouring,
in a style that makes free of every dialect, that borrows expressions
from all the languages imported into Rome, that extends the fron-
tiers and breaks the fetters of the so-called Golden Age, that makes
every man talk in his own idiom – uneducated freedmen in vulgar
Latin, the language of the streets; foreigners in their barbaric lingo,
shot with words and phrases from African, Syrian, and Greek; and
stupid pedants, like the Agamemnon of the book, in a rhetorical
jargon of invented words. There are lightning sketches of all these
people, sprawled round a table, exchanging the vapid pleasantries
of drunken revellers, trotting out mawkish maxims and stupid
saws, their heads turned towards Trimalchio, who sits picking his
teeth, offers the company chamber-pots, discourses on the state of
his bowels, farts to prove his point, and begs his guests to make
themselves at home.

This realistic novel, this slice cut from Roman life in the raw,
with no thought, whatever people may say, of reforming or satirizing society, and no need to fake a conclusion or point a moral;
this story with no plot or action in it, simply relating the erotic
adventures of certain sons of Sodom, analysing with smooth finesse
the joys and sorrows of these loving couples, depicting in a splen-
didly wrought style, without affording a single glimpse of the
author, without any comment whatever, without a word of
approval or condemnation of his characters' thoughts and actions,

the vices of a decrepit civilization, a crumbling Empire – this story fascinated Des Esseintes; and in its subtle style, acute observation, and solid construction he could see a curious similarity, a strange analogy with the few modern French novels he could stomach.

Naturally enough he bitterly regretted the loss of the *Eustion* and the *Albutia*, those two works by Petronius mentioned by Planciades Fulgentius which have vanished for ever; but the bibliophile in him consoled the scholar, as he reverently handled the superb copy he possessed of the *Satyricon*, in the octavo edition of 1585 printed by J. Dousa at Leyden.

J. K. Huysmans, *Against Nature* (1884)
Translated by R. Baldwick

For, while he was but too ready to accept the position that was almost immediately offered to him on his coming of age, and found, indeed, a subtle pleasure in the thought that he might really become to the London of his own day what to imperial Neronian Rome the author of the 'Satyricon' once had been, yet in his inmost heart he desired to be something more than a mere *arbiter elegantiarum*, to be consulted on the wearing of a jewel, or the knotting of a necktie, or the conduct of a cane. He sought to elaborate some new scheme of life that would have its reasoned philosophy and its ordered principles, and find in the spiritualizing of the senses its highest realization.

Oscar Wilde, *The Picture of Dorian Gray* (1890).
Cf. the portrait of Petronius in M. Sienchiewicz's
Quo Vadis (in Polish, 1896).

I send you also Petronius. He startled me at first, but I liked him. He is a gentleman when all is said. I have taken a great dislike to Dostoievsky in *The Possessed*. It seems so sensational, such a degrading of the pure mind, somehow [...] Petronius is straight and above-board. Whatever he does, he doesn't try to degrade and dirty the pure mind in him.

D. H. Lawrence in a letter to Lady Ottoline Morrell
(1 February 1916)

It is prejudice, do you think, that makes us hate the Victorians, or is it the truth of the case? They seem to me a set of mouthing, bungling hypocrites [...] I would like to live for another 200 years (to be modest). The literature of the future will, I see clearly, be amazing [...] To live in those days, when books will pour out from the press reeking with all the filth of Petronius.

Lytton Strachey in a letter to Virginia Woolf
(8 November 1912)

It was when curiosity about Gatsby was at its highest that the lights in his house failed to go on one Saturday night – and, as obscurely as it had begun, his career as Trimalchio was over.

F. Scott Fitzgerald, *The Great Gatsby* (1925)
(originally titled *Trimalchio at West Egg*)

Trimalchio: 'the only figure [in literature before Shakespeare] on whom Falstaff's belt would even slackly have hung.'

Helen Waddell, *The Wandering Scholars*
(Harmondsworth, 1926)

We hold various opinions about Vergil; and we think more highly of Petronius than our grandfathers did.

T. S. Eliot, 'Euripides and Professor Murray,'
The Sacred Wood (London, 1920)

Thus, if you doubt the essential truth of Petronius, you may see his grim comedy enacted everyday.

T. S. Eliot quoting Charles Whibley in 'Charles Whibley,'
Selected Essays (London, 1932)

SUGGESTIONS FOR FURTHER READING

Studies

J. N. Adams, *Latin Sexual Vocabulary* (London, 1982).

G. Anderson, *Ancient Fiction: The Novel in the Graeco-Roman World* (London, 1984).

G. W. Bowersock, *Fiction as History: Nero to Julian* (Berkeley, 1994).

R. Boroughs, 'Oscar Wilde's Translation of Petronius: The Story of a Literary Hoax', *English Literature in Transition 1800–1920* 38 (95) 9–49.

M. M. Bakhtin, 'The Problem of the Text in Linguistics, Philology, and the Human Sciences: An Experiment in Philosophical Analysis' in *Speech Genres and Other Late Essays*. Trans. V. W. McGee (Austin, 1986).

—— *The Dialogic Imagination*. Trans. C. Emerson, M. Holquist (Austin, 1981).

C. A. Barton, *The Sorrows of the Ancient Romans: The Gladiator and the Monster* (Princeton, 1993).

J. Bodel, 'Trimalchio's Underworld.' (See under Tatum.)

E. L. Bowie, 'The Greek Novel' in *The Cambridge History of Classical Literature*, vol. 1. Eds. P. E. Easterling and B. M. W. Knox (Cambridge, 1985).

R. B. Branham, *Unruly Eloquence: Lucian and the Comedy of Traditions* (Cambridge, Massachusetts, 1989).

—— 'Inventing the Novel' in *Bakhtin in Context: Across the Disciplines*. Ed. A. Mandelker (Evanston , 1995).

C. Connors, 'Famous Last Words: Authorship and Death in the *Satiricon* and Neronian Rome' in *Reflections of Nero: Culture, History and Representation*. Eds. J. Elsner and J. Masters (London, 1994).

G. B. Conte, *Latin Literature: A History*, tr. J. B. Solodow (Baltimore, 1994).

P. Dronke, *Verse with Prose from Petronius to Dante* (Cambridge, Massachusetts, and London, 1994).

I. Gozzini Giacosa, *A Taste of Ancient Rome*. Translated by Anna Harklotz, with a Foreword by Mary Taylor Simeti (Chicago, 1992).

A. Grafton, 'Petronius and Neo-Latin Satire. The Reception of the "Cena Trimalchionis"', *JWCI* 53 (1990) 237–49.

T. Hägg, *The Novel in Antiquity* (Oxford, 1983).

W. V. Harris, *Ancient Literacy* (Cambridge, Massachusetts, 1989).

D. Konstan, *Sexual Symmetry: Love in the Ancient Novel and Related Genres* (Princeton, 1994).

F. Lissarrague, 'On the Wildness of Satyrs' in *Masks of Dionysus*. Eds. T. H. Carpenter and C. A. Farone (Ithaca, 1993).

F. Lissarrague, 'Why Satyrs Are Good To Represent' in *Nothing To Do with Dionysus*. Eds. J. J. Winkler and F. Zeitlin (Princeton, 1990), 228–36.

David Lodge, *After Bakhtin: Essays on Fiction and Criticism* (London, 1990).

P. MacKendrick, 'The Great Gatsby and Trimalchio' in *Classical Journal* 25 (1950) 307–14.

M. Morford, 'Nero's Patronage and Participation in Literature and the Arts' in *ANRW* II.32.3 (1985) 2003–31.

W. J. Ong, *Orality and Literacy: The Technologizing of the Word* (London, 1982).

B. Pabst, *Prosimetrum: Tradition und Wandel einer Literaturform zwischen Spätantike und Spätmittelalter*, 2 vols. (Cologne and Vienna, 1994).

C. Panayotakis, *Theatrum Arbitri: Theatrical Elements in the 'Satyrica' of Petronius* (London, 1995).

B. P. Reardon, *The Form of Greek Romance* (Princeton, 1991).

Walter L. Reed, *An Exemplary History of the Novel: The Quixotic versus the Picaresque* (Chicago, 1981).

J. Relihan, *Ancient Menippean Satire* (Baltimore, 1993).

L. D. Reynolds, ed. *Texts and Transmission: A Survey of the Latin Classics* (Oxford, 1983).

S. Richardson, *The Homeric Narrator* (Nashville, 1990).

W. Richardson, *Reading and Variant in Petronius: Studies in the French Humanists and their Manuscript Sources* (Toronto, 1993).

A. Richlin, *The Garden of Priapus*, 2nd ed. (New York, 1992).

G. Schmeling, 'The Satiricon: The Sense of an Ending' in Rheinisches Museum für Philologie 134/3–4 (1991) 352–77.

G. Schmeling, D. R. Rebmann 'T. S. Eliot and Petronius' in Comparative Literature 12.4 (1975) 393–410.

G. Schmeling, ' "Quid Attinet Veritaten Per Interpretem Quaerere?" Interpretes and the Satyricon', Ramus, vol. 23.1, 2 (1994) 144–68.

H. Scullard, From the Gracchi to Nero: A History of Rome from 133 BC to AD 68 (London, 1972).

Niall W. Slater, Reading Petronius (Baltimore, 1990).

W. J. Slater, ed. Dining in a Classical Context (Ann Arbor, 1991).

Martin S. Smith, 'A Bibliography of Petronius (1945–82)' in ANRW II.32.3 (1985) 1628–65.

J. P. Sullivan, The Satyricon of Petronius: A Literary Study (Bloomington and London, 1968).

J. H. Stuckey, 'Petronius the "Ancient": His Reputation and Influence in Seventeenth–Century England' in Rivista di Studi Classici 20 (1972) 145–53.

J. Tatum, ed. In Search of the Ancient Novel (Baltimore, 1993).

A.-M. Tupet, La magie dans la poésie latine (Paris, 1976).

Antonio Varone, Erotica pompeiana: iscrizioni d'amore sui muri di Pompei (Rome, 1994).

P. G. Walsh, The Roman Novel: The 'Satyricon' of Petronius and the 'Metamorphoses' of Apuleius (Cambridge, 1970).

C. Wells, The Roman Empire, 2nd ed. (Cambridge, Mass., 1995).

G. Williams, Change and Decline: Roman Literature in the Early Empire (Berkeley, Los Angeles and London, 1978).

J. J. Winkler, Auctor & Actor: A Narratological Reading of Apuleius' 'Golden Ass' (Berkeley, 1985).

Froma Zeitlin, 'Petronius as Paradox: Anarchy and Artistic Integrity' in TAPA 102 (1971) 631–84.

——— 'Romanus Petronius: A Study of the Troiae halosis and the Bellum civile' in Latomus 30 (1971) 56–82.

Texts and Translations

[John] Addison, tr. The Works of Petronius (London, 1736).

William Arrowsmith, tr. The Satyricôn (New York, 1959).

P. Burman, ed., T. Petronii Arbitrii Satyricon quae supersunt (Utrecht, 1709).

W. Burnaby, *The Satyricon* (London, 1694), based on Nodot's spurious edition of 1691.

A. Ernout, tr. and ed., *Le Satiricon*, 2nd ed. (Paris, 1931).

E. Courtney, ed., *The Poems of Petronius* (Atlanta, 1991).

Héguin de Guerle, ed., *Oeuvres complètes de Pétrone* (Paris, 1860).

Apicius, *The Roman Cookery of Apicius: A Treasury of Gourmet Recipes & Herbal Cookery.* Translated and adapted for the modern kitchen by John Edwards (Point Roberts, Washington, 1984).

W. C. Firebaugh, tr., *The Satiricon of Petronius Arbiter* (New York, 1922).

Allen Lewis, ed., *The Satiricon of Petronius Arbiter in the Translation Attributed to Oscar Wilde* (Chicago, 1927).

K. Müller, ed., W. Ehlers, tr., *'Satyrica'/Schelmenszenen*, 3rd, rev. ed. (Munich, 1983). Cf. p. xxxvii, n. 51, above.

B. P. Reardon, ed., *Collected Ancient Greek Novels* (Berkeley, 1989).

R. Seaford, ed., *Euripides' 'Cyclops'* (Oxford, 1984).

W. B. Sedgwick, ed., *Petronii Arbitrii 'Cena Trimalchionis,'* 2nd ed. (Oxford, 1950).

M. S. Smith, ed., *Petronii Arbitri 'Cena Trimalchionis'* (Oxford, 1975).

J. P. Sullivan, tr., *The Satiricon and the Apocolocyntosis*, rev. ed. (Harmondsworth and New York, 1977).

TEXT SUMMARY

Agamemnon (Chapters 1–15)

Agamemnon and Encolpius debate rhetoric and literature (1–5); Encolpius and Ascyltos quarrel over Giton (6–11); Encolpius and Ascyltos recover their lost cloak in the market (12–15).

Quartilla (Chapters 16–26)

Quartilla enlists Encolpius, Ascyltos and Giton in the rites of Priapus.

Trimalchio (Chapters 26–78)

Encolpius, Ascyltos, Giton, and Agamemnon attend a lavish banquet given by Trimalchio. Trimalchio plays ball, takes a bath (27–8); wall paintings, entering the dining room (29–30); hors d'oeuvres, Trimalchio's entrance (31–2); peahens' eggs, Opimian wine (33–4); the zodiac; Carver (35–6); Hermeros (37–8); Trimalchio's astrology, the boar is served, Dionysus is liberated (39–41); Dama (41); Seleucus (42); Phileros (43); Ganymede (44); Echion (45–6); Trimalchio's stomach (47); Trimalchio and Agamemnon converse (48); gutting the pig (49); Corinthian bronze (50); Trimalchio's story of the unbreakable glass bowl (51); a drinking cup is dropped (52); Report on Trimalchio's estates (53); the acrobats (54); poetry (55); the hardest jobs (56); Hermeros (57–8); the rhapsodes (59); gifts for the guests (60); Niceros' story of the werewolf (61–2); Trimalchio's story of the witches (63); Plocamus, Puppy and Pearl (64); Habinnas arrives (65); Habinnas and Trimalchio converse (66–7); Habinnas' slave performs (68–9); the slaves join the party (70); Trimalchio's tomb (71); a failed escape (72); the baths (73); a bad omen and a quarrel (74); a frugal kiss (75); Trimalchio's autobiography (76–7); Encolpius, Ascyltos and Giton flee (78).

Eumolpus (Chapters 79–125)

Ascyltos and Giton abandon Encolpius (79–82); Encolpius meets Eumolpus in an art gallery (83–4); Eumolpus tells the story of the boy of Pergamon (85–7); Eumolpus decries the decline of culture (88) and recites *The Fall of Troy* (89–90); Encolpius and Giton are reunited (91); jealousy disrupts dinner with Encolpius, Giton and Eumolpus (92–6); Ascyltos comes looking for Giton (97–8); Encolpius and Giton join forces with Eumolpus (98–9); adventure at Sea with Lichas and Tryphaena (100–11); Eumolpus tells the story of the widow of Ephesus (111–12); shipwreck and the death of Lichas (112–15); on the road to Croton (116–17); Eumolpus on poetry (118); Eumolpus recites his *Civil War* (119–24); Things go well in Croton (124–5)

Circe (Chapters 126–41)
Circe's maid, Chrysis, approaches Encolpius/Polyaenus (126); Encolpius/Polyaenus meets Circe (126–7); Encolpius suffers impotence and seeks help from Proselenus (128–33); Encolpius seeks a cure from Oenothea (134–8); a poem on Priapus (139); Philomela and her children (140); Eumolpus' will (141).

ACKNOWLEDGMENTS

First of all, we would like to thank William Arrowsmith and Bryan Reardon for their warm and generous support of this project in its earliest stages. We are also deeply grateful to W. S. Anderson and Niall Slater for reading and commenting on the entire translation; to Edward Courtney for detailed comments on those poems that he has edited as well as on some sections of the prose; and to Stephen Cushman for his acute notes on a draft of the poems. We would also like to thank Gareth Schmeling, Susan Stephens, Jim Tatum and Garth Tissol for reading and responding to the completed typescript, and Mary McKinley, for both checking and pardoning our French. Finally, we would like to thank our students for keeping us in touch with the current vernacular and letting us know where notes were most needed. Last, but by no means least, we would like to acknowledge the vital support that this project received from Emory University and the Stanford Humanities Center.